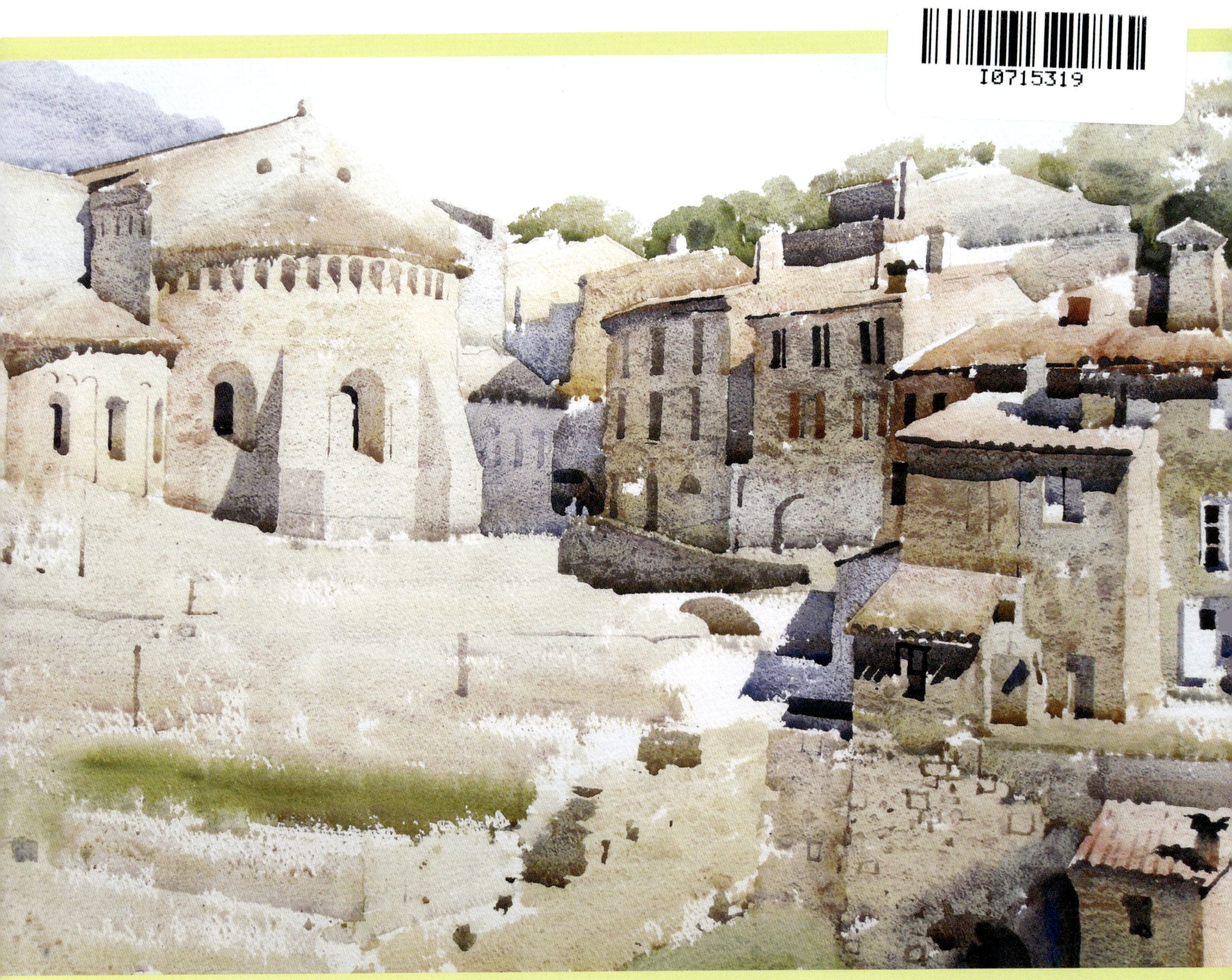

Atmospheric Buildings
in Watercolour

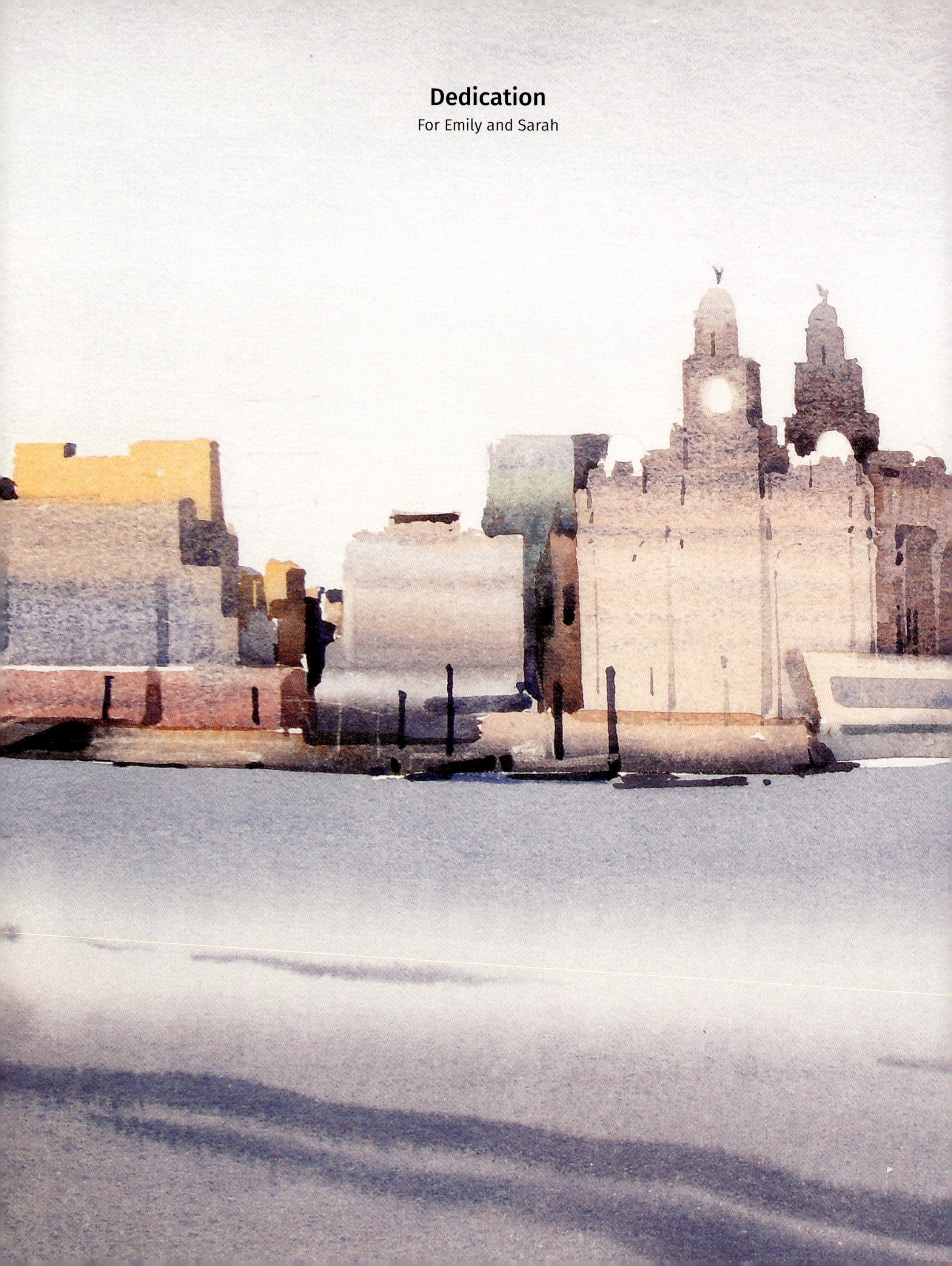

Dedication

For Emily and Sarah

Atmospheric Buildings
in Watercolour

Nicholas Poullis

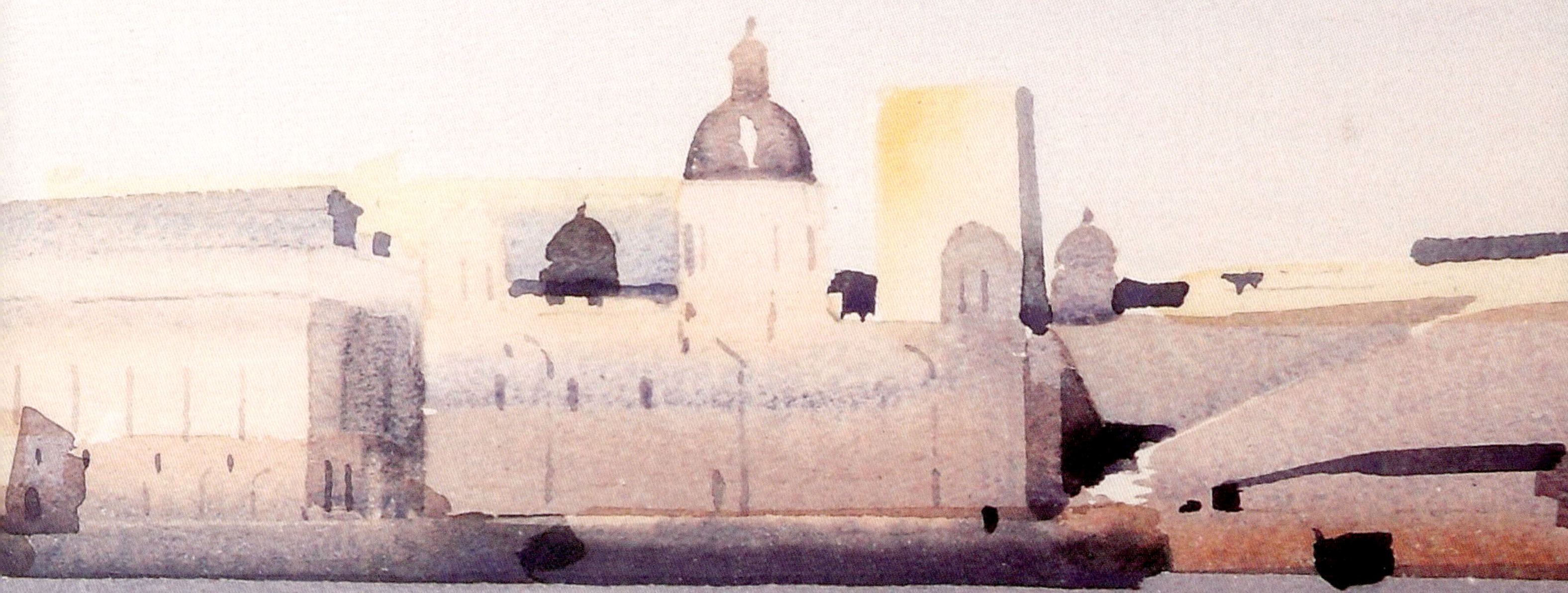

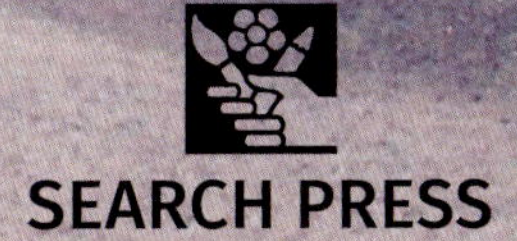

SEARCH PRESS

Contents

Foreword   *by Dr Sally Bulgin*   6

Introduction   8

Materials and equipment   10

THE PAINTING SESSION   16

Pure watercolour techniques   24

Choosing a subject   38

Simplification   48
CATHAR BRIDGE   *step-by-step*   56

Drawing and perspective   64
WATERMILL   *step-by-step*   70
SHADY CORNER   *step-by-step*   84

Painting light   88
MARKET HALL, EARLY MORNING   *step-by-step*   96

The order of painting   104
MARKET HALL INTERIOR   *step-by-step*   114

How to develop your painting   122
ANCIENT BRIDGE   *step-by-step*   134

Afterword   142

Index   144

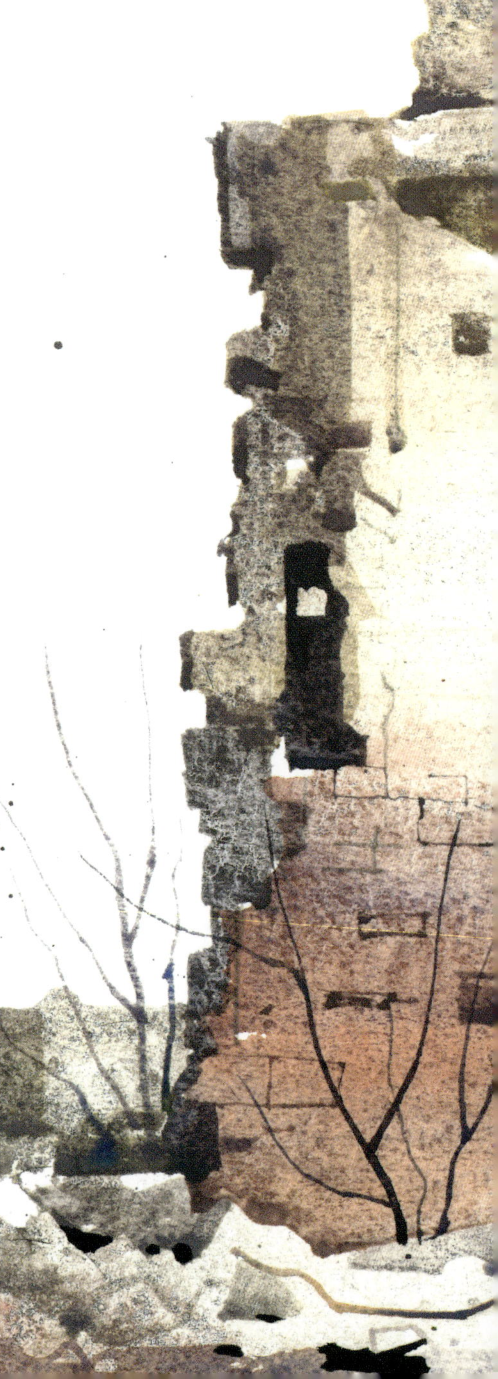

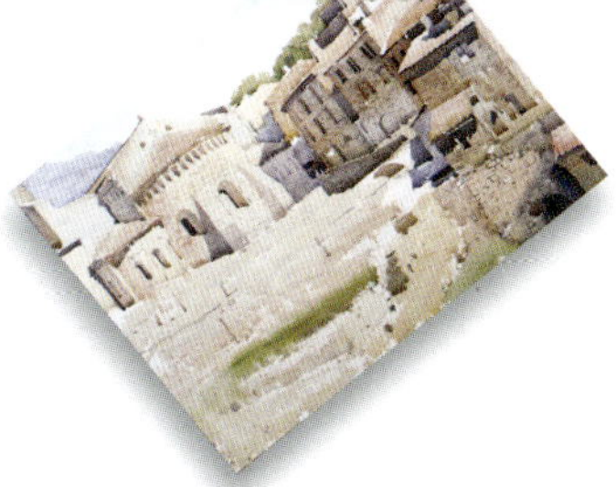

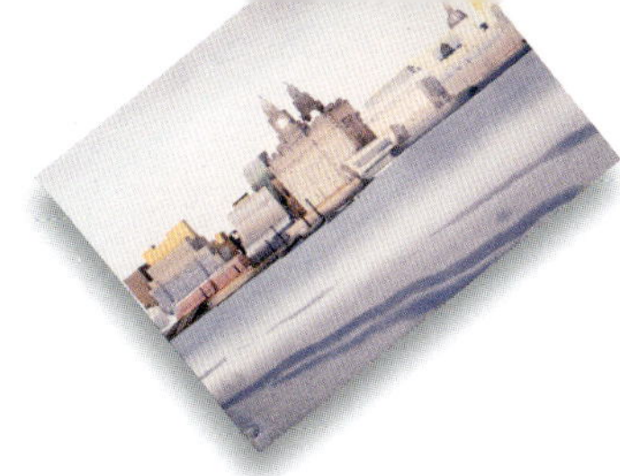

Page 1

Saint-Guilhem-le-Désert

*56 × 38cm (22 × 15in) Millford
300gsm (140lb) Rough surface paper*

*This attractive subject allowed me to explore
light and contrasting architecture.*

Pages 2–3

The Three Graces, Liverpool

*56 × 38cm (22 × 15in) Whatman
300gsm (140lb) Not surface paper*

*In this painting, texture was unnecessary,
so a Not paper surface was ideal.*

Below

Moulin de Bessan Ruins

38 × 28cm (15 × 11in) Arches 300gsm (140lb) Rough surface paper

The various forms made a strong natural design, while texture added contrast.

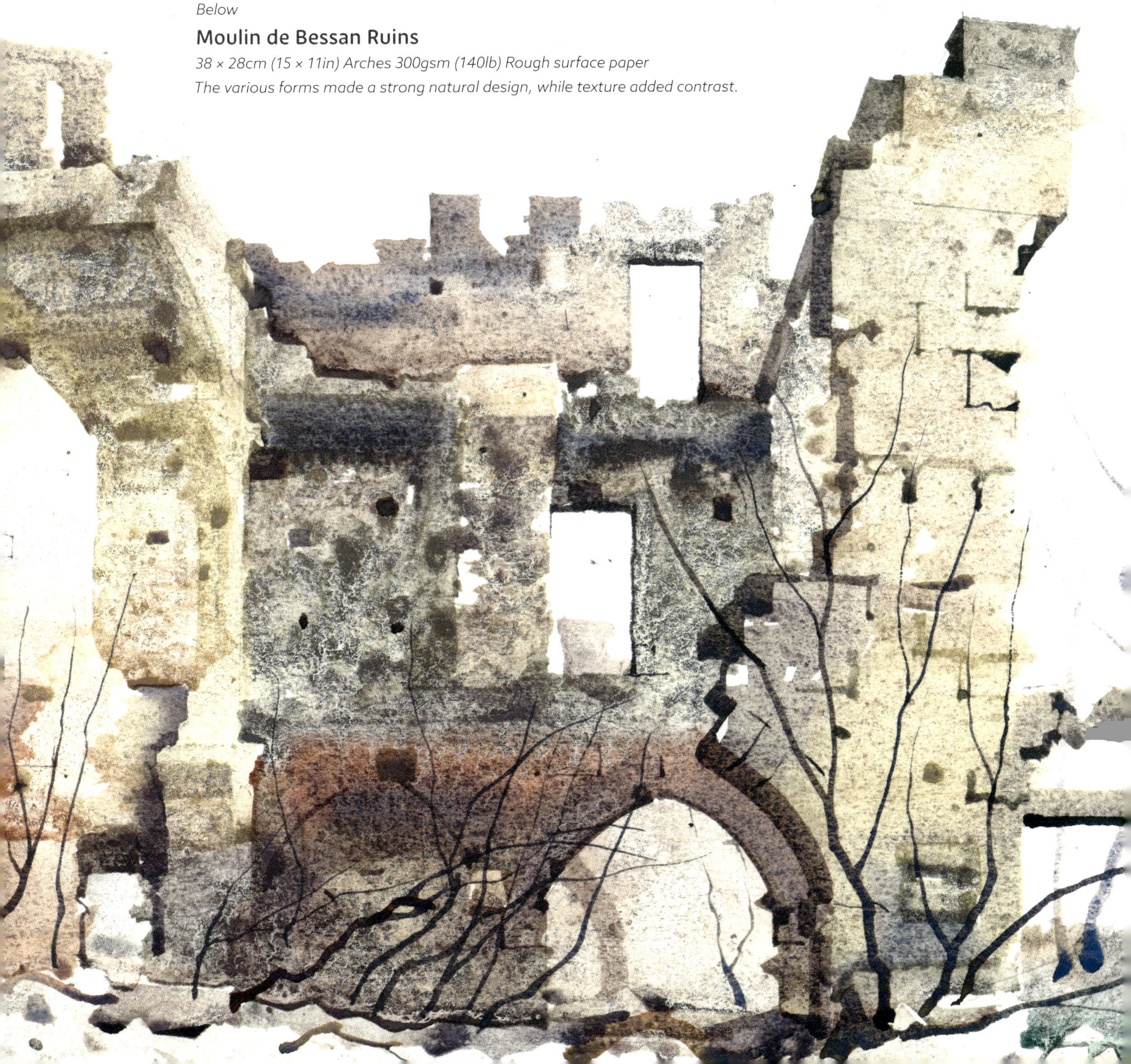

Foreword by Dr Sally Bulgin

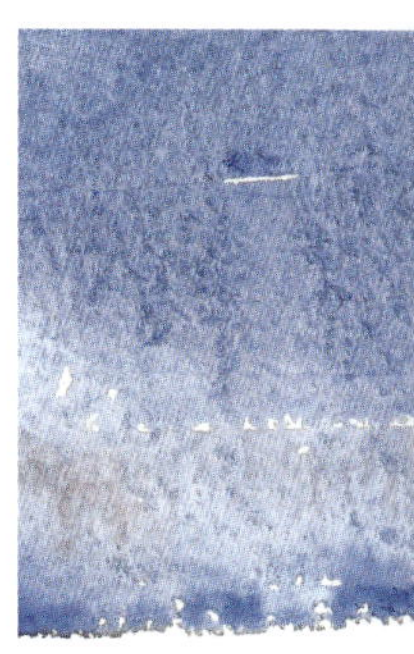

Having worked with Nick and published a variety of inspirational practical articles by him in *The Artist* magazine over many years, I was delighted when he told me about his new book *Atmospheric Buildings in Watercolour*, and honoured to be invited to write this foreword.

Nick is a master *en-plein-air* watercolour painter with a distinct, personal style. He is passionate about painting landscapes and townscapes, expressing himself with bold watercolour brushstrokes that communicate to the viewer his excitement about the beauty of his chosen subject. He is open and honest about what and how he paints and you know directly through his paintings where his interests lie. He sees a view and paints a picture *en plein air*, in direct response to his sensations in front of his subject, conveying the beauty of buildings within the natural environment, the subject of this book, through his favourite medium and exquisite brushwork.

Nick's philosophy towards watercolour painting is simple: every mark made with the medium is definitive, with the freshness of the brushstroke and the capturing of the light and atmosphere of a scene absolutely crucial to a painting's success. His teaching style, like his paintings, is inspirational. As confirmed by the enthusiasm expressed throughout his many practical, demonstration-style articles for *The Artist*, he loves sharing his knowledge and helping other painters practise their techniques, build their confidence and become better watercolour artists.

This invaluable book, illustrated throughout by a range of Nick's magnificent watercolours, is the ideal comprehensive guide. It will help artists to develop their own understanding of the medium, teach them pure watercolour techniques, and also show how to choose a subject, create texture, understand the importance of perspective, and capture the light and atmosphere of the chosen subject matter. It's a masterclass in painting buildings in watercolour that will inspire everyone with an interest in the unique and entrancing qualities of the medium.

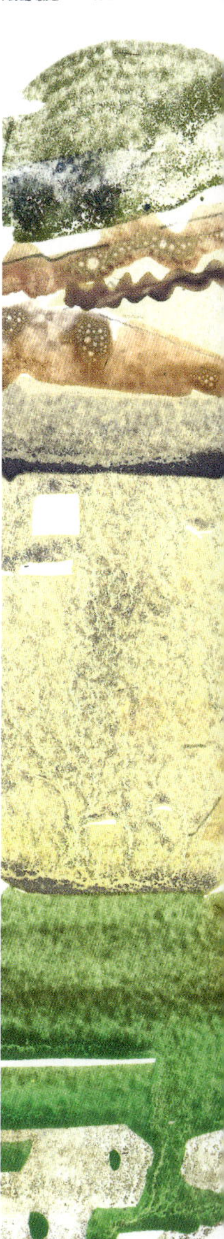

About Dr Sally Bulgin

Dr Bulgin has a BA in painting and art history and an MA and PhD in art history. She has been editor of The Artist magazine for over 35 years, including 18 years as owner and publisher of The Artist, Leisure Painter, StartArt, and the website Painters Online, launched in 2007 as a community hub to inspire, inform and educate artists of all abilities and experience. Sally is also author of four practical art books: Oils Masterclass, Acrylics Masterclass, Light in Watercolour with Lucy Willis and Ken Howard: A Personal View.

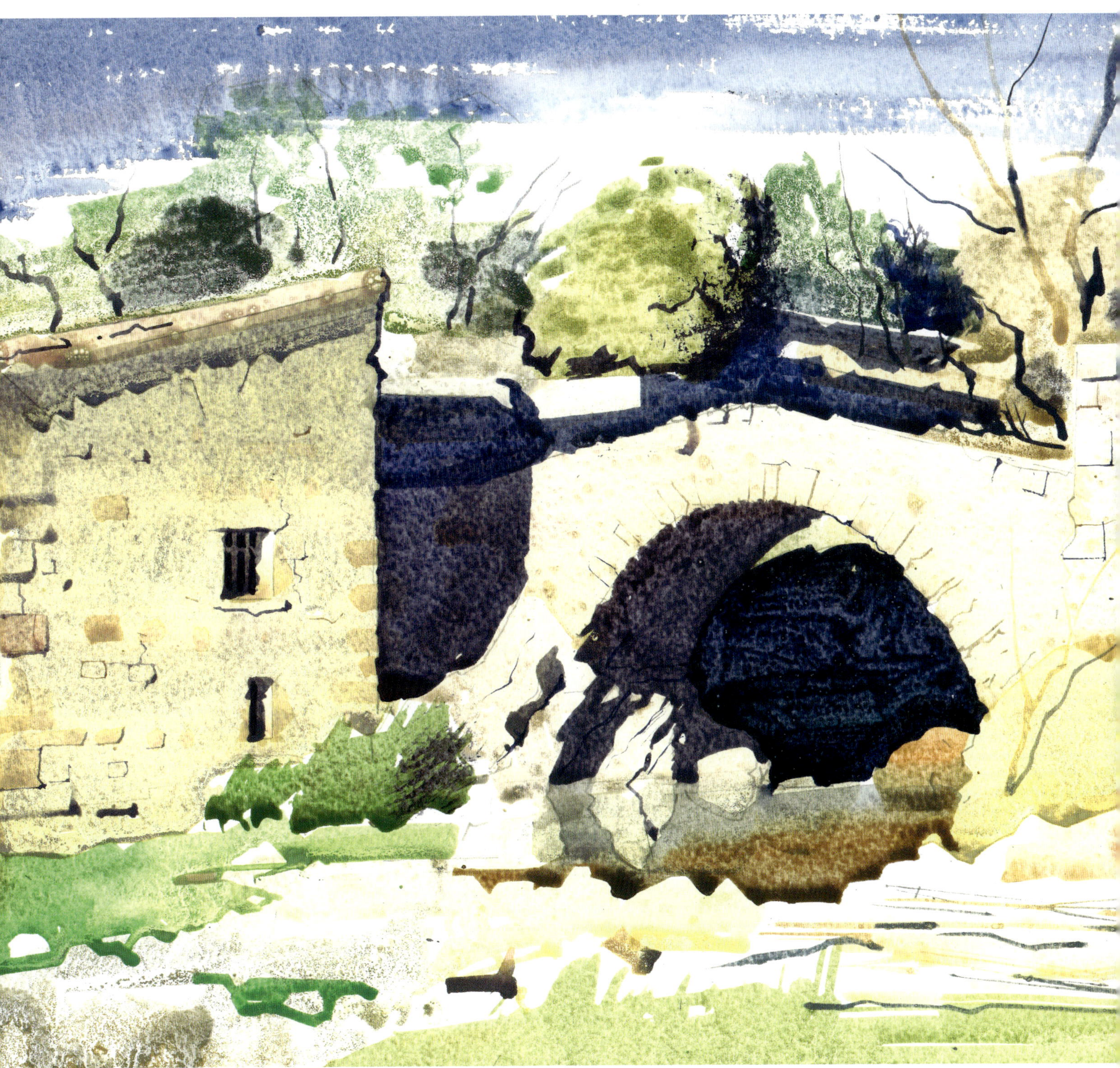

Moulin de Julian

38 × 28cm (15 × 11in) Saunders Waterford
300gsm (140lb) Rough surface paper

*Sometimes architecture is incongruous in its setting.
However, as is often the case with watermills, here the
mill building and bridge sit in the landscape as if they had
been there forever and make an appealing subject.*

Introduction

Subtle, powerful and expressive, watercolour has always fascinated me: the way it moves, mixes and layers is entrancing. I was painting my first watercolours by the age of eleven and painted alongside members of the Royal Birmingham Society of Artists including my grandfather, Arthur Sheldon Phillips RBSA. I'm still using the same easel I used then – though I've since had to fit it with longer legs!

The challenge of painting in watercolour is absorbing, and there is a thrill in it too, particularly on the spot. Watercolour painting is high risk – though even failure can be useful, as we learn far more from failures than from our successes.

When painting an atmospheric building, we are aiming to capture what inspired us: the lighting, ambience, character and essence of the experience. These will all come together into our own personal vision on paper. The ambition with an impressionistic watercolour is to do this efficiently, as this gives the painting impact and focus.

To best express the atmospheric aspect of a chosen view, we must decide which elements need to be kept, and which should be left out. Architecture must be simplified while retaining those distinctive aspects that make it not just any building, but our chosen building.

Much of what makes for successful painting is down to confidence with the medium, painting technique and technical aspects such as drawing, choice of subject, composition, balance and simplification. All of these should ideally become instinctive, and this is only achieved through hard work and regular practice.

For many years I have enjoyed teaching, running painting workshops and holidays *en plein air* – that is, outdoors – and writing practical articles for many of the best art magazines published today. I enjoy sharing my knowledge about what I love doing with a growing number of enthusiastic students, and while so doing, I have become aware of the many issues and problems students face while painting. This book is written with those issues in mind and offers practical solutions with hints and tips.

It is sometimes daunting to paint a watercolour from life. My aim for this book is to provide you with a comprehensive and practical guide to painting *plein-air* buildings in watercolour. I hope to equip you with the tools you need to successfully capture the atmosphere and character of your chosen scene.

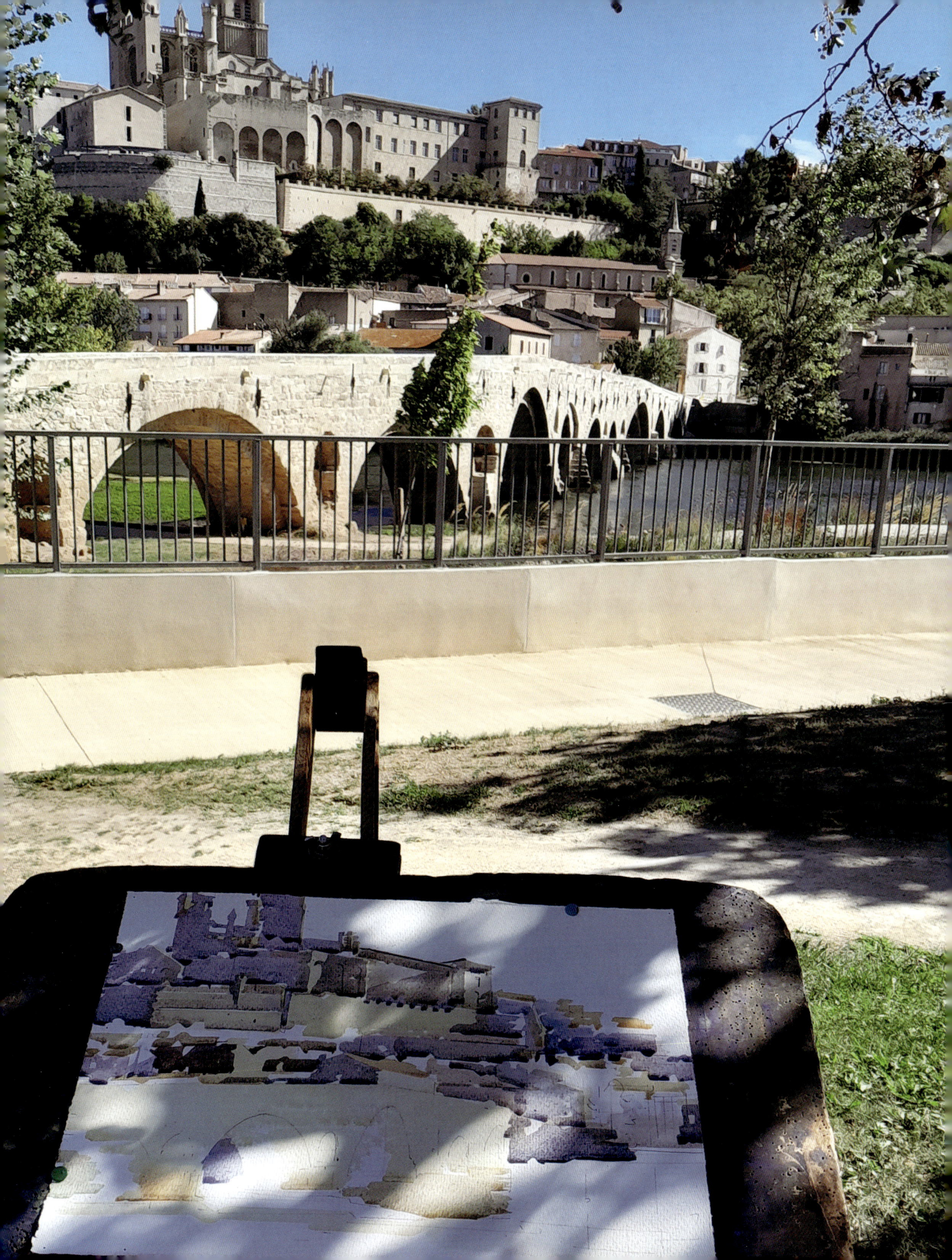

Materials and equipment

Watercolour is an accessible medium that requires less luggage than other painting media. The equipment you use for painting watercolours outdoors has to be practical, lightweight and portable, as you have to carry with you all that you need. The list below will give you a quick checklist of the essential supporting materials you'll need, and the following pages look in more detail at the paints, brushes and paper.

Supporting materials

Easel For watercolour the board must be supported at a slight incline that allows the paint to descend slowly when placing a wash. An adjustable travel easel is ideal for this. These are available from many suppliers and are inexpensive.

Board and pins A flat board provides a solid surface on which you can secure your watercolour paper. Keep it lightweight and ensure that you can press pins into the board – a soft wood is ideal.

Palette You need a space to prepare your paints and mix your colours. I use a paintbox with large mixing areas for large washes. Mine also has places to secure pans of paint (see page 12), making it clean and convenient to transport.

Clean water and kitchen paper You need a water pot that you can attach to your easel, and a bottle of clean water. Kitchen paper or other sturdy tissue is needed for cleaning, and for certain techniques like lifting out.

Pencil and eraser For your initial sketch, I recommend a soft pencil such as a 2B: a harder pencil will score the paper. A soft or putty eraser is best.

Bag with a shoulder strap *(not pictured)* Everything you bring with you needs to be carried, so you need a sturdy bag to transport it all comfortably and securely.

Foundations

- Carry as little as possible – take only what you need.
- Use the lightest equipment possible.
- I cut my own board using wood from a DIY centre.

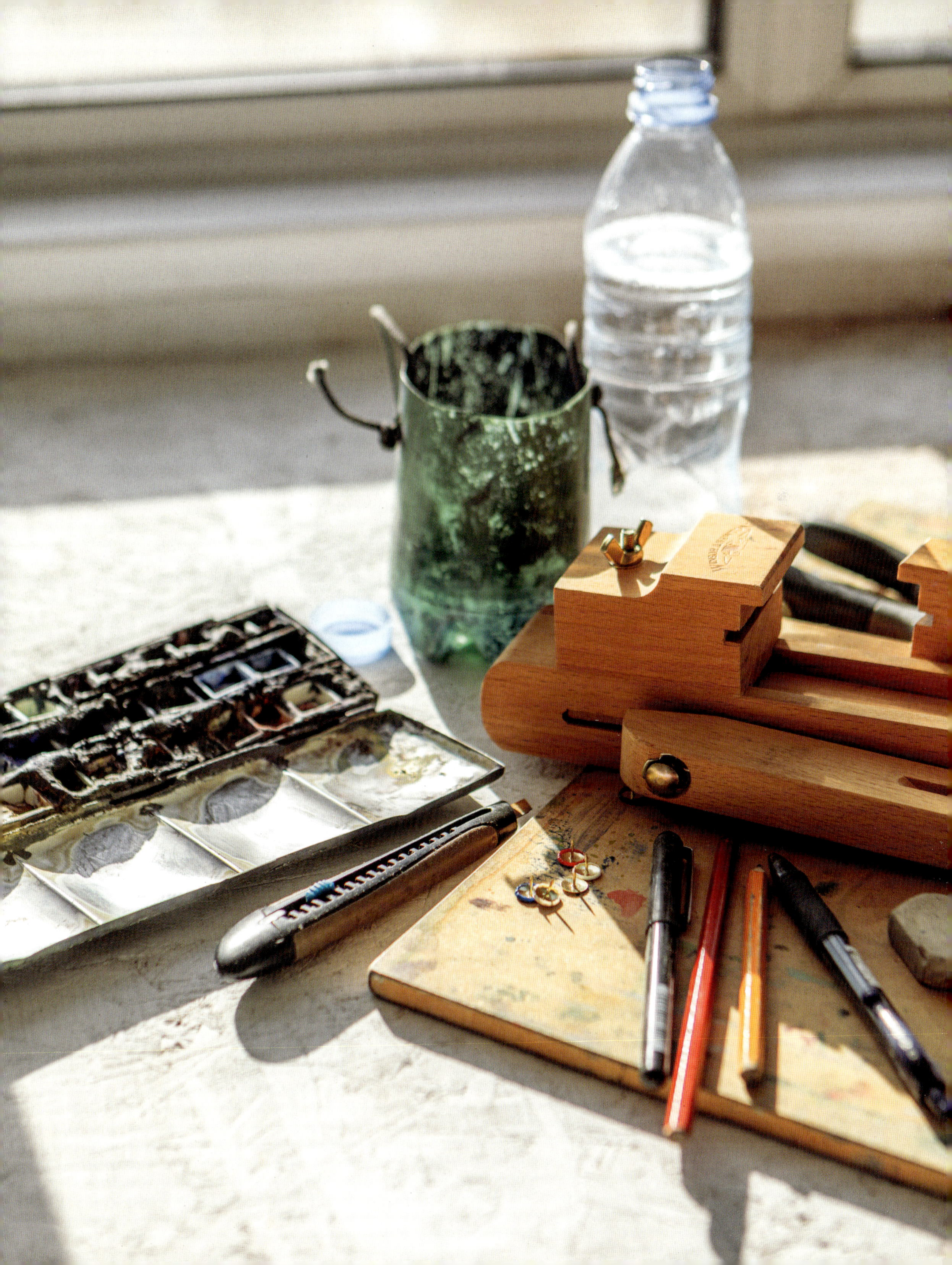

Paints

Watercolour paints are pigments in water-soluble binders. The medium best serves the *plein-air* painter because it is quick to use and suits an economical expression with reference to a scene or atmosphere.

Watercolours can be bought in tubes of soft paint or pans, which are blocks of hard paint. The difference between them is the proportion of gum and glycerine content, which give each type different qualities. The proportions in tube paint help to keep the paint moist in the tube, but also slow drying and mean the paint sits on the surface slightly more.

Pans need to be gently scrubbed with a wet brush to make the paint workable, while tubes offer immediacy as they can be used straight away. This also makes tube paints a little kinder on the brushes. Either type, however, will work, so experiment to see which suits you better.

More important than the type is the quality. Using artists' quality (as opposed to cheaper students' quality) paint is important as the colour is better – deeper tones and purer pigment, which can affect the way the colours mix.

Foundations

- Use artists' quality paint. Other than that, I don't favour any particular brand – there are a number of high-quality manufacturers.
- There is no particular advantage to tubes over pans or vice versa: I use what is available for the colours I want.
- As noted, my paintbox and palette has space for pans – but that doesn't limit you. You can refill these using tube paint when they run out.
- There is more on my choice of paint on pages 18–19.

Brushes

The best paintbrushes to use are natural fibre as they hold the paint better and release it gradually – brushes with synthetic fibre tend to spill the paint out. As a result, natural hair brushes allow better control of the flow of paint.

Kolinsky Sable brushes are considered the best because they keep their shape and point well. Squirrel is also good but the point does not last as long.

You will need a mix of round brushes for applying washes, and smaller rigger brushes for finer details such as trees and their branches. A very large brush is useful for particularly large areas of wash, and a stiffer brush for lifting out.

Foundations

- Choose natural fibre brushes for everything except specialist techniques: for lifting out, a stiff synthetic or hog hair brush will work best as they are more abrasive.
- Carry your brushes tightly packed into wooden boxes so they cannot move inside. This prevents the hairs being squashed and damaged.
- The brushes I favour are listed on page 23.

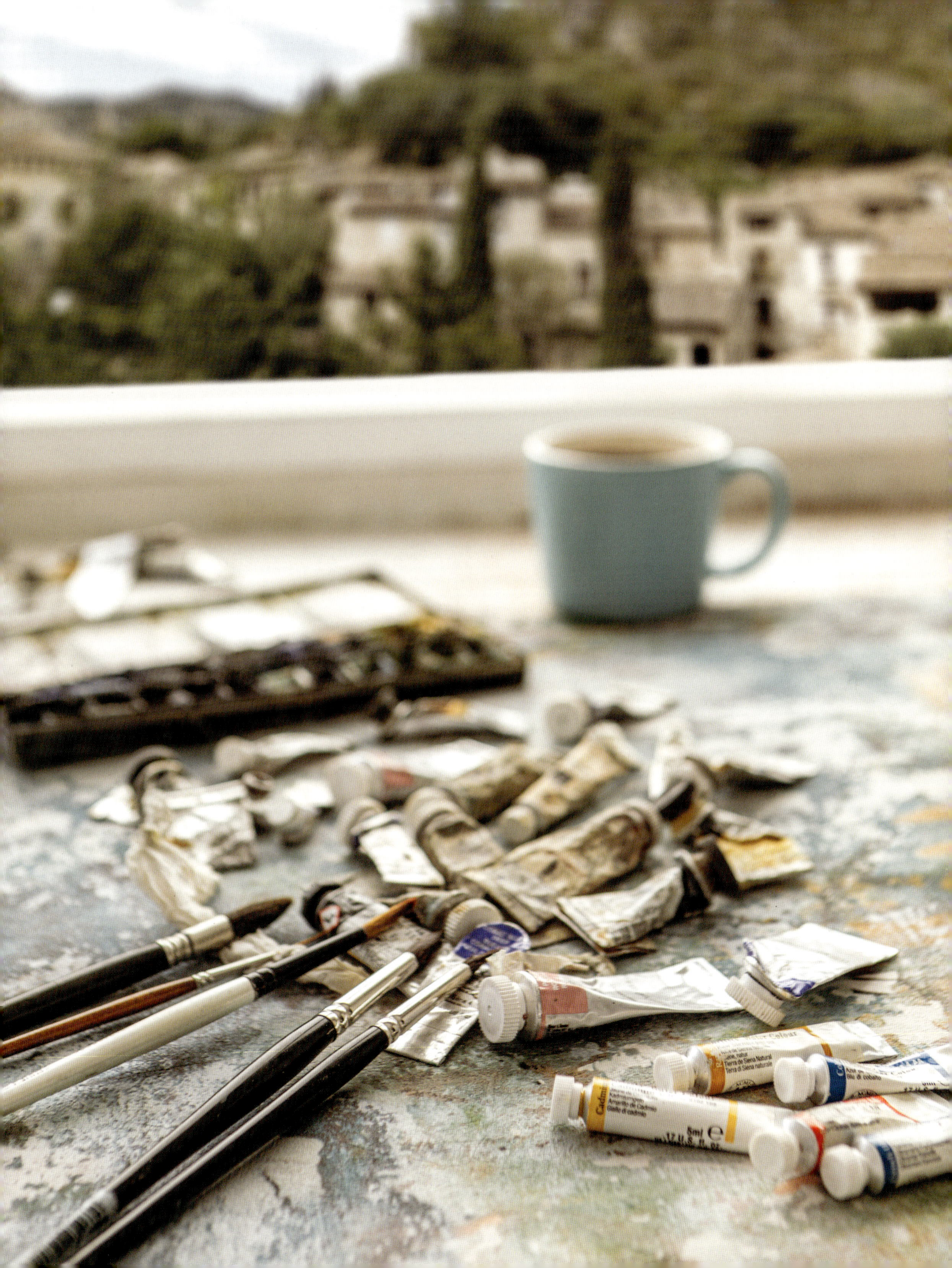

Watercolour paper

The qualities and personality of the chosen paper surface affect how the paint goes on. The paper's character can be described in terms of three qualities – weight, sizing and surface texture. The tint of a paper can also vary.

Weight

Paper thickness is described as weight. It is measured in grams per square metre (gsm) or pounds per ream (lb). Standard machine weights are 190gsm (90lb), 300gsm (140lb), 356gsm (260lb) and 638gsm (300lb). Heavy paper might, depending on surface quality, take more working or scraping or scratching out than lighter papers. I generally use good quality papers of 300gsm (140lb) as this avoids the need to stretch (see page 21); any buckling will flatten out as it dries.

Sizing

The sizing is the resistance the surface has to the paint going on. Paper that will easily accept and absorb paint can be described as soft-sized. Hard-sized paper is very resistant to paint – it can be lively and exciting to work upon.

Surface texture

Rough Rough-textured watercolour paper has a prominent 'tooth' that can accentuate granulation (see page 32). Rough paper will more easily allow dry brushing.

Not Short for 'not hot-pressed', this surface has a moderate tooth. It is a very versatile surface – especially if it is hard-sized. Not surface paper is sometimes called 'CP' or 'cold-pressed'.

HP Short for 'hot-pressed', and also simply called 'smooth', hot-pressed papers have a very fine-grained surface with little or no tooth. Less versatile than Rough or Not surface papers, hot-pressed papers are good for specific things rather than for general use. They suit detailed work if that is your style or intention.

Foundations

- Buying papers in sealed packs is cheaper than as individual sheets – and single sheets have often been handled, which affects the sizing.
- Use acid-free paper so your painting won't yellow. Some papers are pH-buffered, which means that they will counteract the acidic effects of the atmosphere.
- Both sides of all papers can be used – the 'right' side is where the watermark can be read, or the side with more texture.
- If a paper is too hard-sized to do what you want, add a little ox gall (two or three drops per 250ml/½pt) to your water to allow the paint to go on a little easier.
- When a paper is too soft-sized, add some gum arabic to your water and this will help the paint sit on the surface.
- Gum arabic will also increase the drying time which may be useful if you are painting in the sun on a really hot day.

Rough surface

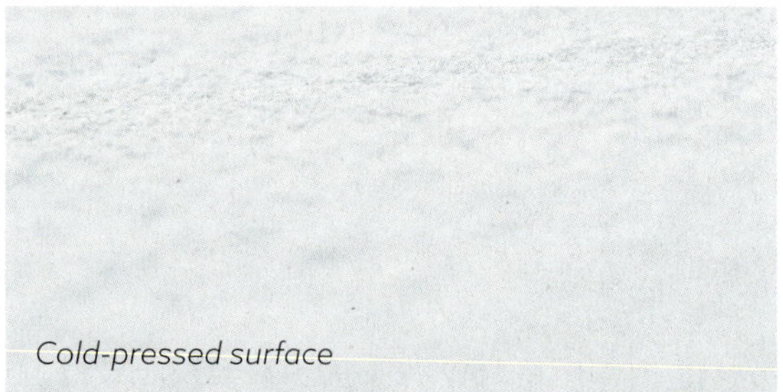

Cold-pressed surface

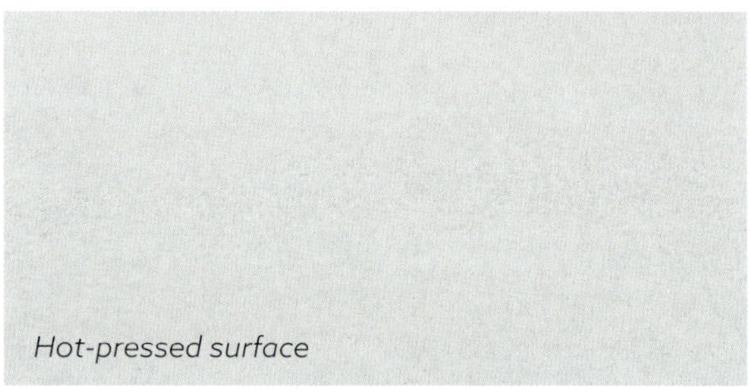

Hot-pressed surface

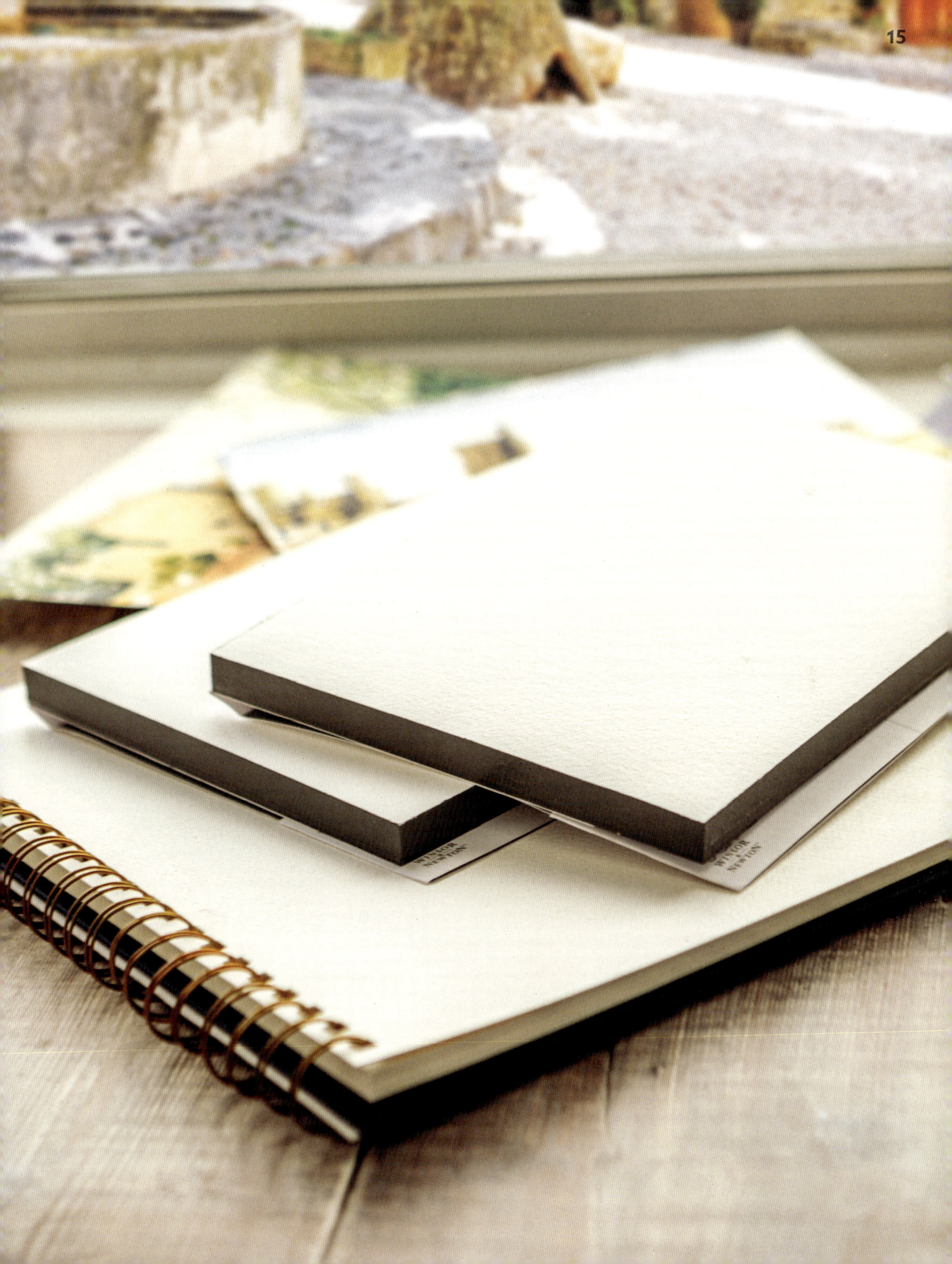

THE PAINTING SESSION

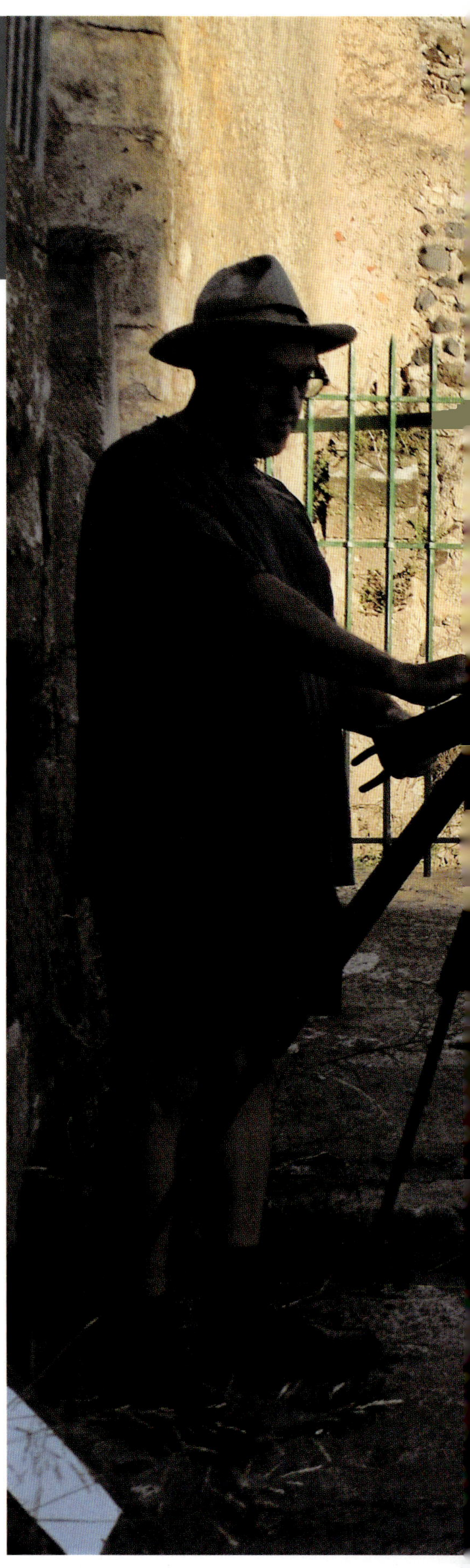

Watercolour is recognized as the most difficult medium to master for good reason and is far less relaxing to use than the non-painter might imagine, because without a clear plan, watercolours can go wrong very quickly! In this part of the book, I'll show you how to properly prepare, so you have the best chance of success and the most enjoyable time possible.

I find it best to work in intensive sessions of about four to five hours – time enough to engage with and finish a painting successfully without becoming exhausted.

Setting up

Setting up properly is often overlooked, and many students quickly resort to sitting and working on their knees. It is, however, important for the best chances of success. Set up so that you will be comfortable working and not struggling with balancing boards and spilling paint.

Always use an easel at the right height and at the right incline, and ensure you position yourself directly in front of the subject that you want to capture. You can only paint what you can actually see, so make sure you set up in full view of what you wish to paint. It's all too common to realize too late that something that you know is beautiful is sadly hidden from view!

Make sure the paper is properly pinned down. Any grease from your fingertips will affect washes, so handle it as little as possible to help keep the surface clean. If there is strong sunlight, angle the board on the easel so you can see the marks you are making.

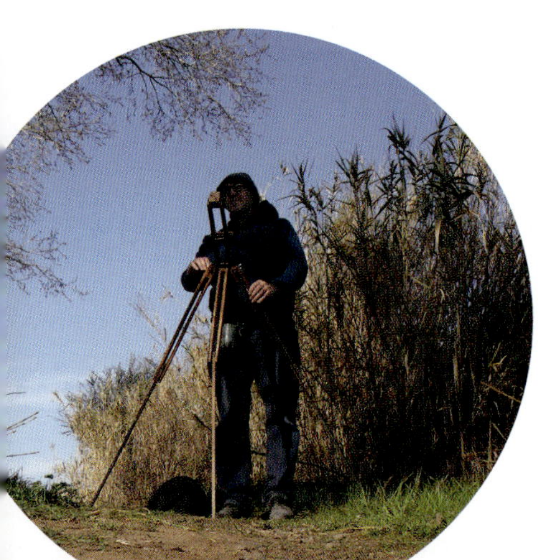

I work standing up as it allows for better arm movement. Also, when sitting, I find the perspective can easily become a little extreme and over-dramatic.

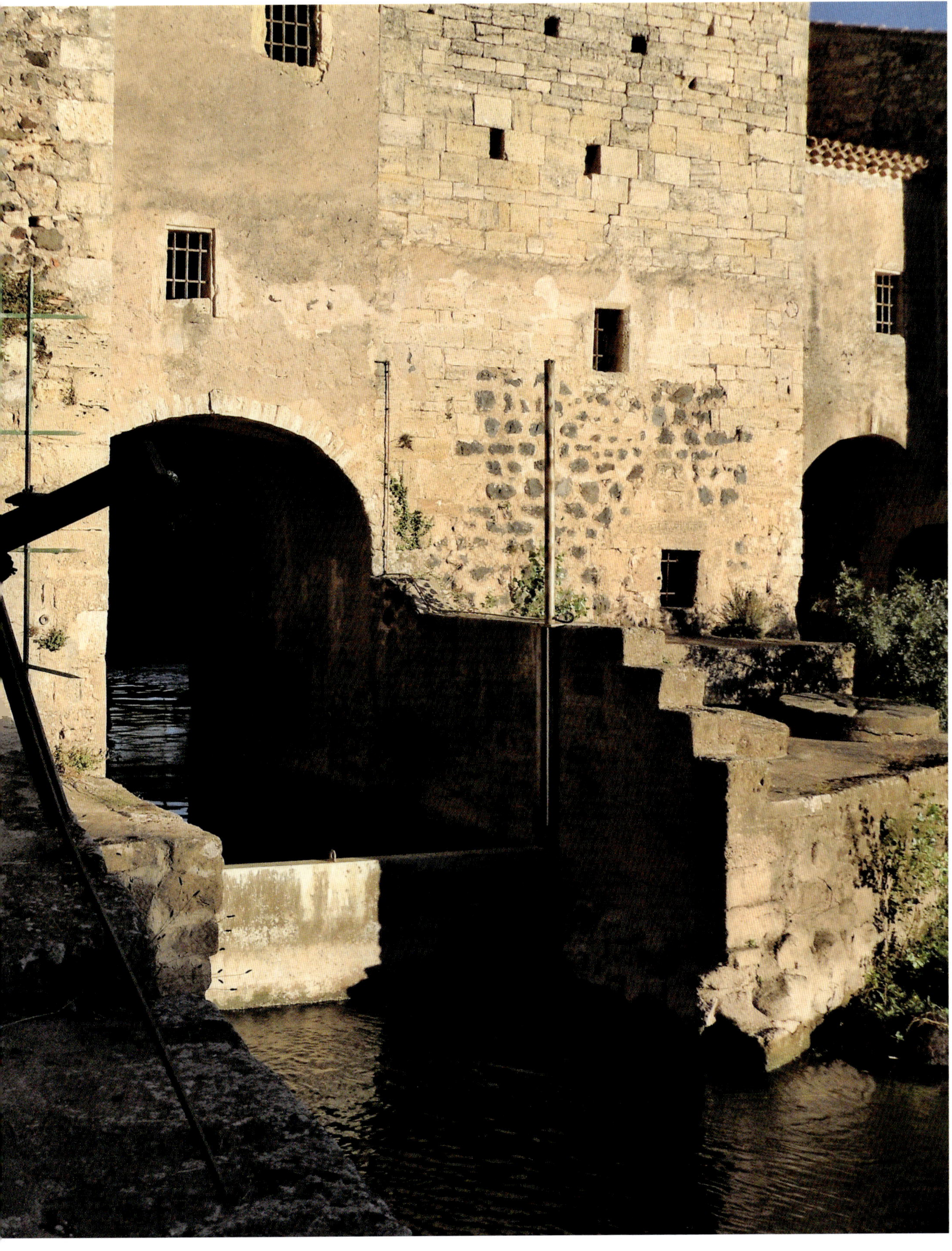

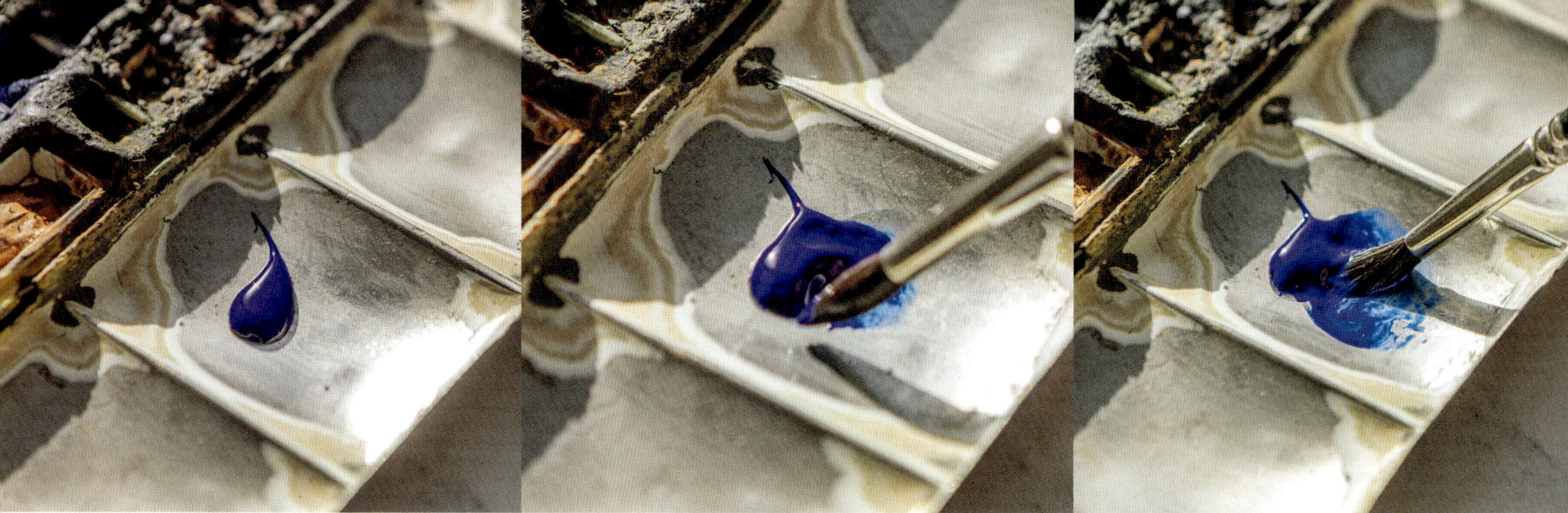

Ensuring fresh paint

Watercolour works by sitting on the surface of the paper: the light shining through the semi-transparent pigment is reflected from the white surface to give the distinctive clean, bright look of the medium. Because of this characteristic it can easily become obliterated with subsequent layers.

For a 'fresh' finish, it is important to be decisive and put down colour close to what we want in as few layers as possible. I aim to use no more than three in total, including all finishing and details: two wash layers plus a much darker layer used for detail.

Picking your colours

The paints in your palette should broadly correspond with the colours of the subject, although the colour mixes we make are usually translations of the true colour in the subject – it makes for more harmonious pictures if particularly vivid colours in reality are slightly muted in the painting.

For the landscape, architecture or marine palette, I have a warm and cold version of most colours – comparatively, Naples yellow for cool and raw sienna for warm, as an example. Having a warm and cold version of each colour is useful as this increases the range of tone and colour available. Importantly, the warmth of a colour once put down is also determined by the amount of water in the mix.

Apart from in the very light areas of a painting, the pigments are mixed with each other, so a livelier version of a colour is sometimes useful too. I favour cadmium yellow as a third yellow, for example. This is particularly important for greens. Pre-mixed green paints need to be mixed with something else – otherwise they can easily dominate the picture.

Finally, avoid colours that are too acidic: acidic colours can be a little difficult in terms of colour harmony and can 'jump out' at the viewer.

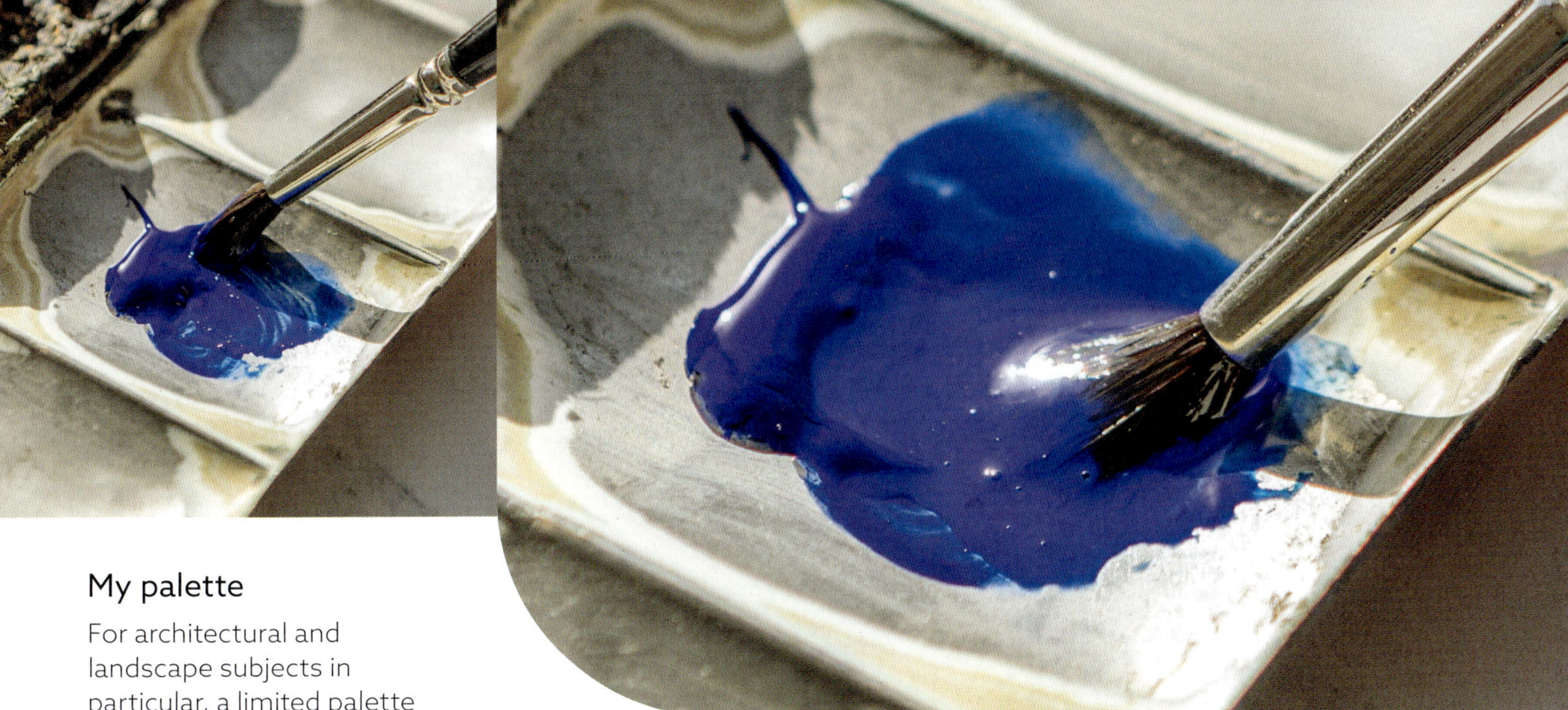

My palette

For architectural and landscape subjects in particular, a limited palette works best and will help to give the painting unity.

I avoid using overly vivid colours in my palette – these are better suited to flower painting than the landscape.

There are thirteen colours in my regular palette. The number could be further reduced, but this range allows for a huge variety in colour and tone:

• Cadmium yellow deep
• Naples yellow
• Raw sienna
• Cadmium red
• Light red
• Potters pink
• Cobalt blue
• Cobalt blue deep
• French ultramarine
• Manganese blue
• Viridian
• Brown madder
• Ivory black.

Keeping colour clean

Use plenty of clean water when preparing paints – particularly when mixing the lightest colours, as these can be easily contaminated. In particular, I do not place blue next to yellow in my mixing palette. Likewise, I have no white paint, which has a habit of finding its way into the surrounding colours and effectively turns them into body colour. Instead of adding white, we should use the white of the paper.

A common question is 'how many colours can we mix together while maintaining freshness?' This depends on which colours are being mixed, how concentrated they are and how they are applied – but as a rule of thumb, use no more than three paints. More than this will tend to result in a muddy mix.

Foundations

• Work on an incline and allow each wash to dry on an incline to avoid 'treeing' – where pooling wet paint flows back into partially dry paint.

• Use the right brush. Natural fibre brushes work best as you can control the flow and hold the paint well. Use a large brush to cover a large area.

• Mix the colour well beforehand and make sure you have enough mixed. Avoid having to mix more in a hurry halfway down the area you wish to cover.

• A lightweight portable easel will allow you to support your painting on a slight incline is crucial. This will give a better, more comfortable painting position. While sitting, your arm movement is restricted.

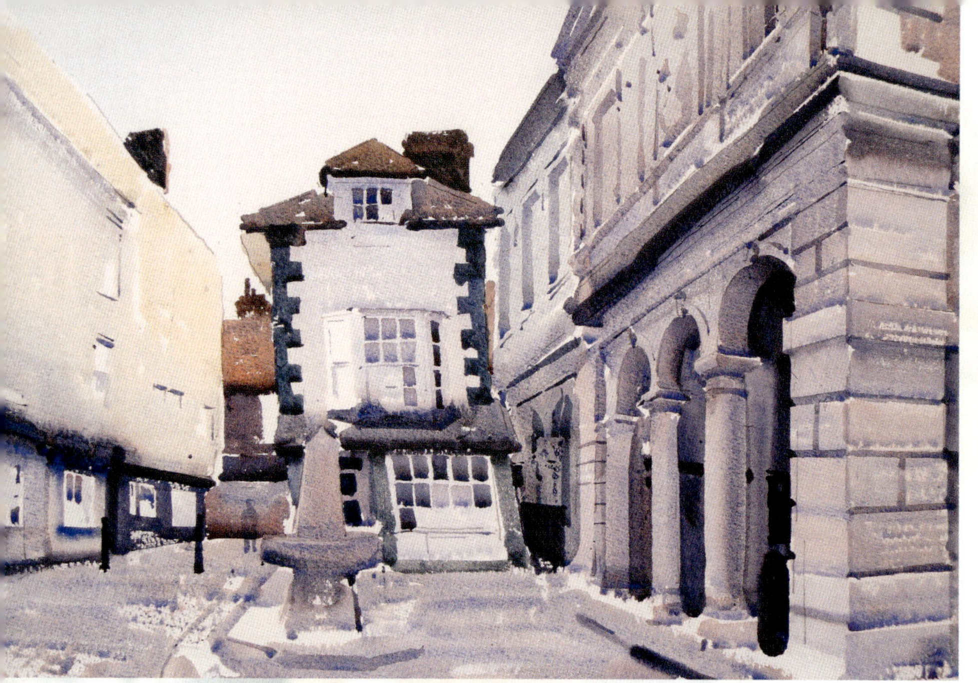

The Crooked House of Windsor

56 × 38cm (22 × 15in) Saunders Waterford 300gsm (140lb) Not surface paper

Not surface papers can be extremely versatile – in this painting, a range of effects were needed and the paper used allowed for some detail.

Fitting the paper to the subject

Think about what sort of marks/effects you might make to capture the subject. This will help you to decide on what tools and techniques you will need, and inform your choice of paper.

As a rule of thumb, when painting a subject where a lot of texture is required, use a highly textured surface or a hard-sized smoother paper. When little or no texture is required, use a paper with a Not or HP surface (see page 14).

Your way of working will also affect you choice of paper – see page 36 for more on direct and indirect painting. Some papers will allow both ways of working and these papers will obviously permit a broader range of expression.

My choice of paper

I tend to use medium-priced machine-mould-made paper. These papers have a distinct surface pattern and therefore texture. Some, like the example to the right, have a pronounced parallel texture and because of this characteristic they can buckle – that is, curl up when wetted – more along their length. This doesn't matter, as good paper will flatten out once dry.

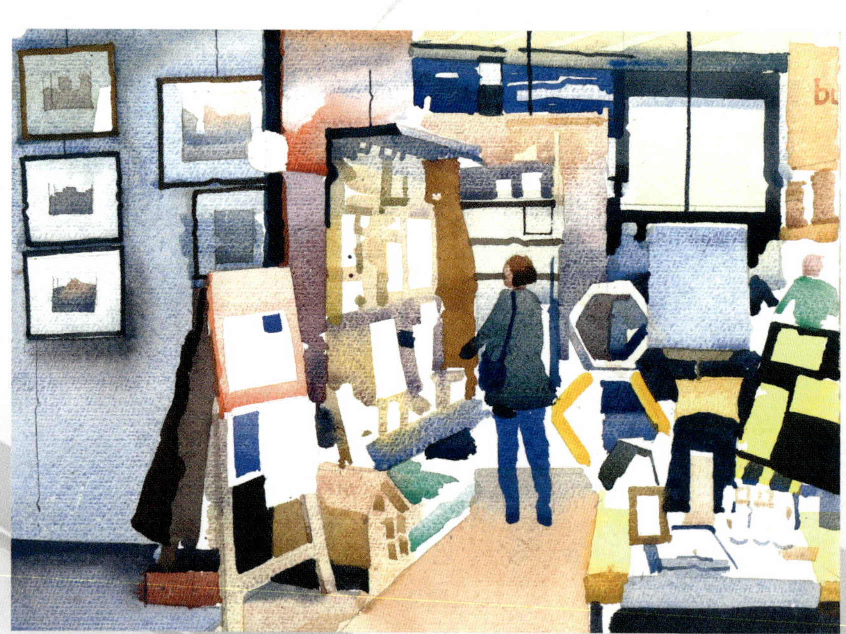

Can't Stop Shopping, Cultura Béziers

38 × 28cm (15 × 11in) Hahnemühle 300gsm (140lb) Rough surface paper

The bright surface of this highly-textured paper suited this subject and helped when creating contrasts. Note that you can see the machining. This can be incorporated into your picture, on a particular scale with a particular subject.

Exploring papers

Most watercolourists find it useful to keep a stock of papers of different weights, surfaces and makes. The different characters of paper will sometimes limit or demand different handling. For example, some papers accept washes easily, some don't, some may punish you with treeing (see page 19) for leaving tiny puddles, some won't.

You will quickly find your favourites, but do keep exploring: I have found it a useful exercise to use a paper that is extremely punishing, where treeing occurs easily, as this can help reveal faults and so I can improve my technique.

Try using different papers for the same subject, as this forces you to adapt to your materials and hopefully control them. This will push you creatively and you may find that you can reveal something new in a subject. Very often the first painting on a new paper is a little tentative as you feel your way forward, but this approach can be an exciting way of better understanding the medium.

Instead of stretching the paper, use a drawing pin in each corner to keep it secure on the board.

Stretch or not?

Whether you stretch probably depends on the size at which you wish to work on and weight. I personally never stretch paper – even very lightweight papers don't need it unless working on pictures larger than 30.5 × 20.5cm (12 × 10in). Stretching paper is useful if you want a soft-edged effect or for very detailed work. Soak the paper with clean water and secure it to a board with gum tape all around. As the water evaporates, the fibres in the paper will shrink and tighten the surface to a drum-tight finish. However, stretching paper removes some of the sizing from the surface and will reduce the nice resistance that some surfaces have.

You need only stretch paper if it is very lightweight. Paper weights of 300gsm (140lb) or more – and even smaller paintings on lightweight 165gsm (90lb) paper – do not benefit from stretching.

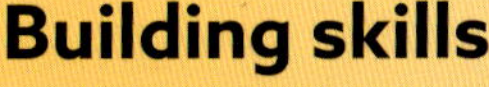

Building skills

- Some techniques will only work (or work differently) on particular textures. Dry brushing, for example, will give striking effects on Rough surface paper, be less obvious on cold-pressed paper, and likely not work at all on hot-pressed paper.
- Likewise, granular effects can be achieved on all papers but will appear differently on the various surfaces.
- A small amount of buckling is not detrimental to the look of a painting and is often barely visible once framed.

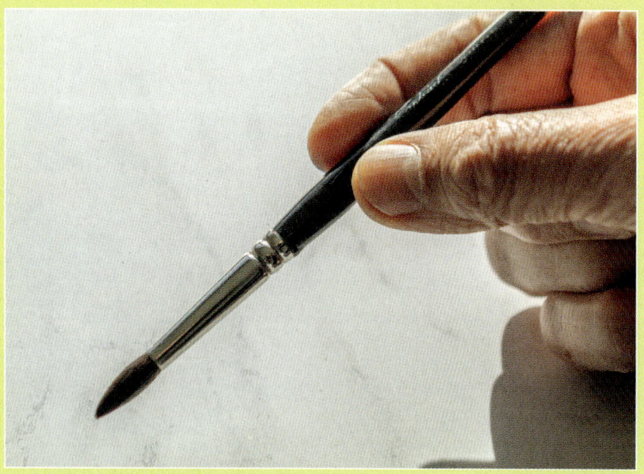

Holding the brush between the tips of thumb and forefinger will give the most sensitivity.

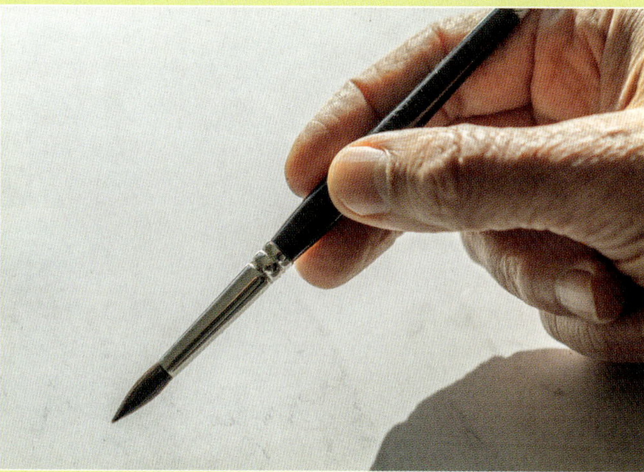

Holding the brush between the tips of thumb and fingers, as though holding a pen, gives us most control.

Handling a brush

When we paint in watercolour, we need to judge sensitively the pressure exerted on the brush. You can best judge the pressure and control the brush if you hold it between the tips of your thumb and forefinger, as shown above left.

For larger areas of wash, or if you need to put the paint down with some vigour, such as when dry brushing (see page 28), hold it in the same way with the additional support of your middle finger, as shown above right.

Watercolour will naturally run down the paper, with the working edge at the bottom of the wash.

When we put down a wash, the brush should be drawn along horizontally: that is, we should not put a wash down with the brush held like a pen (that way of holding the brush is better suited for painting details).

Foundations

- If you're struggling to hold the brush in the correct position, let me reassure you that regular painting practice will likely resolve things as you become more comfortable painting.

- If the problem persists, try drawing with an old-fashioned dip pen. This will only allow a correct holding position – if held incorrectly you will either bend or break the nib, or tear a hole in the paper. More importantly, the position you're forced to use is identical to that needed for watercolour painting.

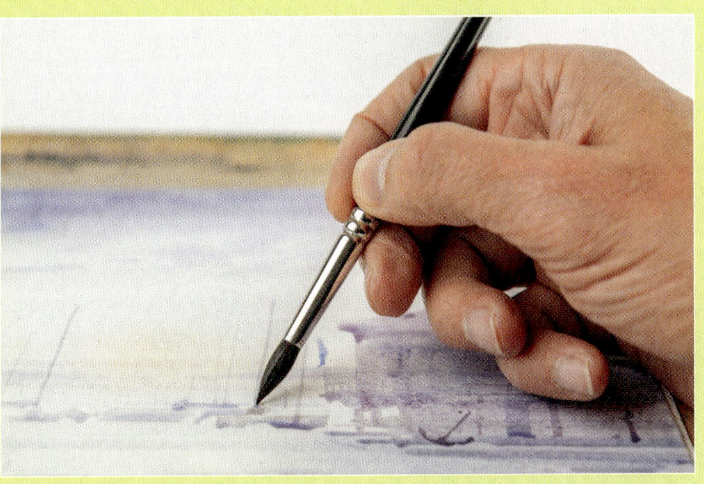

When painting in detail it's fine to rest your hand on the paper surface as shown – just be careful not to rest your hand on a wet area of paint.

Brush care

In watercolour the quality of the brush is important, and the best brushes will keep their shape, point and springiness for as long as possible. Rinse them thoroughly with clean water and reshape them after each painting.

The point of a brush is important. Keep rigger brushes in the protective plastic sleeve that they are supplied in – this offers quite a good protection.

My brushes

The brushes I favour are shown here. From left to right:
- Sizes 4 and 8 natural fibre riggers
- A small hog hair (a synthetic brush is a good alternative)
- Sizes 6 and 8 natural fibre rounds
- A large squirrel hair round.

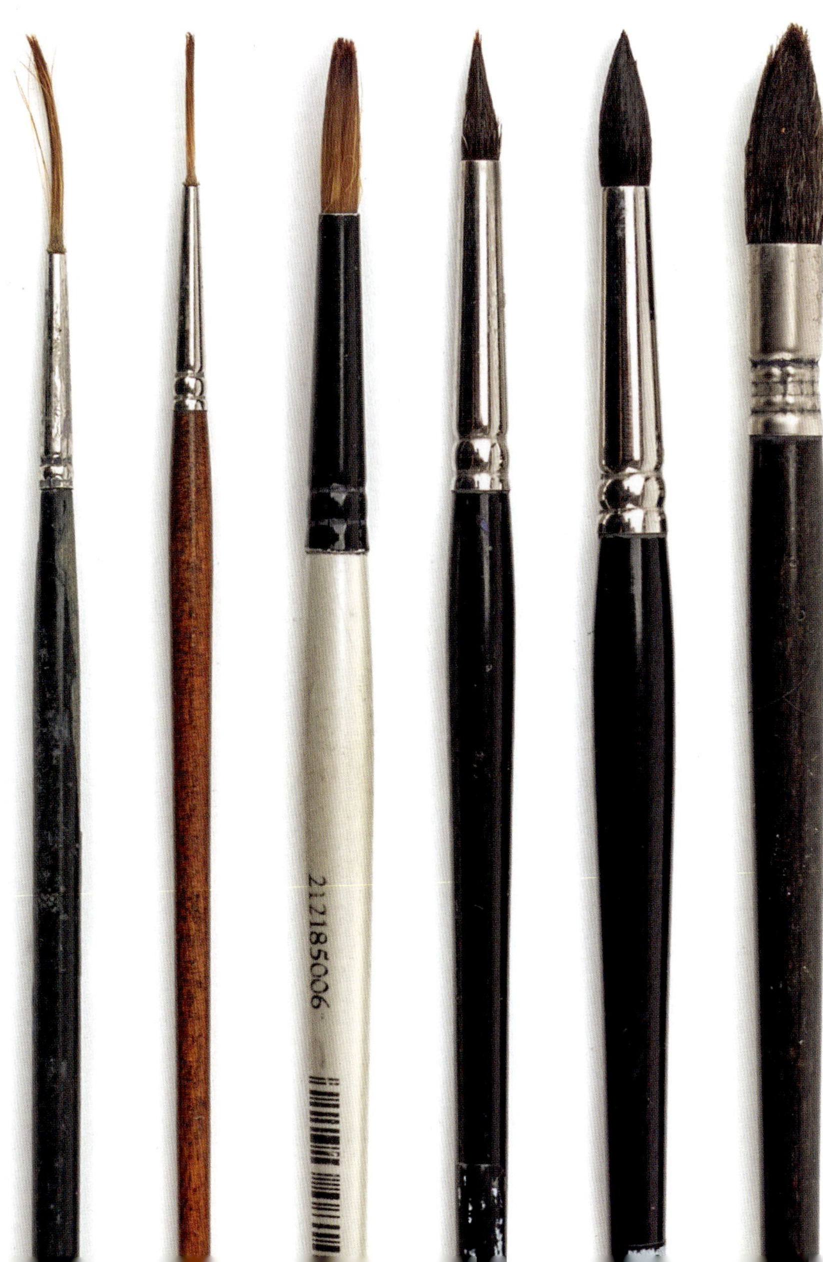

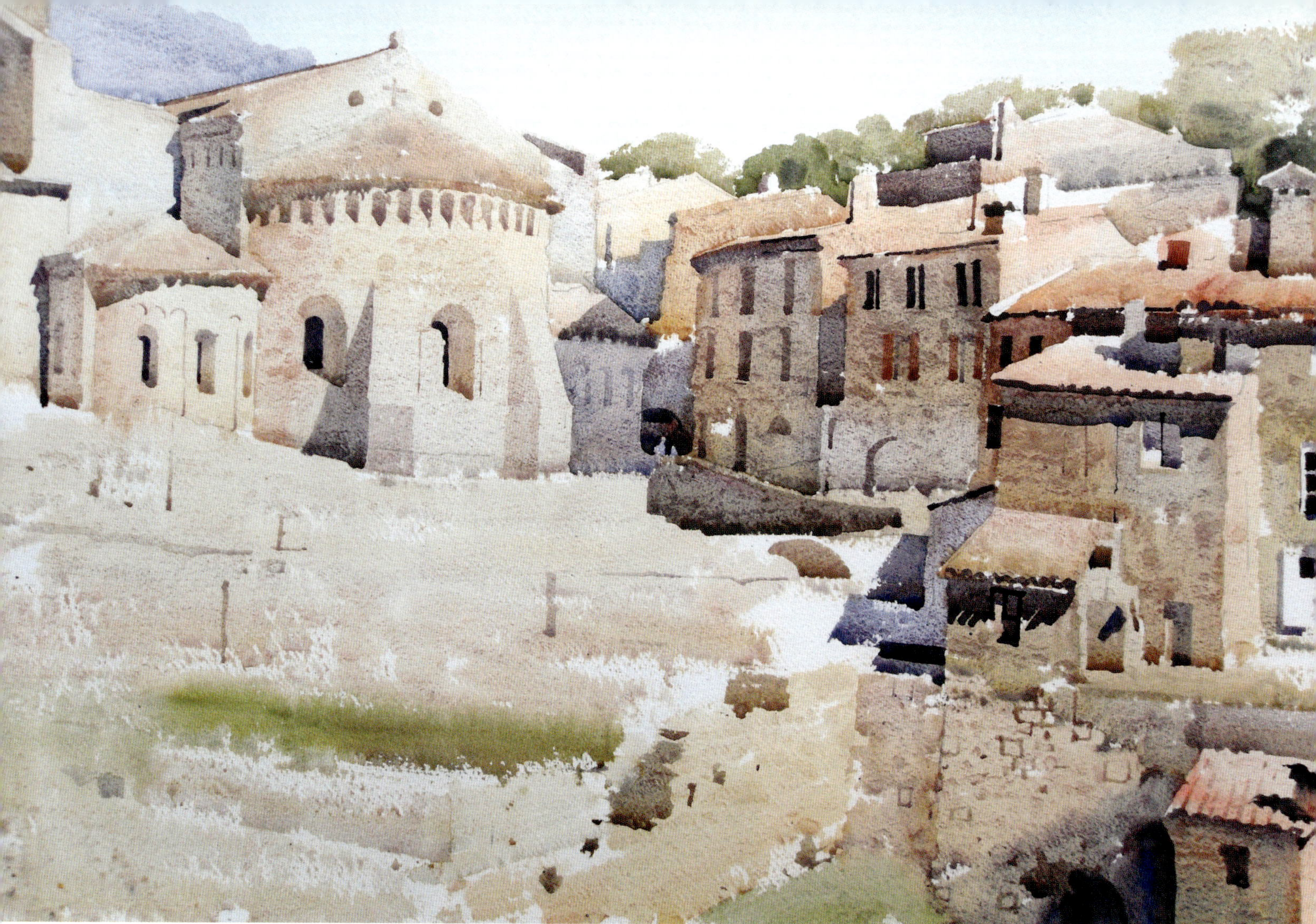

Pure watercolour techniques

It is essential to master these basic techniques, so that you can choose and apply the techniques that will work well with your chosen subject, the paper you are working on, and your own preferred approach.

Because of the range of marks we might wish to make, it is best to use an all-purpose paper that has a little tooth to practise these techniques. Take time to mix up plenty of the colour you want before you try each technique – but apply it as quickly as you can do carefully. Most areas of paint take seconds, not minutes, to put down.

How you use the techniques, and in what combination, is what will give you the freedom to paint whatever you wish.

Vue de Saint-Guilhem-le-Désert

56 × 38cm (22 × 15in) Millford 300gsm (140lb) Rough surface paper

This painting incorporates a variety of the techniques explained over the following pages, including washes and wet on dry.

Wet on dry flat wash

This technique is used for filling in shapes on the paper. It is a fundamental technique; used so broadly and so often, and in so many ways, that it is crucial to master.

Starting at the top of the area you want to fill, draw the loaded brush in a broad horizontal strokes across the paper. The wet paint will gather at the bottom of the brushstroke, forming a 'bead' at the working edge.

When you reach the edge of the area, take the brush downwards and begin working back the way you came, overlapping the previous stroke and drawing the bead along so the colour flows together.

Foundations

- Set up properly. All wash techniques rely on the paper being tilted at a slight angle so the wet paint (or water) forms a slight bead at the bottom of each horizontal brushstroke.
- Don't rush: work steadily, and reload as necessary.
- Always work at the working (bottom) edge of the wash.
- Work from the top of the shape to the bottom.
- For crisp edges, allow the wash to dry before moving on to an adjacent area – or leave a thin gap of dry paper between the areas.

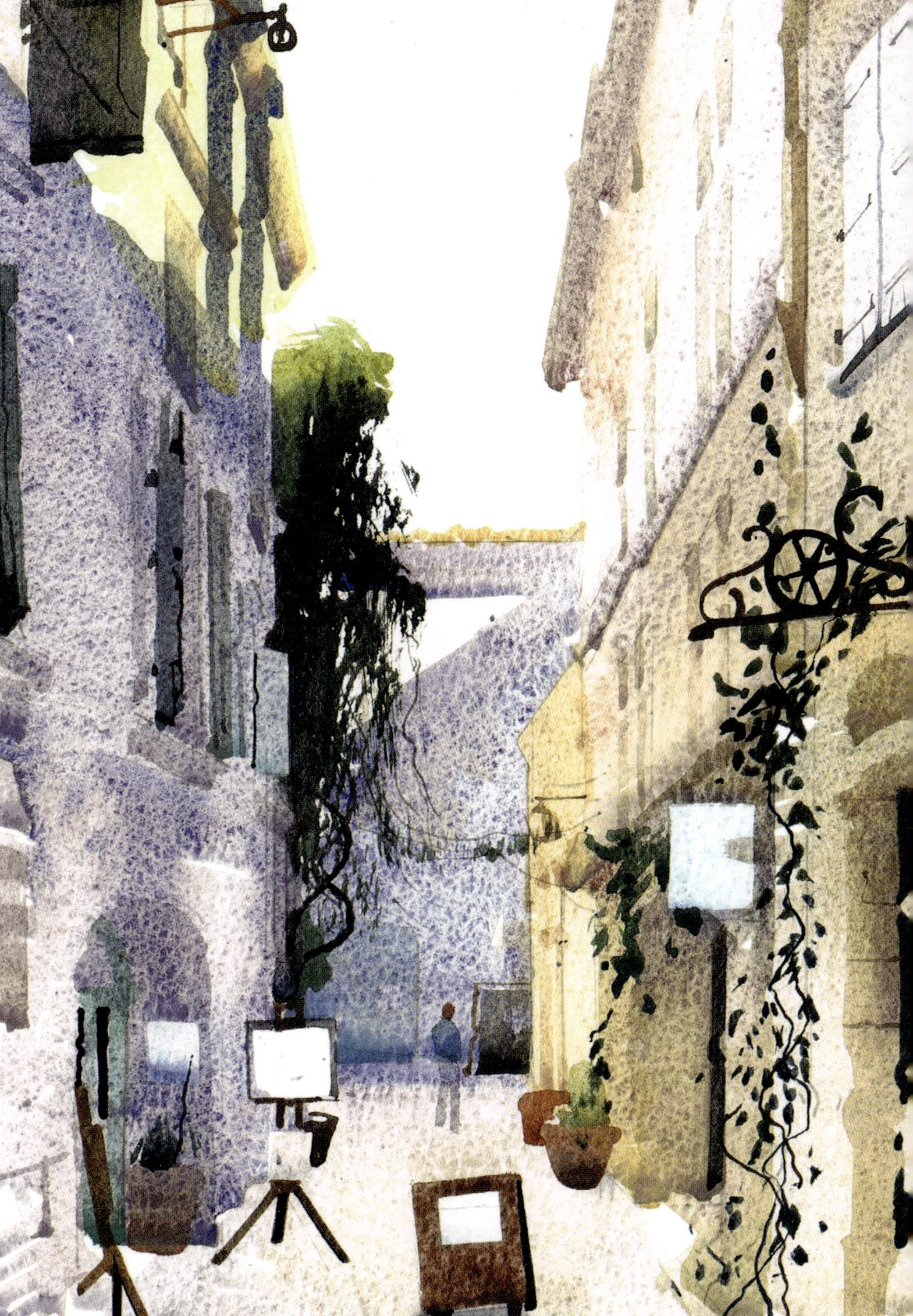

Pézenas Galerie Poullis

18 × 28cm (7 × 11in) Bockingford 300gsm (140lb) Rough surface paper

In this view of my old gallery there is a lot of reflected light and shadows. It was important to retain crisp edges and contrast, so I divided up the picture by only applying washes next to areas that had dried properly.

Graduated washes

Graduated washes are a group of related techniques that all involve moving from one colour or tone to another by working down the paper. As with the flat wash, starting at the top of the area, you draw the brush across the surface of the paper to lay in a broad horizontal brushstroke, then lift the brush away and repeat a little lower down, picking up the bead each time.

The difference between a flat and graduated wash comes from how you load your brush. As you progress, you can load your brush with more water, more paint, or another colour, as you require for the effect you want to achieve.

Graduated wash: colour to paper

Mix up the colour then, working from top to bottom, apply the wash while adding more and more water as you progress so the colour gradually blends away entirely to clean paper. An extremely useful technique for sky and water.

Reverse graduated wash

This is worked in an identical way as colour to paper, except that instead of adding more water as you descend, you start with a brush loaded with pure water and gradually add more pigment as you progress. As with the previous technique, this is especially useful for sky and creating space.

Graduated wash from one colour to another

With this variation you start with one colour, and instead of adding water as you progress, you begin to add more of the secondary colour.

This is the most useful variation on the technique on any scale, and has a wide variety of applications for any subject. It can be used in a landscape to create depth, for example, with cobalt blue in the distance blending smoothly into a warmer colour in the foreground.

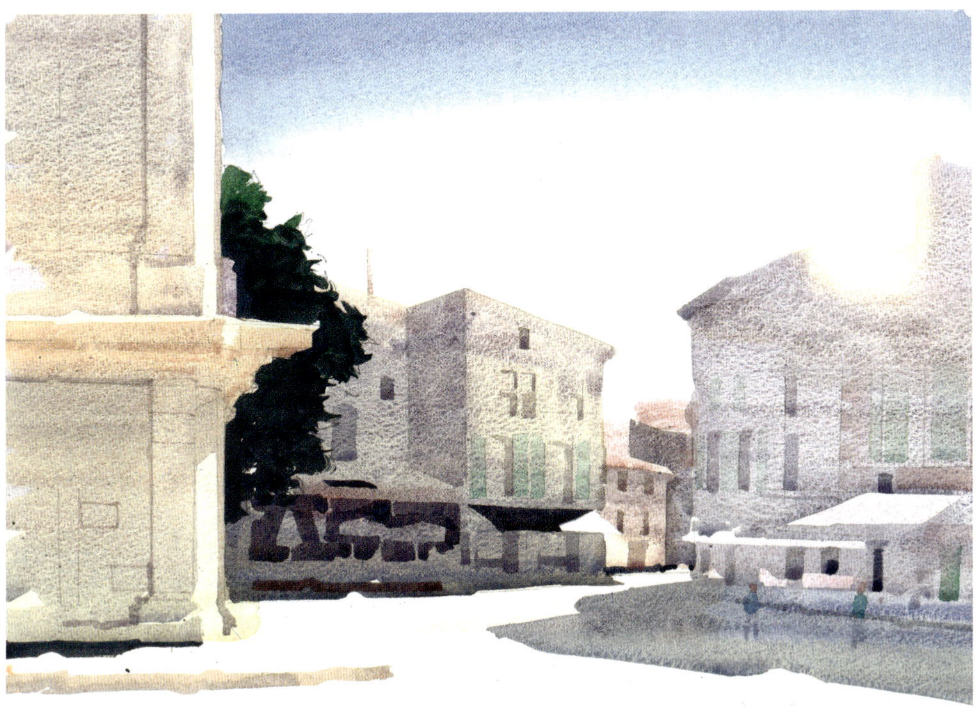

Pézenas

38 × 28cm (15 × 11in) Millford 300gsm (140lb) Rough surface paper

The sky here is a good example of a graduated wash that starts relatively dark and then becomes lighter towards the horizon. Note how this helps both to silhouette and define the edges of the buildings – but also assists in selling the idea of bright sunlight from the right-hand side.

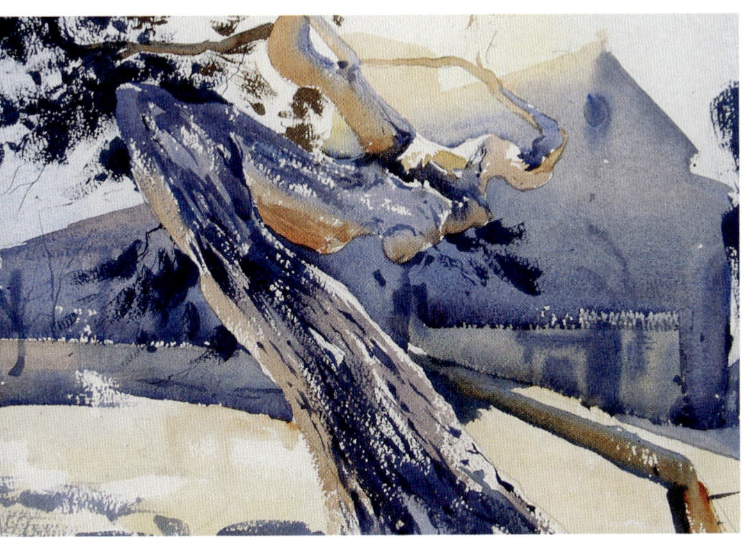

Conas

56 × 38cm (22 × 15in) Saunders Waterford 300gsm (140lb) Rough surface paper

In this complex painting it was important to divide up the picture into manageable shapes. Graduated washes were used to create the effect of sunlight, while darker areas of dry brush provided important contrast in tone and texture.

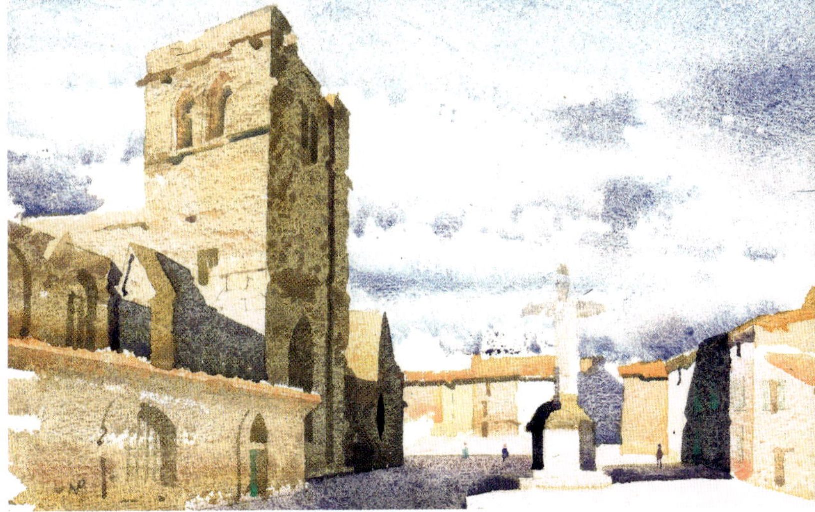

Tourbes

23 × 18cm (9 × 7in) Millford 300gsm (140lb) Rough surface paper

A graduated wash using both dry brush and wet in wet techniques was used for the sky here, while wet on dry washes were used for much of the rest of the painting. The background used a vaguer approach of wet against wet and this helped create distance.

Using a dry brush

This technique involves creating a thick mix of paint, loading the brush, then squeezing out the majority of the paint. Working lightly and quickly, you then drag the side of the brush across the paper to pick up the tooth of the paper.

This can be highly effective in creating texture, especially on a Rough surface – and is even more striking if the paper is hard-sized.

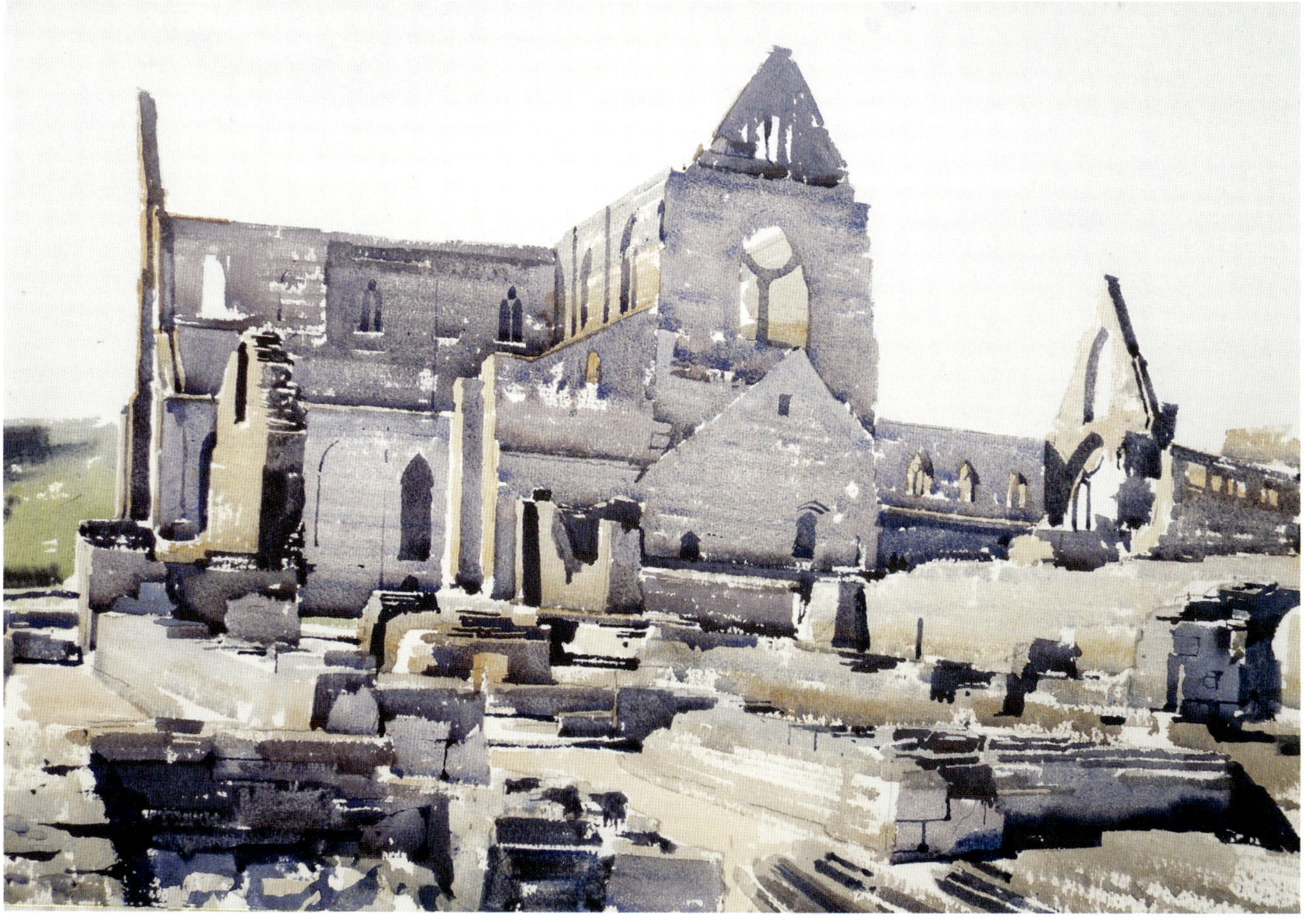

Tintern Abbey

56 × 38cm (22 × 15in) Saunders Waterford 300gsm (140lb) Rough surface paper

I had a definite aim for the surface effect in this painting, and used dry brush techniques alongside pigments that would create a 'granular' stony effect.

Building skills

- The dry brush technique is usually executed with the side of a brush, but you can use the point, too.
- Dry brushed broken lines can also be created by applying a very thick mix with the point of a brush.

Lifting out

To lift out, you use a damp, stiff brush to gently rub an area of dry paint. This will reactivate the paint, which can then be dabbed lightly with tissue, lifting away the pigment from the area and leaving a space.

Lifting out can be used to lighten areas, to soften sharp edges, and it can be quite subtle. The soft edges it gives are ideal for creating rounded forms.

Building skills

- Experiment with your colours to see which are best suited to the technique. How easy watercolour paint is to lift depends on the gum arabic content of the paint – more gum makes lifting more difficult. When artists mixed their own paint, they could control the gum level and therefore how easy it would be to lift out.
- On lightweight and some types of heavier papers this technique can cause damage to the surface.
- The technique was used to great effect by the artist Russell Flint (1880–1969), in his romantic, sensuous figures.

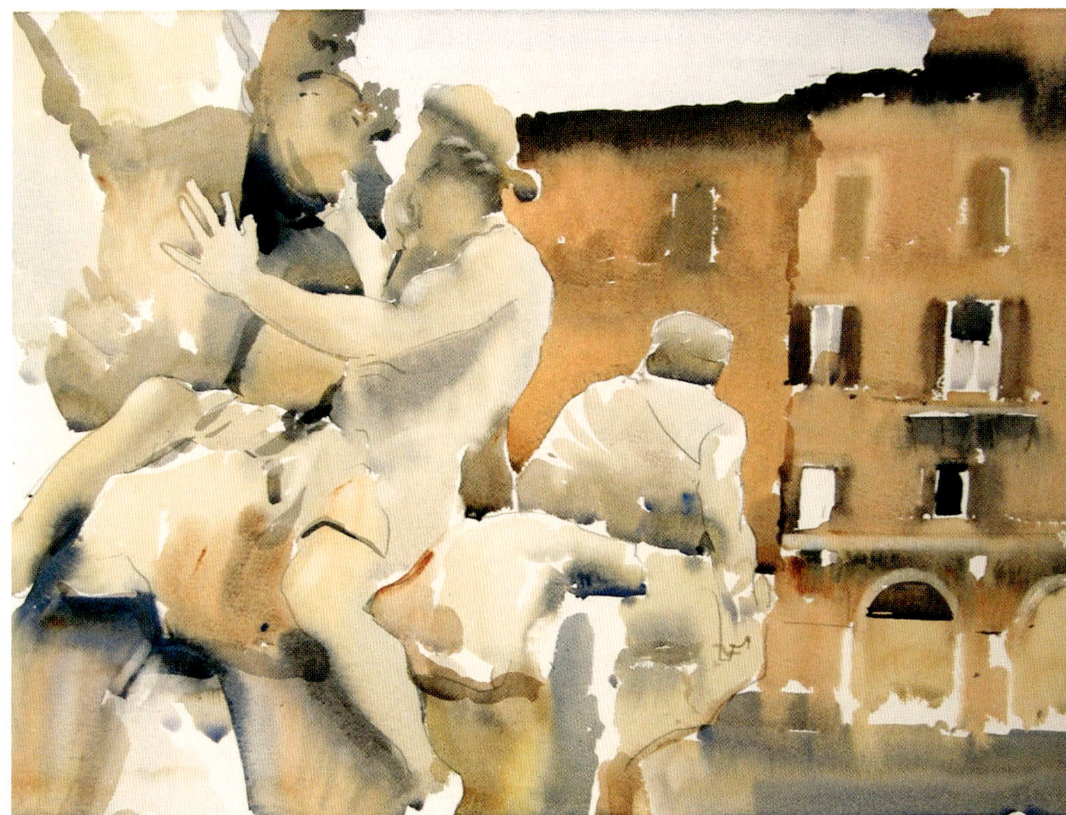

The Fountain of the Four Rivers

56 × 38cm (22 × 15in) Whatman 300gsm (140lb) Rough surface paper

The darker buildings behind this fountain, in Piazza Navona, Rome, helped to define the shapes of the sculpture. Form was given to the sculpture through the use of separated areas of graduated washes. Once dry, some paint was lifted out to add shaping, detail and contrast.

Wet in wet

On a wet area, add a thicker/stronger mix or colour – that colour will diffuse (spread out). The wetter the wash, the more diffusion there will be. For more control you can wait until the area is almost dry, but if the initial wash is too dry, nasty marks will appear. You therefore have a small window of opportunity.

The technique has to be done quickly to avoid 'treeing' – when a cauliflower-shaped mark appears as wet paint creeps into a semi-dry area.

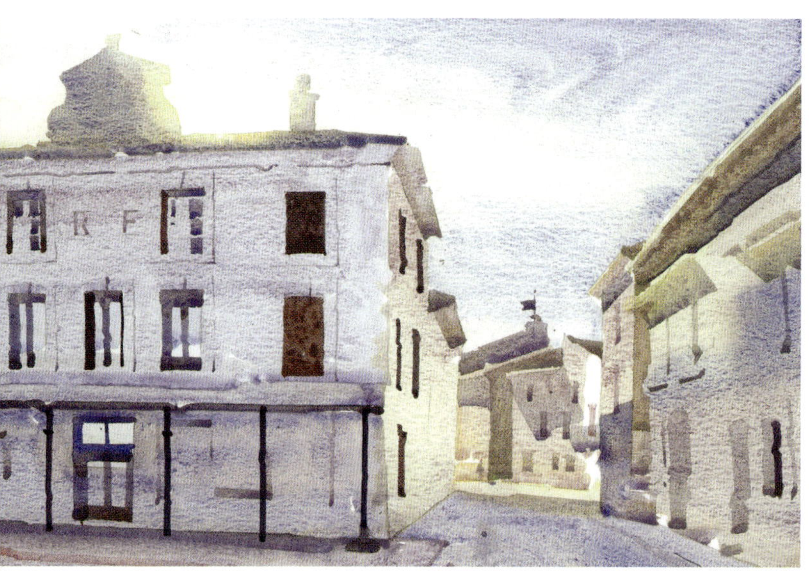

Pinet

30.5 × 25.5cm (12 × 10in) Hahnemühle 300gsm (140lb) Rough surface paper

This is technically quite a complicated painting, looking directly into the sun. As with all the paintings produced on the spot, I used several wash techniques. Wet in wet and graduated washes were used in the sky.

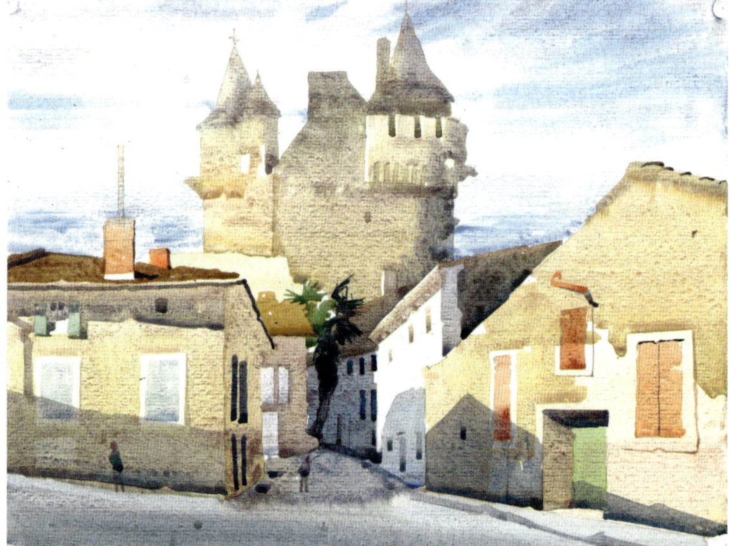

Margon

30.5 × 25.5cm (12 × 10in) Hahnemühle 300gsm (140lb) Not surface paper

Wet in wet was used for the sky. For more control over the marks made, I waited for the initial wash to approach dryness then used a small brush to apply a not-too-wet paint mix. With this approach, you have more control but less time to work.

Building skills

- Wet in wet can be used to add colour variation in a flat or graduated wash – colour variations on a wall for example.
- Treeing can be avoided by working on a slight incline, allowing the paint to dry at the same rate and lifting out excess water at the bottom of the wash with a tissue. Some papers will tree more than others.

- To add a shape with a soft edge, such as a cloud in a sky, allow the initial wash to dry then wet the surface with clean water and drop pigment into this new layer.
- Do not touch the paper to judge how dry a wash is. Instead, look at the paper from an angle so you can see the sun reflected in the gloss – this will show you how wet it is.

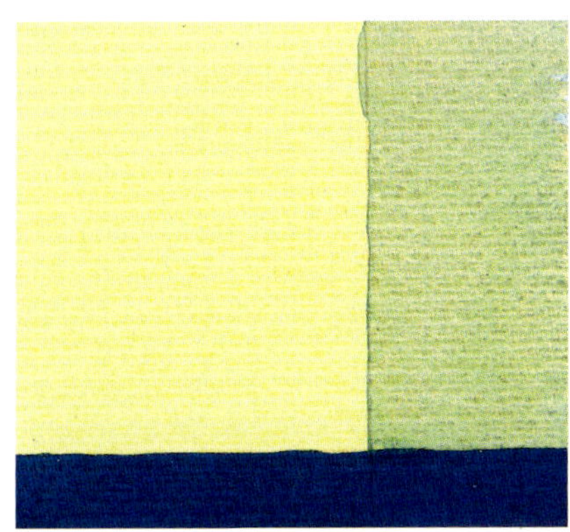

Wet over dry: overpainting and underpainting

When painting on top of a wash, any subsequent layer of paint strong enough to hide the undercoat is 'overpainting'. Where the subsequent layer is light enough – that is, transparent enough to allow the undercoat to shine through – we are using 'underpainting'.

Overpainting is typically used to paint around a lighter shape. Where using underpainting effectively, the second coat is light enough so that the initial layer (or undercoat) shines through. This is especially useful for painting areas of reflected light on, for example, the side of a building.

Building skills

- In oils or acrylics, a lighter shape can just be applied on top of a darker tone – in watercolour, we need to reserve the light colour for the whole painting.

- The dark side of a building (for example) can be painted in a number of ways: directly, with a mix that matches what you see; or indirectly using a bluish-grey wash over the top of the underpainting of 'local colour', as shown here.

- Overpainting is associated with a direct approach and the use of underpainting with an indirect approach (see page 36).

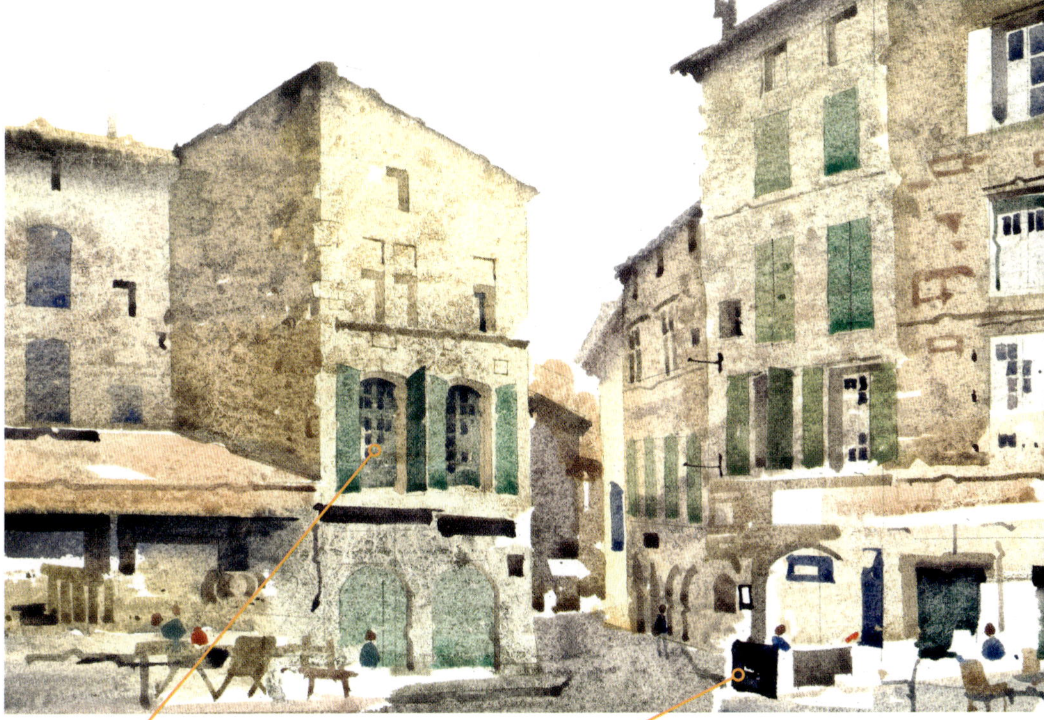

Underpainting

Here, a dilute mix of cobalt blue, raw sienna and potters pink has been painted over the neutral brown of the wall to suggest the shadow of a window – note that the texture of the initial layer is visible through the wash.

Overpainting

In contrast, here a stronger mix of blue has been applied, which completely obscures the layer beneath.

Pézenas
38 × 28cm (15 × 11in) Arches 640gsm (300lb) Rough surface paper

Granulation

While not a technique *per se*, the tendency of some watercolour paints to granulate when mixed is one of the many attractive features of the medium, and can be useful in the expression of texture. Granulation occurs when metals in the pigment form a precipitate, so the pigment particles clump together. These heavier clumps of pigment sink into the recesses of the paper surface, creating a grainy appearance.

Granulation will form on the paper surface with the right mix and a slow drying time; and the results can be controlled by varying the thickness of the mix used and how long the granulation is left to form. As to which colours create these effects it is worth experimenting, but an established mix would be cadmium red and French ultramarine, as shown in the example below.

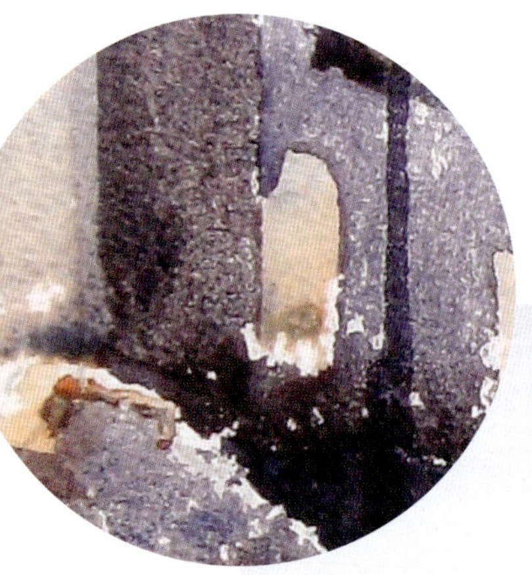

Here, French ultramarine has reacted with cadmium red to create a precipitate that looks granular.

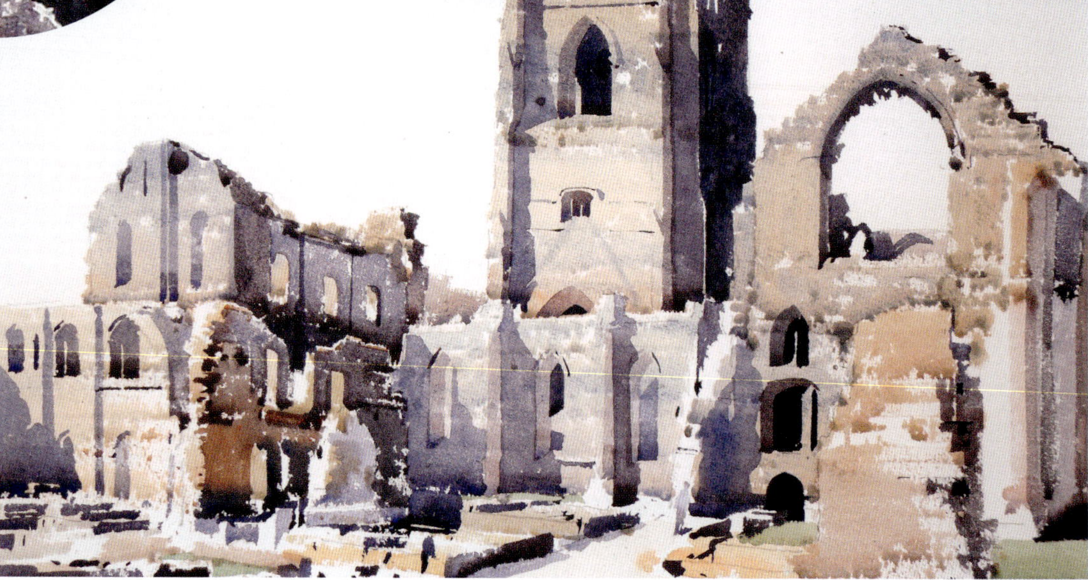

Fountains Abbey
56 × 38cm (22 × 15in) Saunders Waterford 300gsm (140lb) Rough surface paper
Granulation was extremely useful here as it suited the nature of this subject, the ruined abbey in Yorkshire, UK.

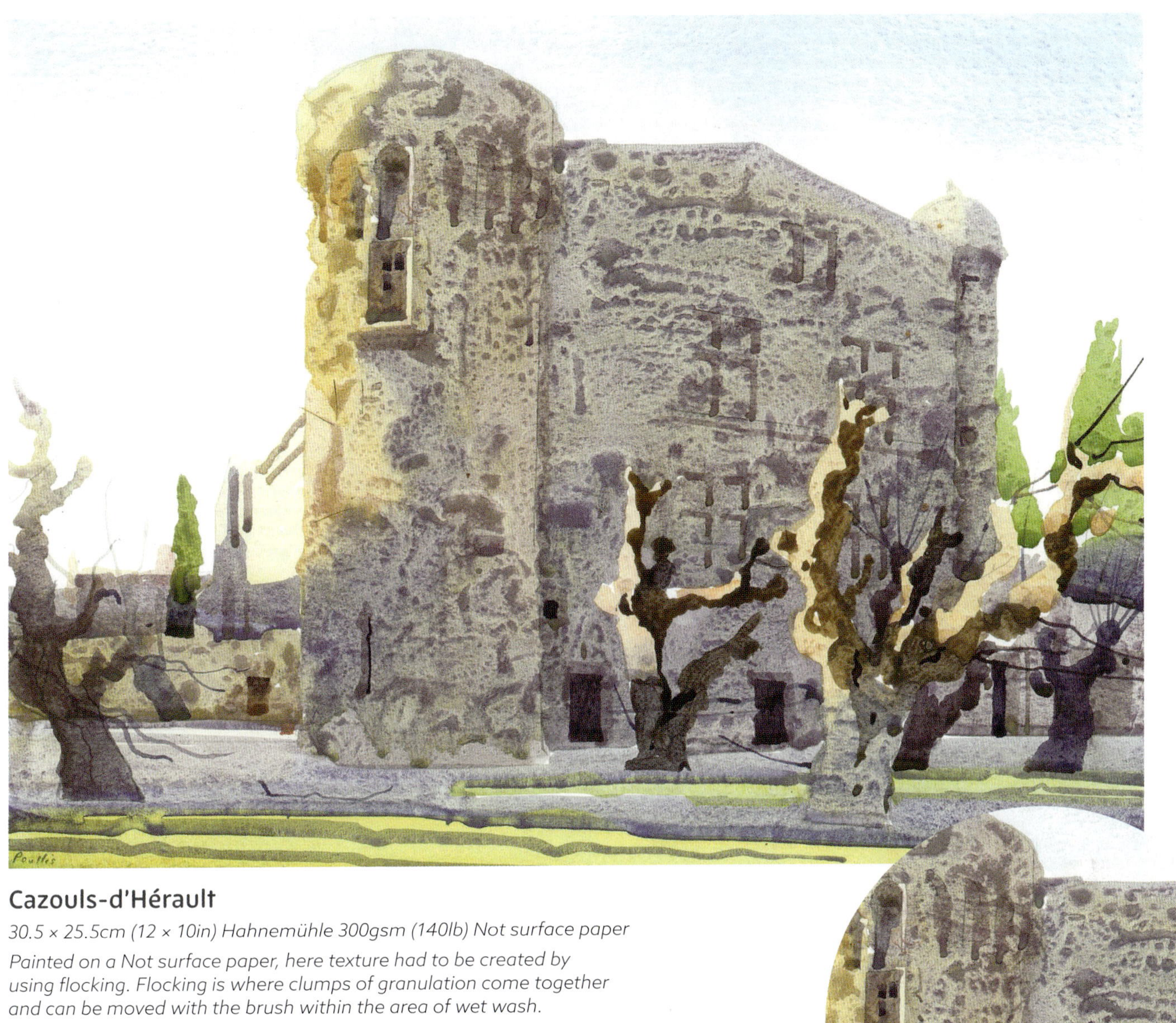

Cazouls-d'Hérault

30.5 × 25.5cm (12 × 10in) Hahnemühle 300gsm (140lb) Not surface paper

Painted on a Not surface paper, here texture had to be created by using flocking. Flocking is where clumps of granulation come together and can be moved with the brush within the area of wet wash.

Applying and combining the techniques

A major part of mastering techniques is learning how to apply them to our subject, and this is where the biggest challenge begins. Painting while respecting the character of the paper is an important aspect of this and will dramatically affect the look of the finished painting. For example, dry brushing (see page 28) is especially useful in the expression of texture and foliage, but for obvious reasons will only work on paper with tooth. To attempt this technique on HP paper or smooth paper will result in a smudge or smear.

Any technique can become limiting if you exclude all others. Use a range determined by the subject and what you wish to say about it. It is your judgement of how and when to use each technique that will make your picture distinctly your own.

Bolton Abbey
56 × 38cm (22 × 15in) Saunders Waterford 300gsm (140lb) Rough surface paper

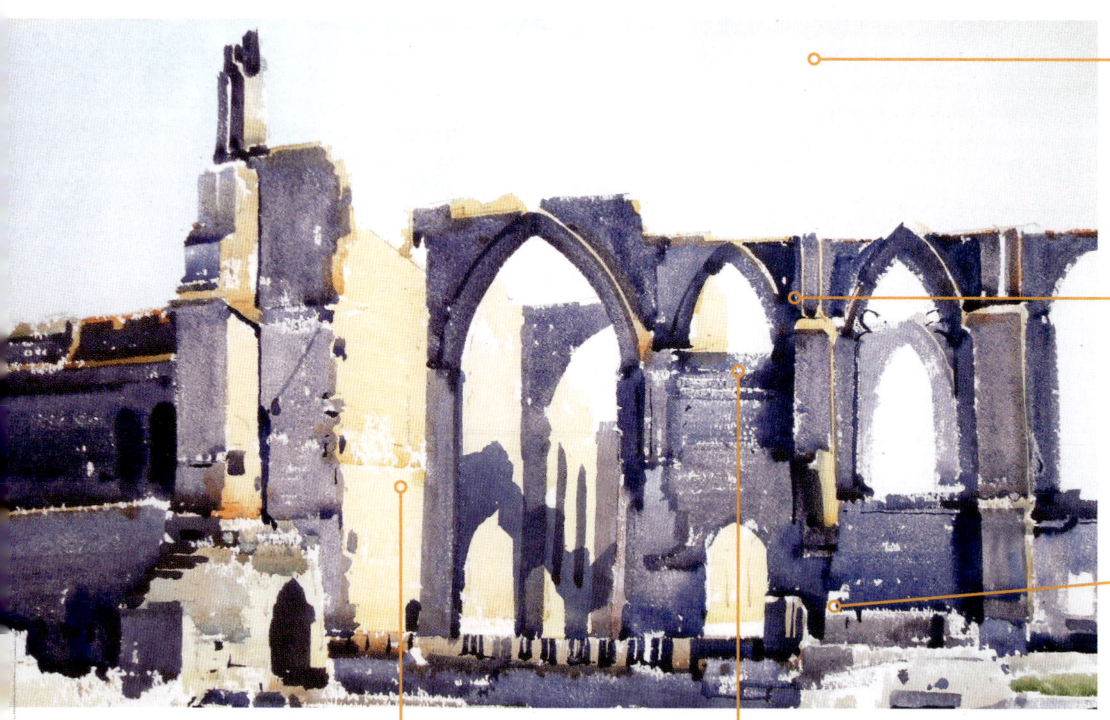

Graduated wash
The sky was painted with a pale wash that fades to clean paper. The subtle, uncomplicated sky helps to set off the complex subject.

Overpainting
Finer details are added over the top of dry washes to add shading and crisp shapes.

Clean paper
The brightest highlights you can achieve are the white of the paper – so sometimes the right technique to apply is nothing at all.

Wet on dry flat wash
The bright, fresh appearance of the finished painting relies on making clear statements early on, then leaving them untouched.

Dry brush
Texture, rather than details, is used to describe these crumbling walls. The overall effect is more important than showing the exact number of stones and where they are.

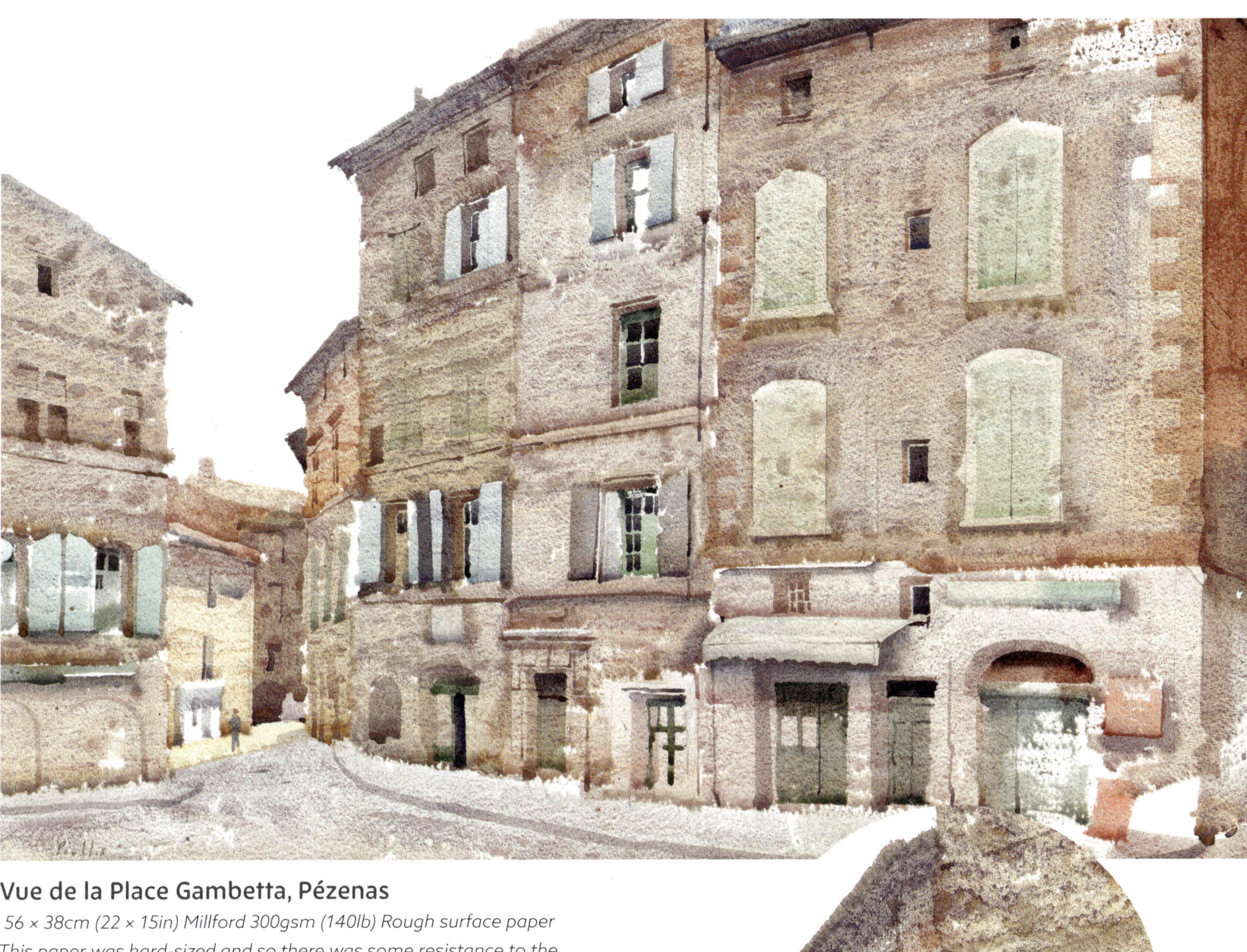

Vue de la Place Gambetta, Pézenas

56 × 38cm (22 × 15in) Millford 300gsm (140lb) Rough surface paper

This paper was hard-sized and so there was some resistance to the paint going down. This made smooth washes difficult but had the advantage of expressing texture – as you can see from the detail.

Sometimes the surface on an older paper will lose its resistance but you can make the paint sit on the surface by adding a little gum arabic to your water.

Direct and indirect painting

Broadly speaking, there are two ways of painting with watercolour: direct and indirect. Working in an indirect way is where colour and tone are built up in translucent layers, allowing each to dry before moving on to the next; while a direct way of working means mixing colours in your palette and laying them down in a single layer on virgin paper to achieve the desired colour in one go.

Fundamentally, both approaches are put down the same way and use the same techniques and types of washes, but they result in different finishes that affect the experience of the viewer. Direct painting tends to give brighter, less subtle results, with greater depth to the colour, while the indirect approach allows a more subtle range of effects as colour shines through subsequent layers. The method you choose will affect the 'feel' of a painting – and hence its atmosphere.

Which approach to use?

The approach you use will depend on what you wish to do with the subject – and what the subject demands. In the top and middle images shown opposite, one method is dominant, while the bottom image shows both used in harmony.

Both approaches are useful, and happily, the two can also be used in combination. In fact, most of the paintings in this book were painted using a combination of approaches.

Foundations

- A direct approach can give the work great impact and freshness, and will result in a more painterly and spontaneous artwork.
- The indirect approach allows for subtlety and nuance, and rewards the use of an underpainting.
- The indirect method makes use of underpainting (see page 31). As an example, a layer applied over the light side of a wall or under a roof can create a shadow: just make sure the second coat is thin enough for the undercoat to shine through.
- Some effects are only achievable with a direct approach; others only with an indirect approach.

Opposite, top to bottom:

Direct – Puissalicon

28 × 18cm (11 × 7in) Saunders Waterford 300gsm (140lb) Rough surface paper

Strong, bold colour mixes contrast well with clean areas of white paper – and are a feature of this style of painting.

Indirect – Marseillan

28 × 18cm (11 × 7in) Fabriano Artistica 140gsm (90lb) Not surface paper

The indirect painting approach lends itself to ethereal mists and subtle lighting effects, as you can build the tone and colour gradually in a considered manner.

Combination – Colyton

28 × 18cm (11 × 7in) Saunders Waterford 300gsm (140lb) Rough surface paper

In this example, direct painting has been used for the bolder foreground areas, while indirect painting has been used in the background – notably for the church tower.

The first warm layer of the tower was painted directly over the sky, creating natural recession. Once dry, a second cooler, bluer layer was painted over the stone to create shadow.

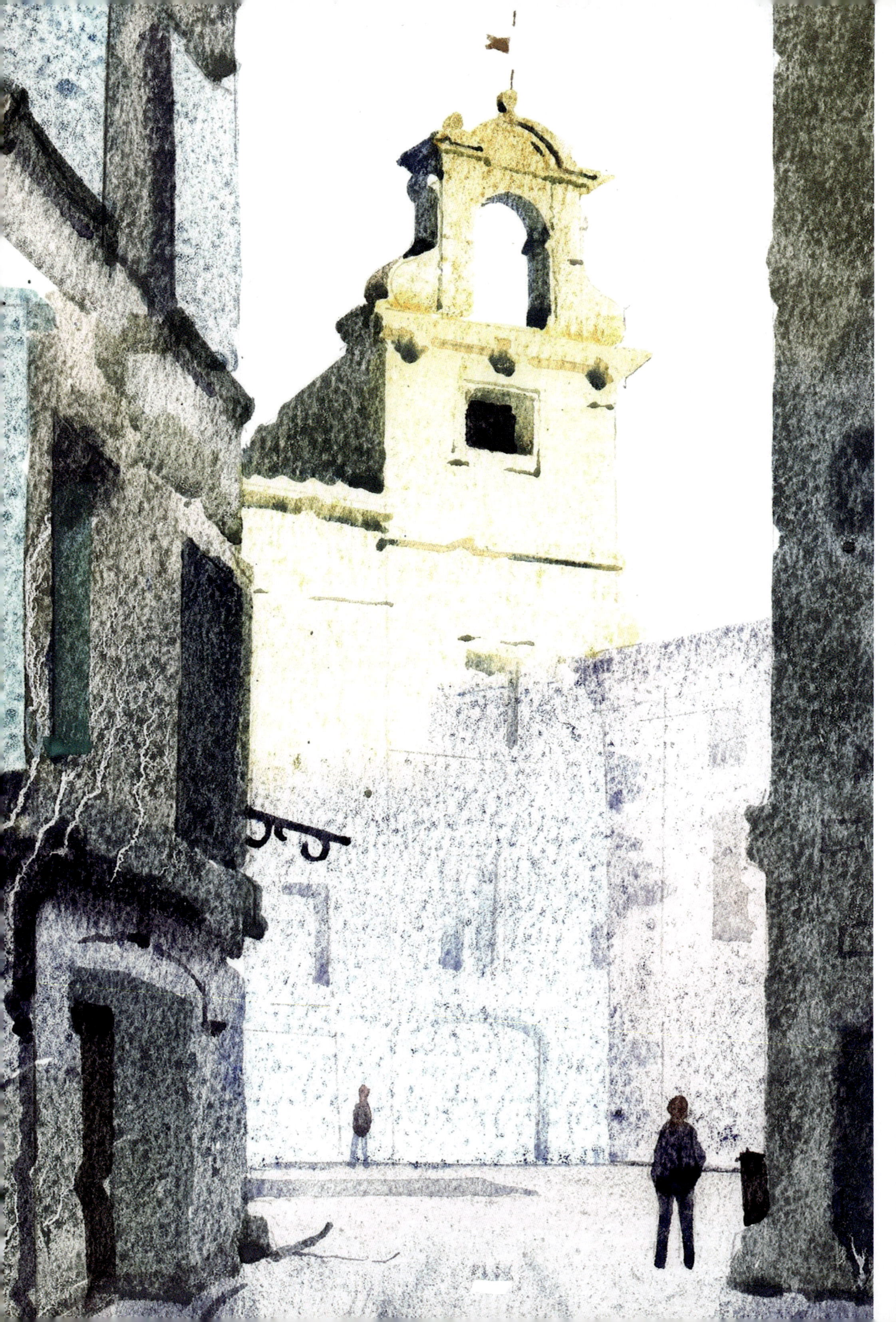

Choosing a subject

The first stage of a painting is the choice of subject. Much of a subject is its setting – the surroundings you find yourself in – and it is helpful to use that in the painting. However, while it is important to choose something that is simple (at least to begin with), it must have enough content to keep you interested while painting it. However much we might enjoy being in the setting, paintings evidently need content as well as a setting.

   The choice of a subject can affect your odds on producing a successful painting. In this chapter we will look at approaches and ideas of how to communicate something about the subject by ensuring the picture-making components come together in a coherent way.

Opposite

Tower Pézenas
18 × 28cm (7 × 11in) Bockingford 300gsm (140lb) Rough surface paper

The detail and shape of the iconic feature of the tower is the focus of this painting, and the natural composition leads to it.

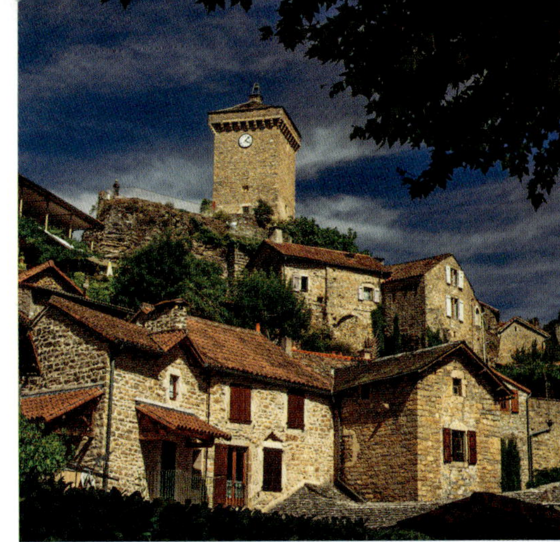

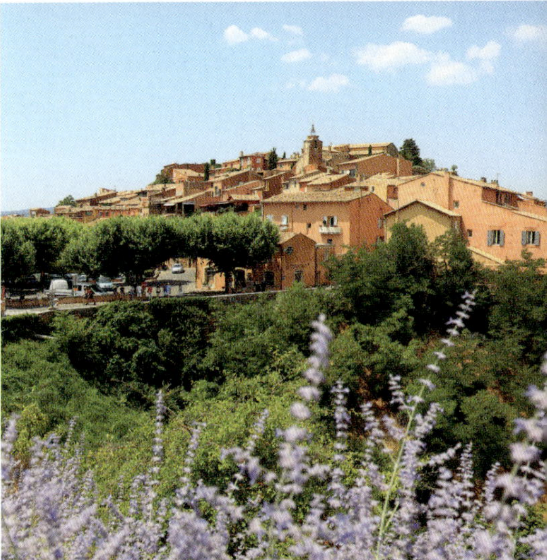

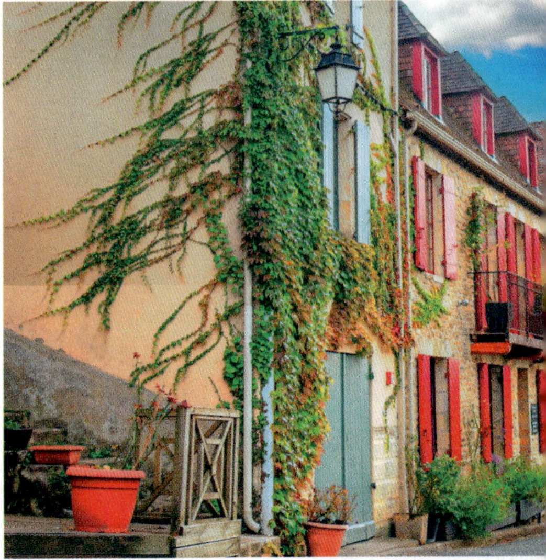

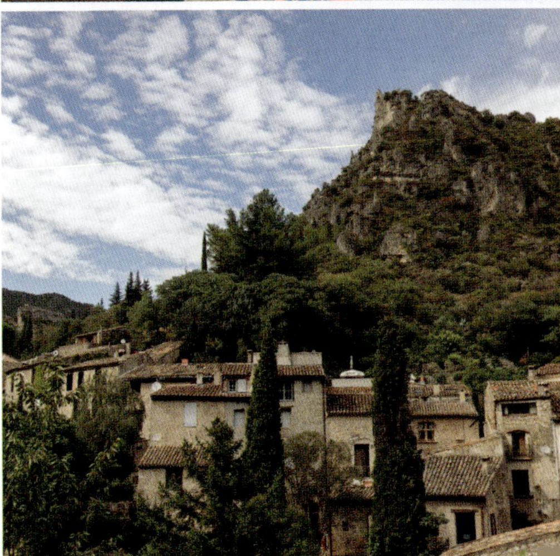

What makes an architectural scene?

In landscape or marine art, shapes are often vague, and because the objective is usually to capture a sense of depth, light and atmosphere rather than detail, precision is not as critical as it is in architectural art. Landscapes thus form a more general interest 'all-over' type of composition, whereas architectural art usually has a specific focal subject.

Architectural art also differs from portraiture – there we deal less with depth and atmosphere and more with the character of the sitter and so details can become more important again. To accurately capture the geometric forms with which we are confronted, perspective, which we look at on pages 64–83, becomes an essential tool.

For successful paintings of architecture, we need to combine all the elements needed in landscape with some of the accuracy and sensitivity to character of portraiture. All of these art forms require specific skills – and happily, there is a great deal of crossover between landscape, marine art and architectural art: some of the elements overlap, as do the experiences of painting each; as you can see in the example below.

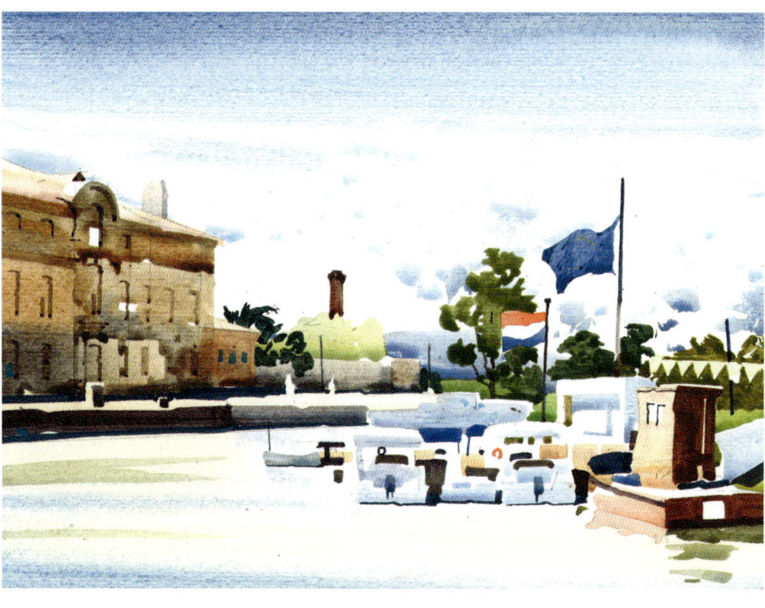

Basin d'Agde

30.5 × 25.5cm (12 × 10in)

Hahnemühle 300gsm (140lb) Rough surface paper

This painting combines landscape, architecture and marine art – these closely related genres often overlap fluidly.

The boats are the focal features here due to their position, but the architecture provides a crucial element to the landscape setting. The distribution of detail across the painting is therefore quite even and ensures the buildings do not become mere supporting actors.

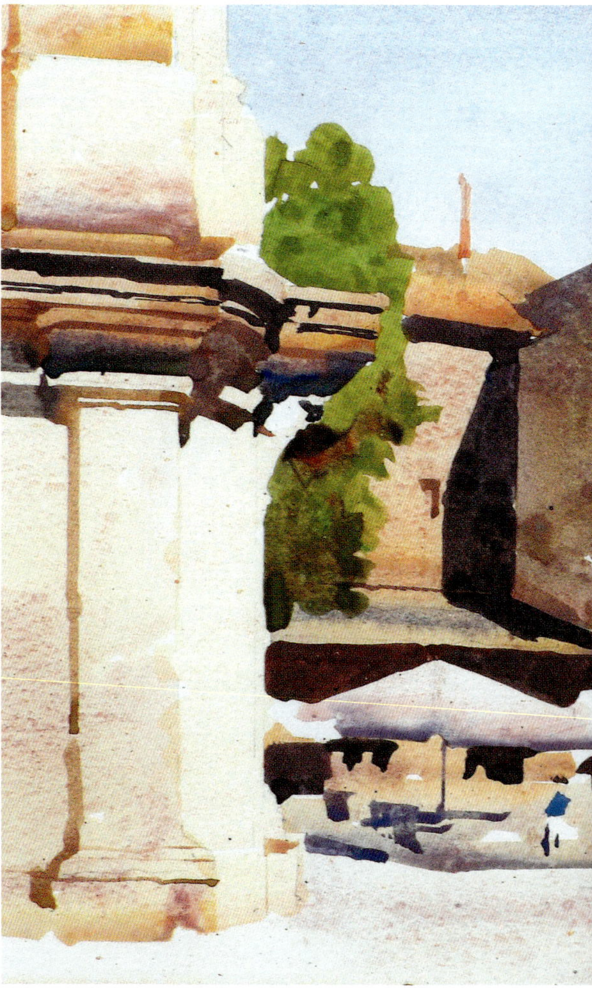

The importance of lighting

A clear light direction will give form to the subject, no matter what that is, but it's a particularly important consideration for architectural work. Look for a subject with a clear light side and a side in shadow.

You may find a subject or setting that seems promising but is lacking something – if possible, come back at another time of day or time of year to see how the light changes it.

Foundations

- Ordinary subject matter can become great in the right lighting.
- A great subject can become dead and flat in poor lighting, so it is worthwhile getting to know potential subject matter.

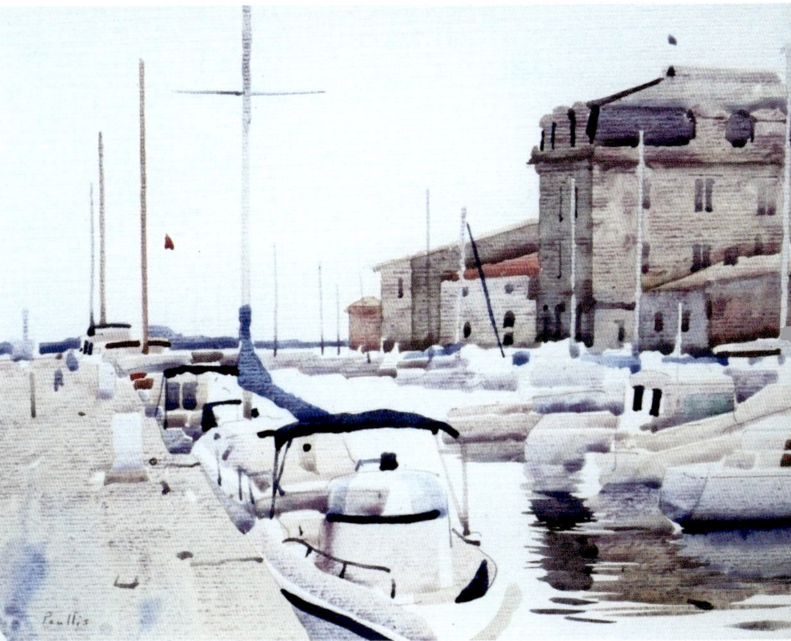

Grey Morning, Marseillan

30.5 × 25.5cm (12 × 10in) Hahnemühle 300gsm (140lb) Rough surface paper

Even in poor lighting there can be enough contrast within the subject for the painting to work. In these instances, the design becomes very important.

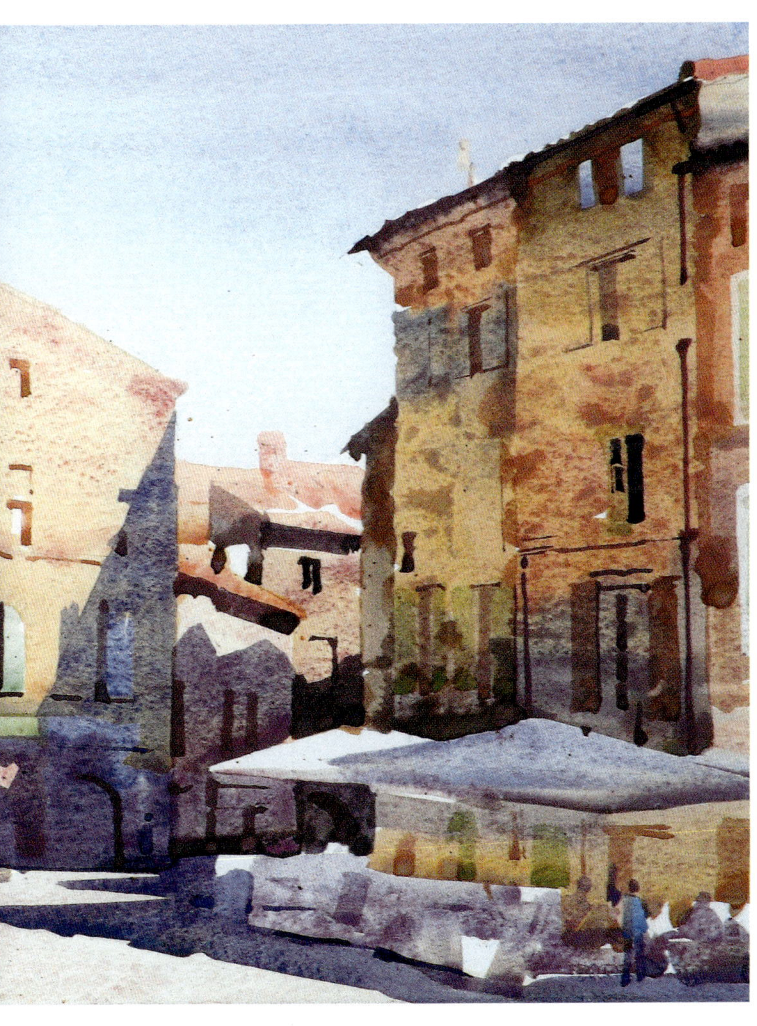

Pézenas Centre

38 × 28cm (15 × 11in) Saunders Waterford 300gsm (140lb) HP surface paper

This scene presented a very natural composition with all-over interest and pleasing areas of contrast. The lighting helps to draw the eye towards the central area, where there is a nice contrast formed by the shadow on the surface of the building facing us.

This page

Self-portrait in Collioure

25.5 × 25.5cm (10 × 10in) Bockingford 300gsm (140lb) Not surface paper

The focus of this piece is the silhouetted reflection of me painting in Collioure – but it's clearly still firmly in the architectural genre, rather than portraiture or figurative work.

The painting came about as I was trying to find an original view of the much painted and well-known tower of the church whose reflection can also be seen in the window.

Opposite, top

View over Montagnac with Building Site

30.5 × 25.5cm (12 × 10in) Hahnemühle 300gsm (140lb) Rough surface paper

This painting has areas that were clearly defined as foreground, middle distance and distance, creating a distinctly layered result.

Natural variations and contrasting colours proved very useful tools here. Aerial perspective also helped in defining the different areas and in creating depth.

The distribution of detail and balance is crucial in getting this type of composition to work. Dividing the picture up into its different areas provides the painting with a clear design.

Opposite, bottom

Ladder in the Library RAC

56 × 38cm (22 × 15in) Millford 300gsm (140lb) Rough surface paper

The ladder provided a focus in this otherwise general 'all-over' type composition. The various features and textures provide important points of contrast and interest.

In this interior space (see page 95) both artificial light and reflected sunlight from buildings on the opposite side of the street were present.

Subject matter

Some compositions aim for general interest, with details dotted throughout to encourage the eye to roam the painting. Others are more focused on a particular area of interest with space around – perhaps with little leads up to the subject.

I find it helpful to find natural compositions that do not require 'tinkering with' or too much artistic interpretation or invention. Ideally, you will find a subject that has some sort of lead into it, a natural line that helps the viewer arrive at whatever the subject or area of interest is.

Unusual subject matter

Good subject matter should not be confused with aesthetically pleasing or beautiful subject matter. The view of the building site opposite may not be conventionally beautiful but it is nonetheless interesting. Although of course highly subjective, experience will teach you that a lot of subject matter falls into this category.

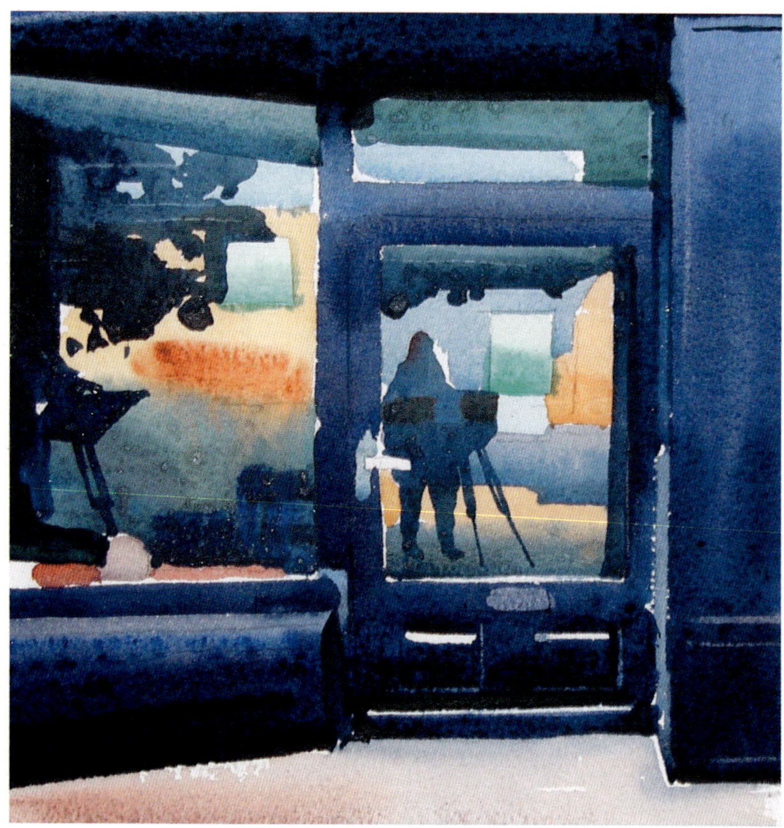

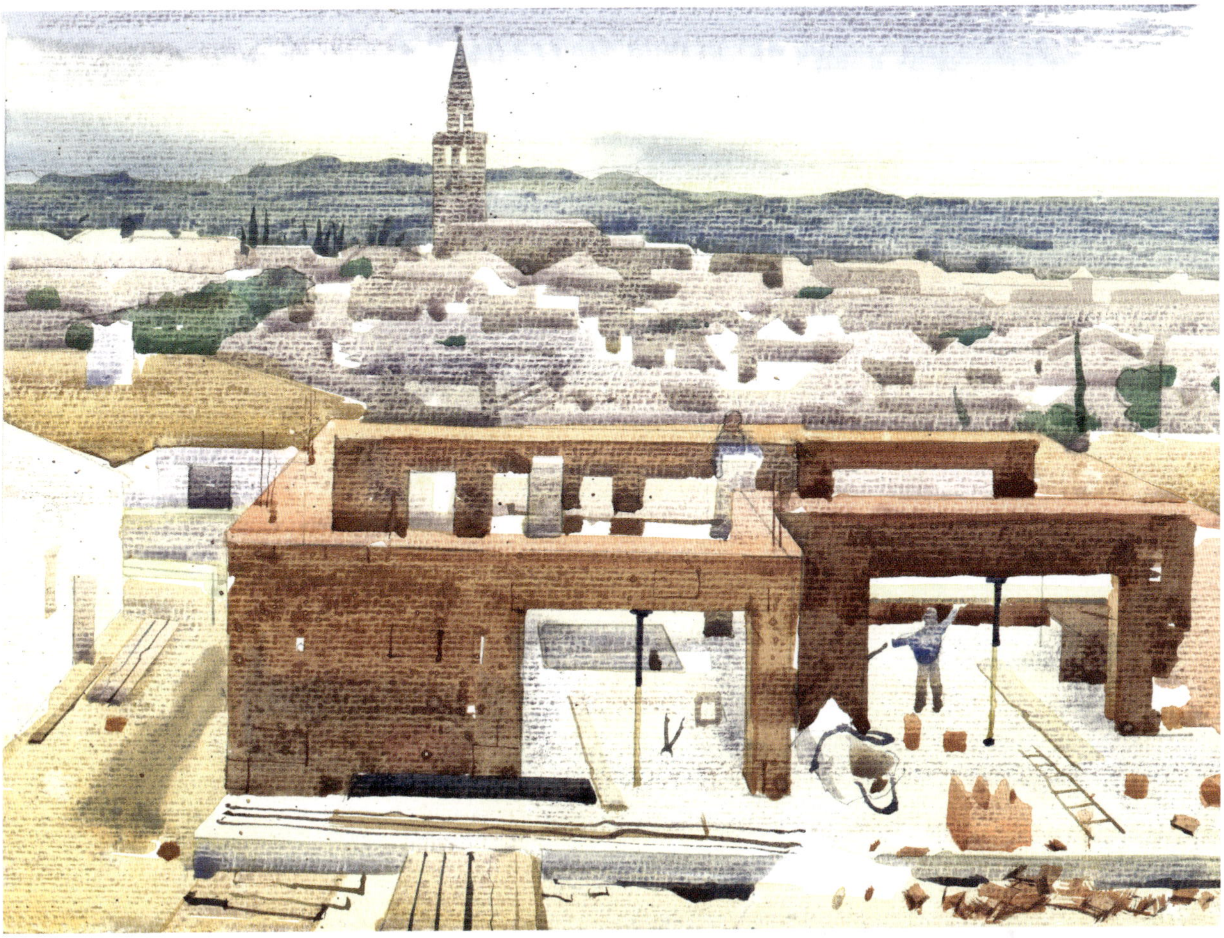

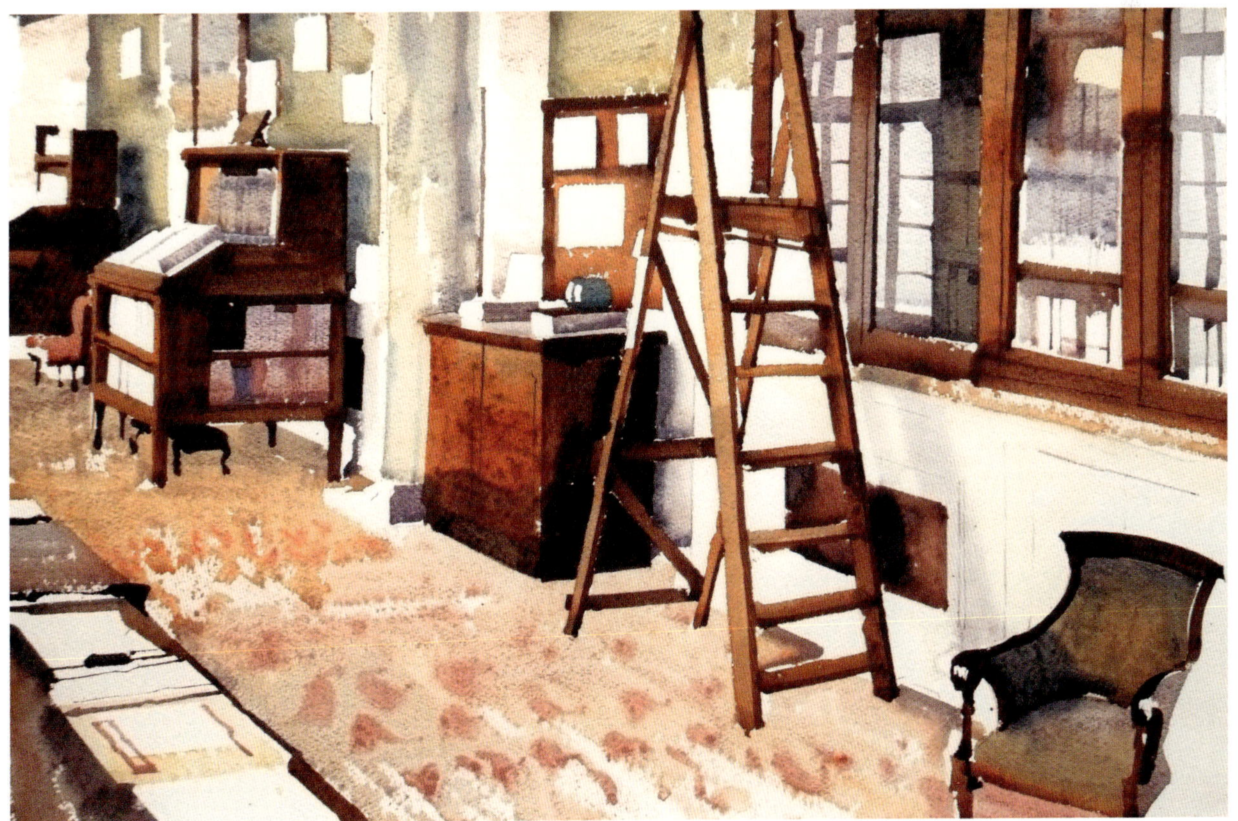

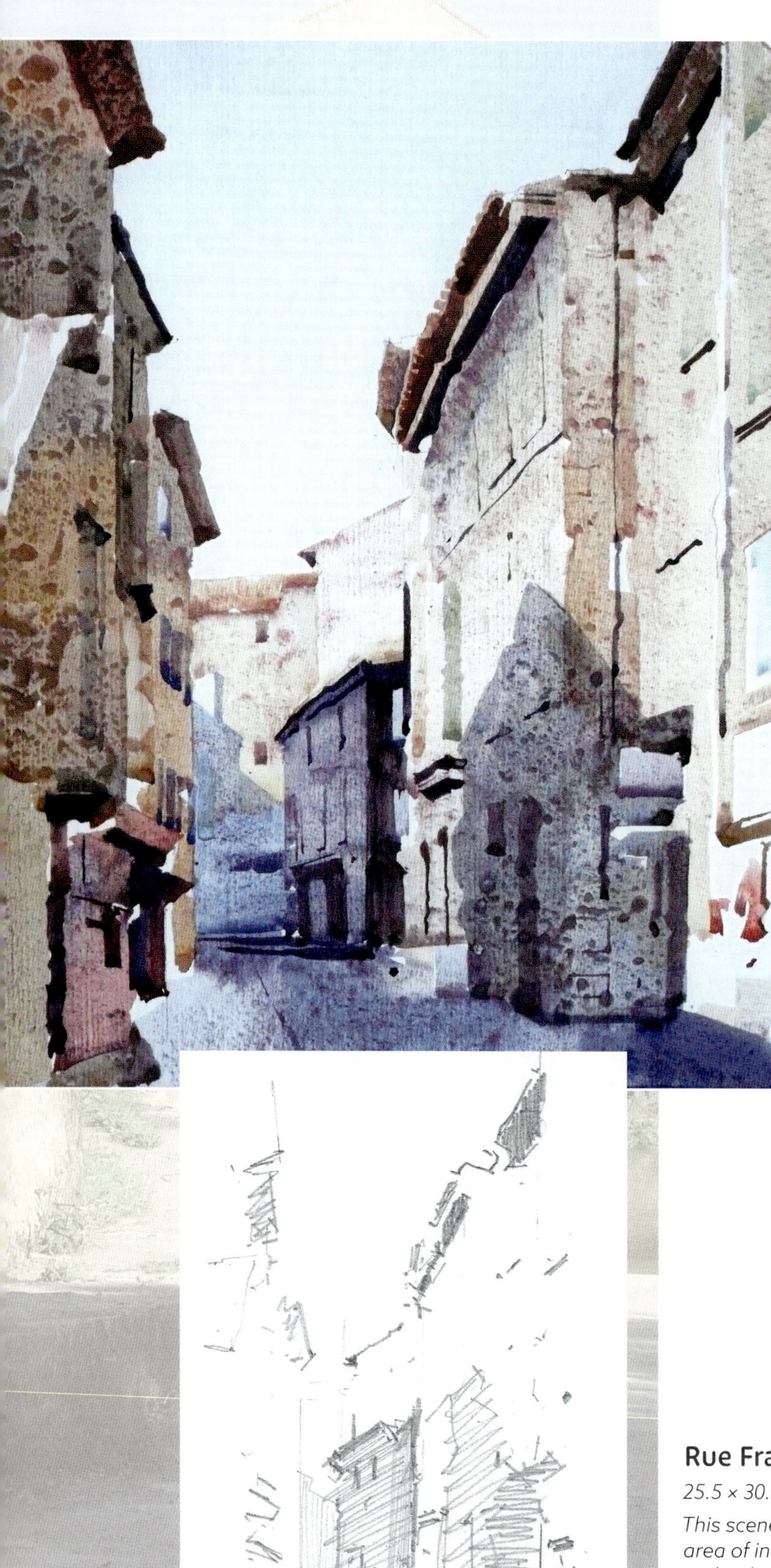

Balance in composition

The composition is the positioning on the paper of the various elements – the design of the image. Balance is the distribution of the features that give weight. The two are intrinsically linked.

Compositions usually have a busy area counter-balanced with flatter or emptier areas. Balance can also be given by the distribution of detail – more detailed areas read as 'heavier' and draw the eye.

If you are working in a representational manner, when the composition fails, perhaps as a result of poor initial drawing or poor balance later on, the painting will fail.

A good composition just looks right, and while you can sometimes make adjustments to rescue a painting, it is best to set it on good foundations before you commence painting.

Compositional sketches

Try to identify the area of interest and key elements, in the view under consideration – including these is obviously crucial to the composition. Making a sketch will help you to focus upon the main features and shapes and explore options of where to place them. Likewise, a tonal sketch can help you to work out the weight of different shapes in the composition.

As you can see in the example to the left, a sketch can help just as much in the selection and identification of smaller details and features as it can with the main shapes.

Rue François Oustrin, Pézenas

25.5 × 30.5cm (10 × 12in) Hahnemühle 300gsm (140lb) Not surface paper

This scene forms a natural composition, where lines lead to a central area of interest. You can see how darker tone and more fine detail in the distant building help to draw the eye into the painting.

The sketch helped to identify and explore these ideas and ensure that the result was properly balanced.

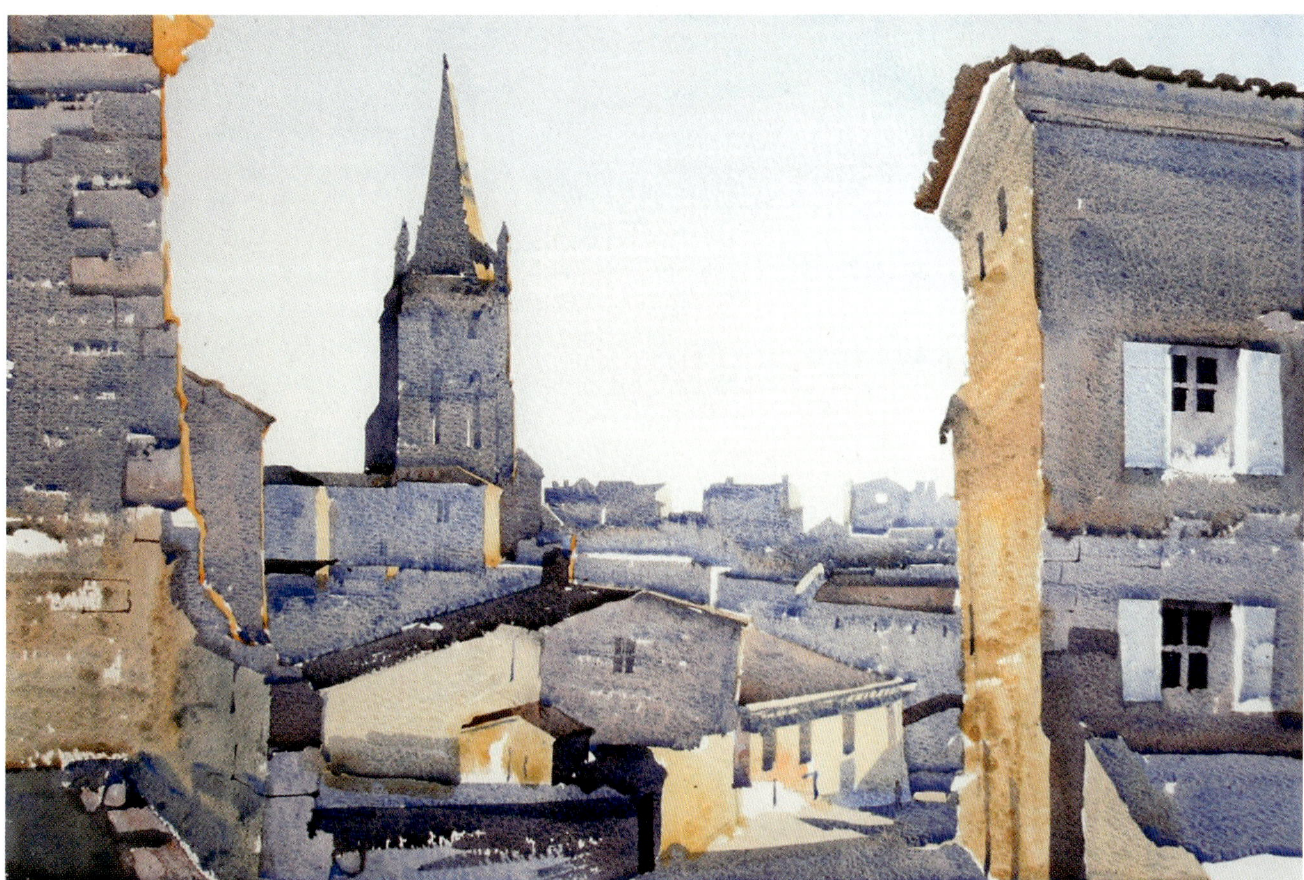

Saint Émilion

56 × 38cm (22 × 15in) Saunders Waterford
300gsm (140lb) Rough surface paper

This is a painting primarily focused on atmosphere, but in addition to the overall appeal, I included a feature – the tower – to draw the eye in and to act as a focus from which the eye can wander to other details.

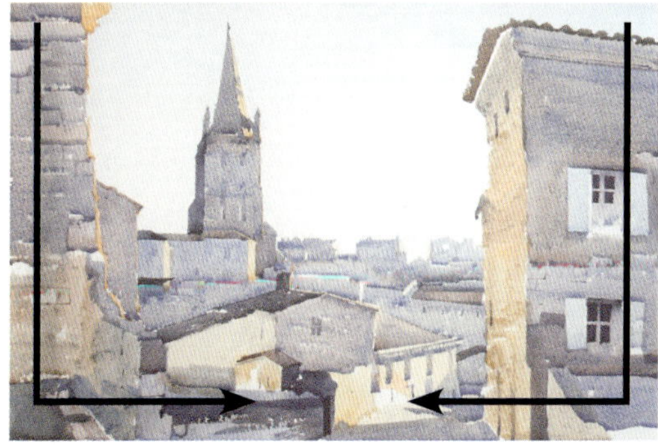

L and reverse L

I refer to this type of composition as the 'L and reverse L type'. This perspective creates depth and contrast. The area of interest is largely central and is usually best balanced just off-centre – in this example, the tower helps achieve this.

Foundations

- Balance refers to the relative strengths, contrasts and those things that draw the attention of the viewer.

- A stark demonstration of balance would be to get a blank piece of paper with a grey shape in the middle and put a bright red shape at one end – just stand back to observe the effect.

- Balance is affected by anything that will draw the eye including complementary colours, bright colours and sharp contrasts or lines.

- Bear in mind that any detail will draw the eye and can help make the composition work.

- Balance can become instinctive because it is about adjusting the picture to 'look right' – sketches can help ensure you get off to a strong start.

Constructing your painting

Once you have found what you want to paint, and got a composition in mind, you need to get the drawing onto the surface. We look in more detail at perspective and drawing later on, so here we focus just on how it relates to composition.

The initial drawing will establish your composition. While drawing we are defining the subject as well as working out and placing areas of interest within the painting. It is important to consider all aspects of composition as you make your drawing: the setting, subject, lighting, and balance – these will all depend on the type of composition you decide to pursue.

In watercolour, the drawing is usually done in pencil or ink or sometimes a brushed-in line of ink. As ink forms indelible and evident lines and marks in the finished painting, I prefer to use a soft 2B pencil as it doesn't smudge and the marks can be removed easily once the painting is dry.

With your composition in place on your paper, you are ready to begin painting.

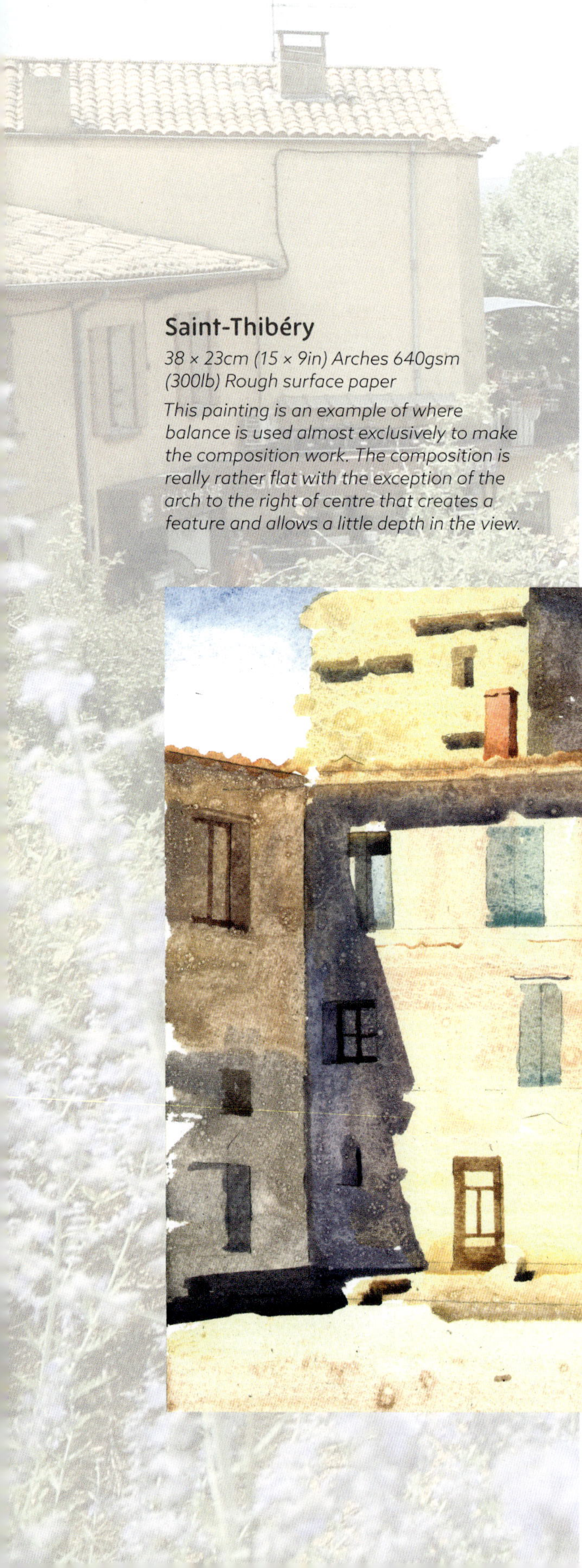

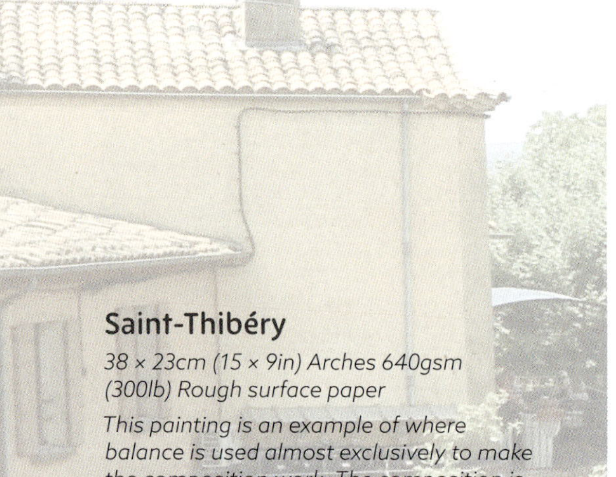

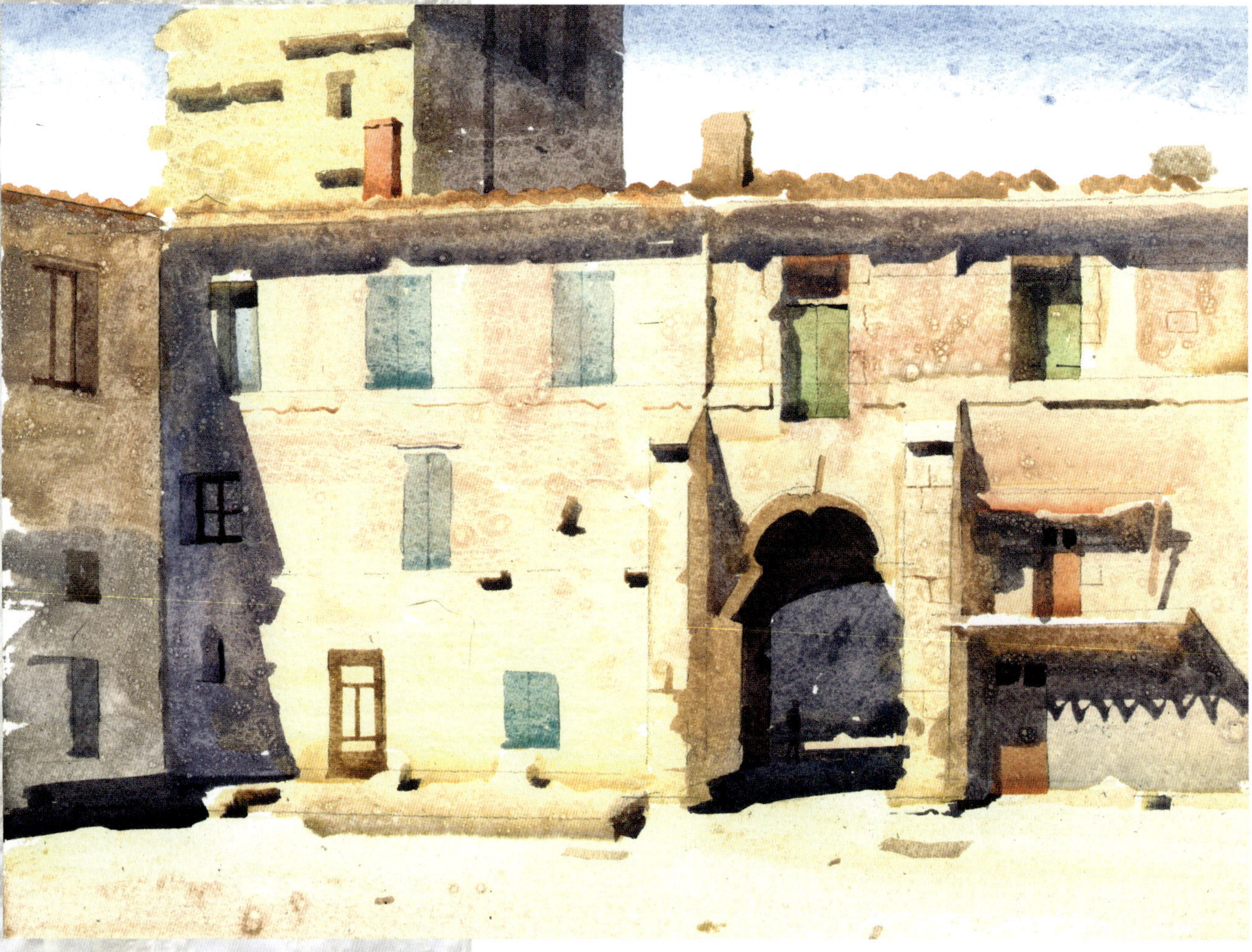

Saint-Thibéry

38 × 23cm (15 × 9in) Arches 640gsm (300lb) Rough surface paper

This painting is an example of where balance is used almost exclusively to make the composition work. The composition is really rather flat with the exception of the arch to the right of centre that creates a feature and allows a little depth in the view.

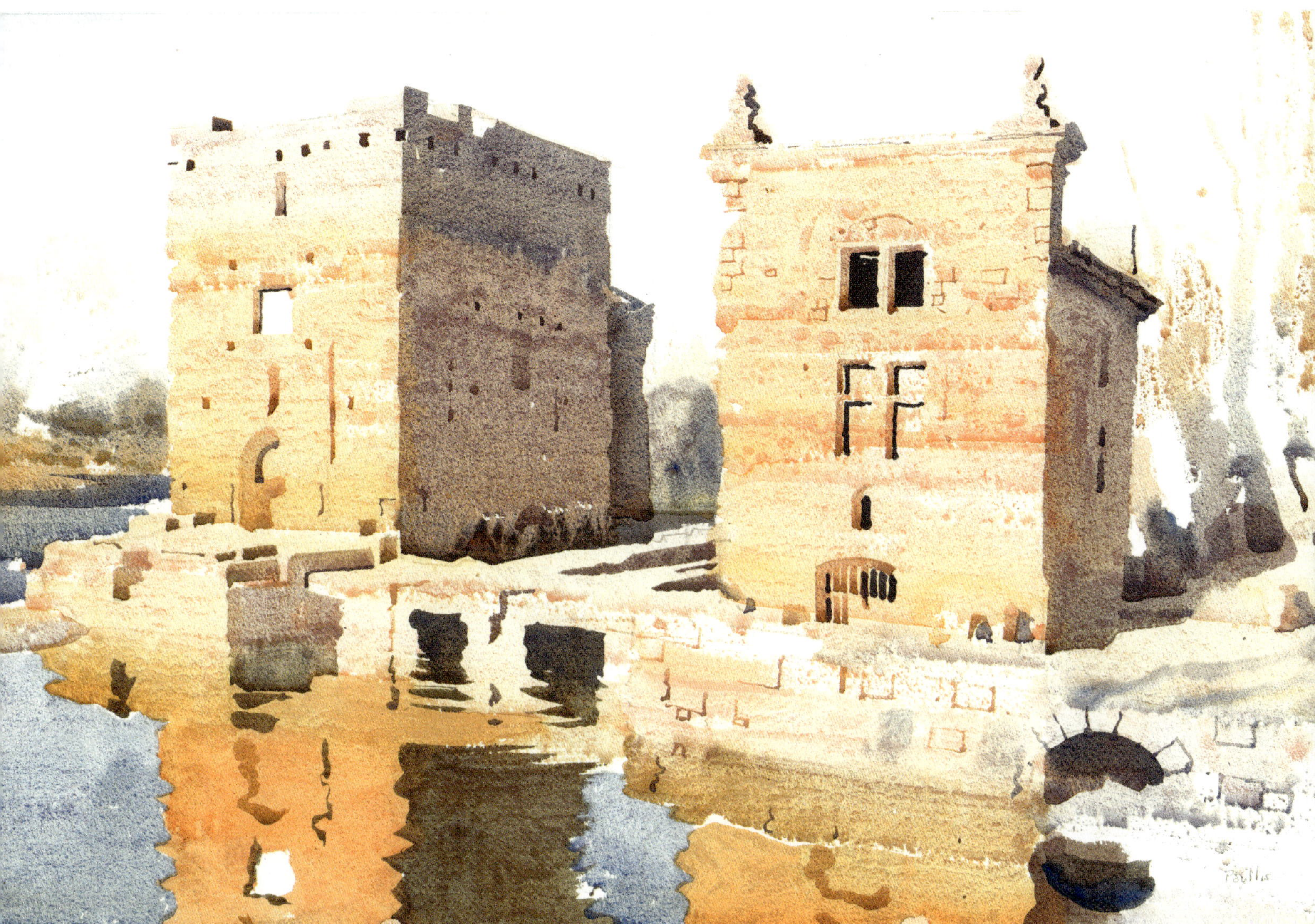

Foundations

- A good subject will usually have contrast, form and, even if not to every taste, will show some interest and passion from the artist.
- Once you have chosen your subject you will have to decide on what the best view is.
- Try to find an unobstructed view. If painting a tall subject, try to position yourself slightly further back to avoid distortion.
- Choose a position from where you can see a light and dark side. Usually, a number of options will become apparent, and you really have to decide quickly, as the light will change.
- Choosing a fairly compact subject will help with placement on the paper.

Roquemengarde

56 × 38cm (22 × 15in) Millford 300gsm (140lb) Rough surface paper

This is a natural composition that brings all the focus to the structure of the subject through the use of drastic simplification of the background, balance, and the distribution of detail.

Drastic simplification of the background is a compositional device where, using the tendency of the viewer's eyes to be drawn to areas of detail, all the focus will go to more defined areas or objects.

Here, the eye is drawn to the structure on the left because of its accompanying reflections and position on the paper. The rest of the painting is simplified as much as possible, which ensures it provides crucial context, depth, and lighting to the subject.

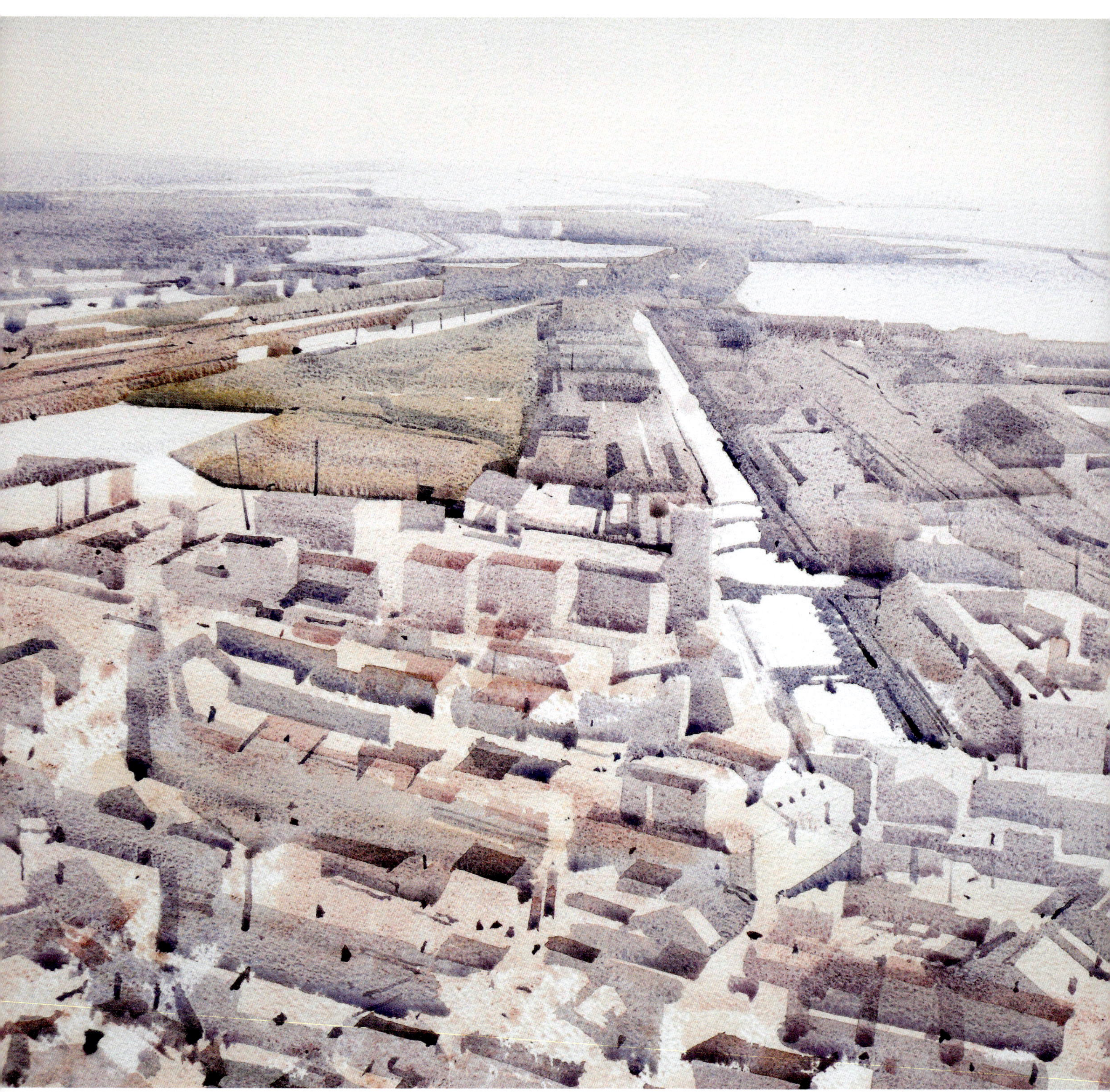

Simplification

Watercolour is in many ways a paradox. It is the most accessible medium for anyone to start painting – but is challenging and requires dedication. It is also counterintuitive; it is logical to think that the more work done on a painting the better it gets, but in watercolour this is never the case. There is a point at which things get progressively worse. Nor can watercolour be corrected, so each touch or wash must be carried out with conviction.

Counterintuitively, we can express much more about our subject if we miss out details and simplify – and by simplifying, we also remove the temptation to fiddle, adjust, and correct. This is the route to successful watercolour painting.

How, what, and to what degree we simplify will affect the whole painting – and it is a profound consideration for the impressionistic painter.

Successful paintings of buildings take a broad approach which concentrates on light and depth while also including key elements of the subject to define character. They are often very descriptive while omitting much detail. Simplification refers to how we distil a scene and, to the impressionist painter, is of fundamental importance.

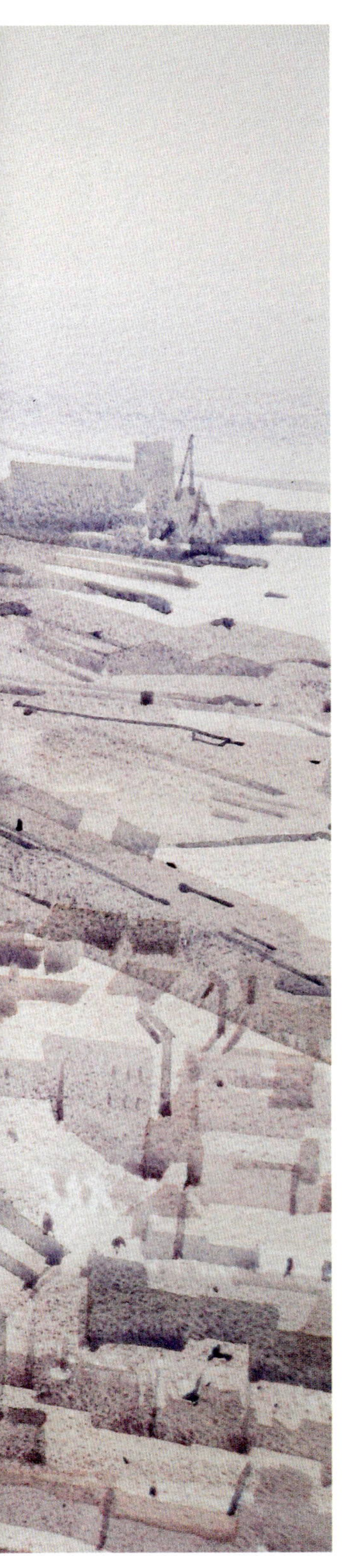

Sète

56 × 38cm (22 × 15in) Millford 300gsm (140lb) Rough surface paper

While there was a great deal of underlying structure to this painting there was also a lot of simplification involved with the painting of the buildings and roofs in the foreground and mid-distance. While complex, the nature of the subject meant that it could be balanced with just a little more detail here or there to give contrast or weight.

To add detail without changing the overall balance, shapes were added using the same tone as the first layer. To change the balance and increase the weight of an area, I could have instead used a stronger mix to add details or form.

Keeping the character

Simplification helps to give a focus to the painting by omitting details. When we simplify architecture, the objective is to retain the character and identity of the subject while making the subject more digestible and more easily read.

The first and most crucial step in any simplification process is observation. Within the area to be simplified, look for shapes, patterns and areas of similar tone that would also describe the object or area.

In this first step we must also identify what is descriptive and what is superfluous distraction. The objective is to use shapes that describe the subject without need of detail.

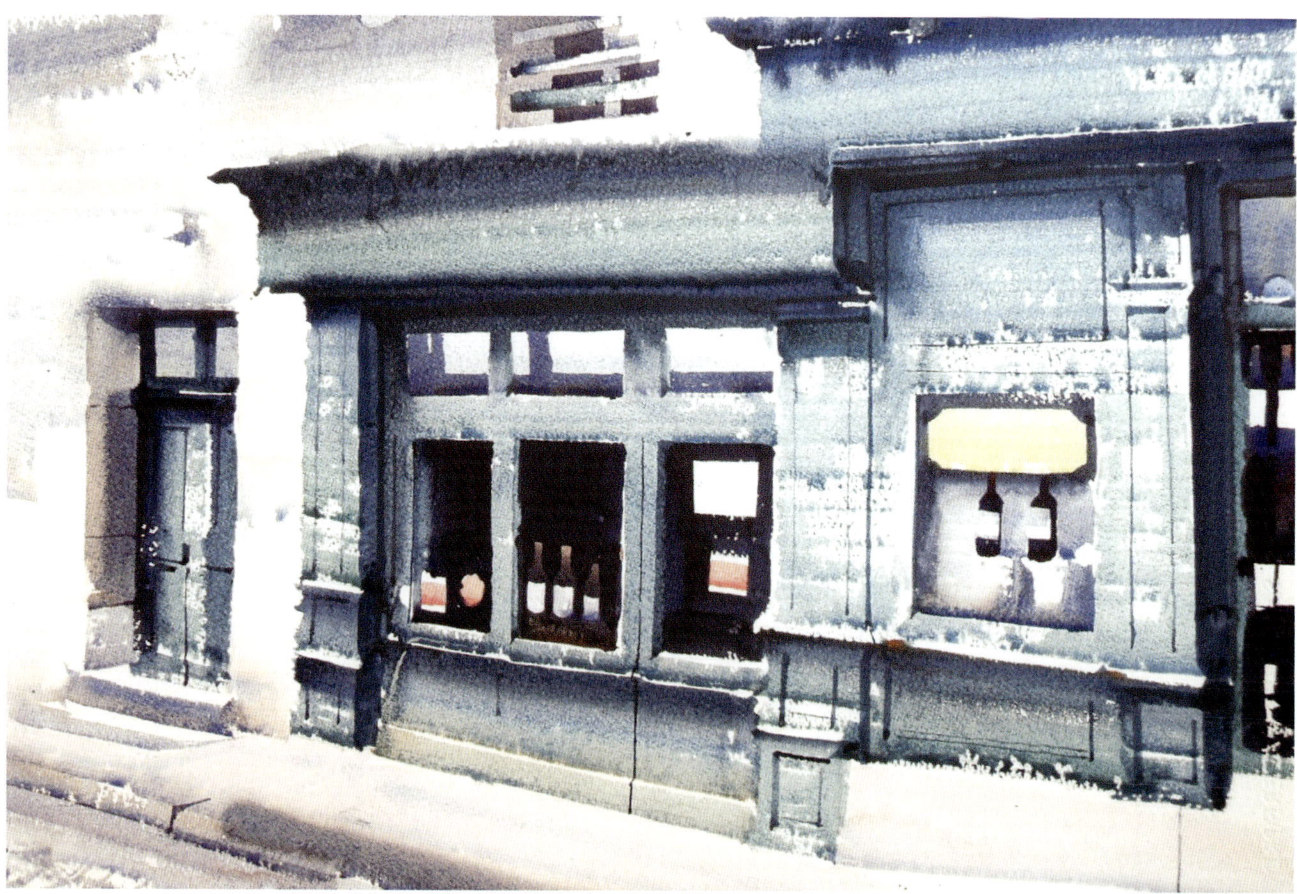

Wine Shop, Saint-Émilion

56 × 38cm (22 × 15in) Saunders Waterford 300gsm (140lb) Rough surface paper

The shapes of the shop front are clear and intact, while the surrounding walls are treated much more loosely. The nature of the produce in the windows is clear – the red foil and clean paper labels on the bottles let them read as wine without needlessly over-complicating them.

Selective detail for character

Some elements within a painting can be simplified by using pattern to capture the nature of it. This method is commonly used when painting skies, water, or trees.

In painting architecture, we can hint at details: a wall can be painted in with a simple wash before a few shapes of stone or bricks could be picked out to say something about the material.

The amount of simplification will depend on the role of the element, and where in the painting the element is. To take an example; part of the background near the edge of the painting, the role of which is to create depth, would certainly be more effective drastically simplified. The foreground is another area that is commonly simplified so as to avoid obstructing the eye's journey into the painting.

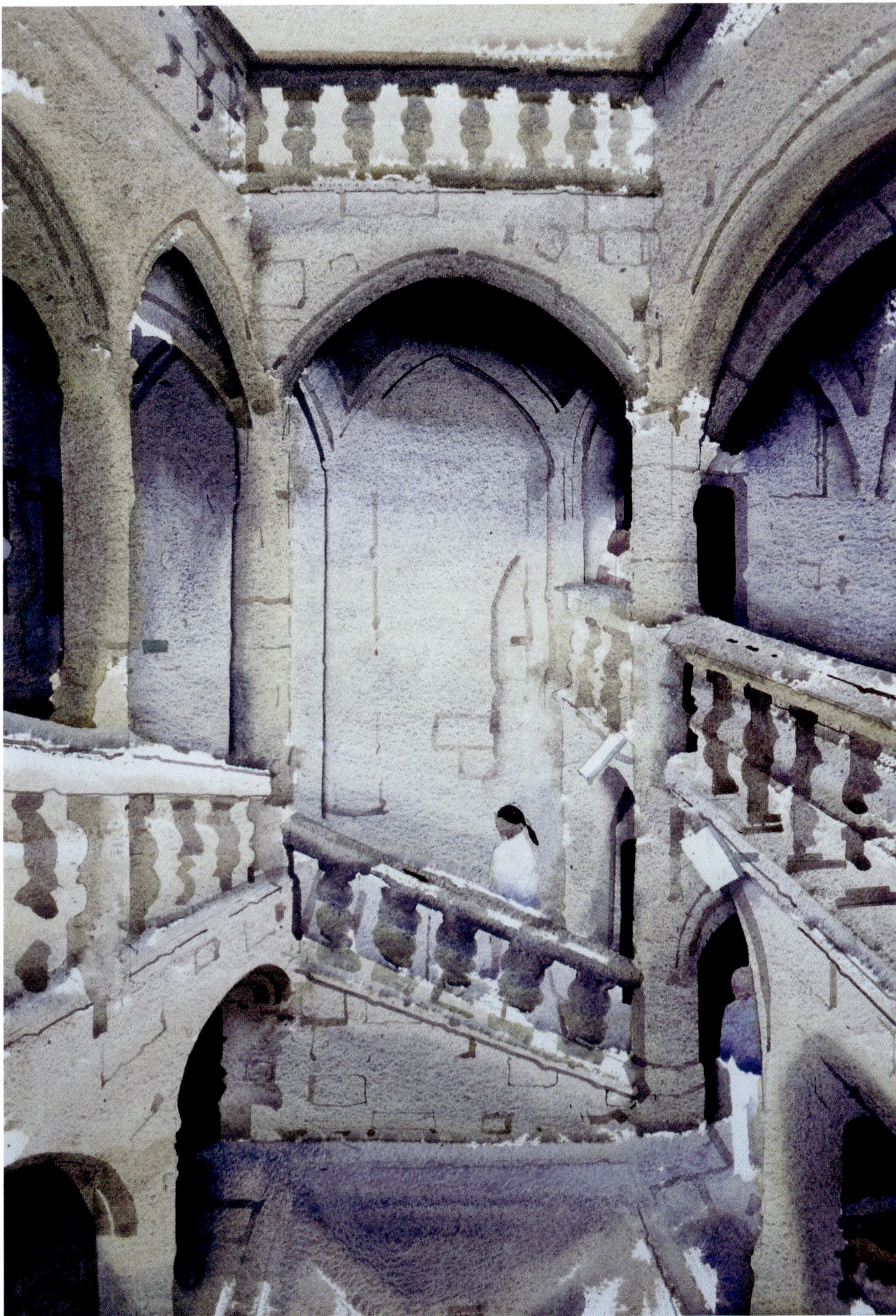

Hôtel des Barons de Lacoste, Pézenas

38 × 56cm (15 × 22in) tinted 300gsm (140lb) Rough surface paper

Note how just a few marks help the back wall read as being made of large stones. Even something as simple as the paper choice can help simplify. Here, a tinted paper suited the lighting of the courtyard subject – and contributed to the low-key tones.

How much to simplify

There are degrees of simplification, and we could simplify so much that the image becomes completely abstract. However, that shows none of the specific character of our building. Conversely if there is a great deal of detail the painting becomes arbitrary, like a photograph.

Handling the paint

The handling of the watercolour is very important in simplification. In the early stages, details and precision are less important, and painting in a loose way that allows the paint more freedom is all we need. Use of broad washes will naturally omit details, which is key to capturing atmosphere, character, lighting, and depth.

The technique we use to paint areas can be highly effective in suggesting form. For example, working wet in wet will create forms devoid of hard edges – useful both for simplification and losing detail. Where we want detail, we can make use of contrasts by overpainting wet on dry.

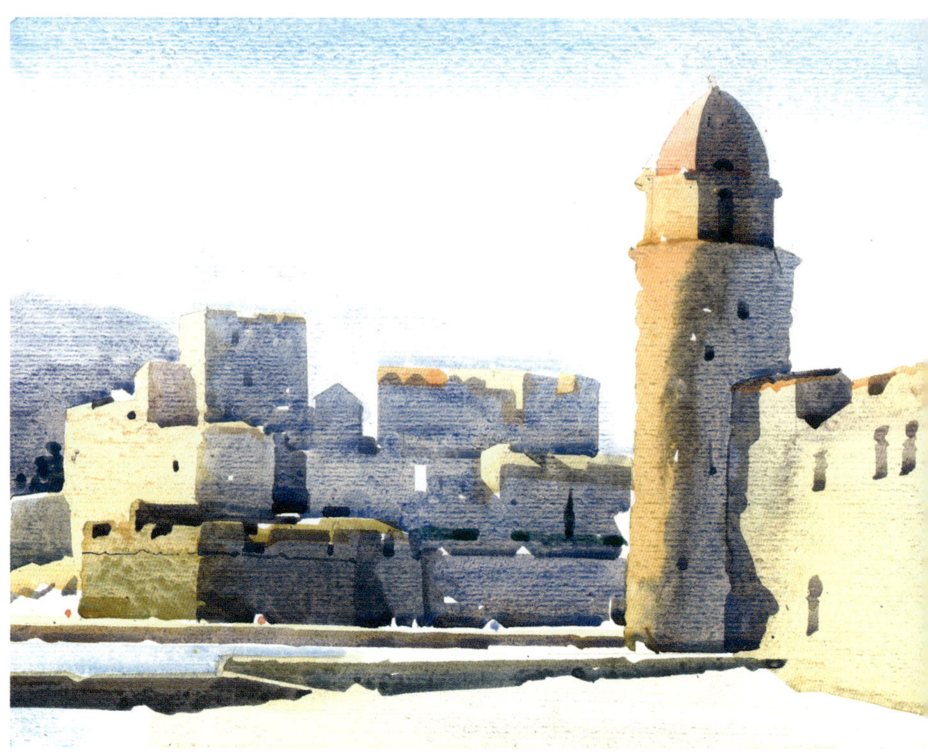

Collioure

30.5 × 25.5cm (12 × 10in) Hahnemühle 300gsm (140lb) Rough surface paper

What you wish to express about a building begins with the choice of angle and the lighting on it. Depending on the lighting you can show details and features or represent the 'mass' of the building with less detail.

Here, the round shape of the tower and the more angular forms of the surrounding buildings are shown through how the light falls on each part, rather than painstaking drawing.

Foundations: simplifying

- Stay faithful to the subject – omit but do not add detail.
- Edit the scene ruthlessly. Look for details in the subject that are relevant to what you wish to express and disregard the rest.
- Look for and retain key features that characterize and identify the subject.
- When simplifying complicated features such as trees and reflections in water, think in terms of pattern and texture. Pick out defining shapes to describe the whole mass.
- The background is usually where we simplify the most, and a simple background can be very effective in creating depth.
- Backgrounds can often be simplified with use of wet in wet to give more vague outlines.
- The level of simplification you apply can depend on where in the painting the object is. Distant objects and shapes, along with those off to the sides of any focal feature, will suit a broader approach.
- The moment you put in a detail, the eye will be drawn to it.

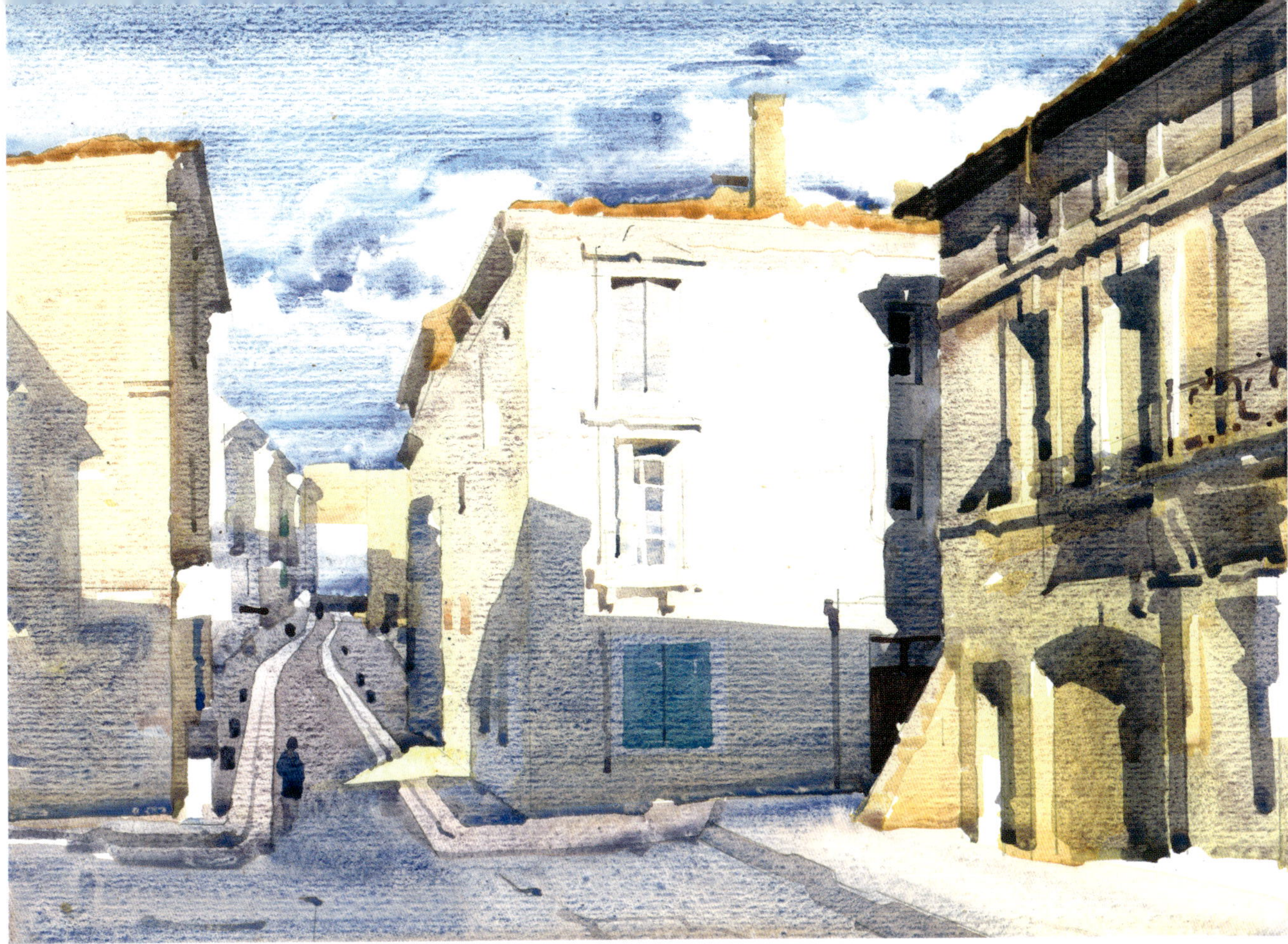

Simplicity, balance and making changes

Balance and simplification work hand in hand but have different roles in making a composition work. Balance refers to the distribution and relative strength of features or details which draw the eye. We can use the placing of these to make compositions work.

The moment we put in detail, the viewer's eye will go to it and 'travel' from detail to detail. We can use this very effectively in our compositions. Art is like a sport in which the viewer plays a role.

Figures and later additions

Unlike composition, which can't really be changed once the painting is done, elements can be added if the painting looks out of balance. You can add shapes to a building's surface to suggest brick or stone, or transitory elements like figures could be included.

Since figures can be added later to animate and add colour, you can put most of your focus on painting atmosphere. It's useful to note the height of passing figures so if you choose to add any later, they will make sense in terms of scale. Nevertheless, it's best to add them at the time of painting and not back in the studio.

Rue Conté, Pézenas

30.5 × 25.5cm (12 ×10in)
Hahnemühle 300gsm (140lb)
Rough surface paper

The eye-catching brightness of the sun-bleached surface of the central building almost causes you to squint – but there's virtually nothing there. For success In watercolour, what you leave out is often more important than what you put in.

As mentioned earlier, the surface of watercolour paper often has a slight resistance, so the paint sits on and dries on the surface. This characteristic can be very useful. For this painting I used the 'wrong side' – the smoother side – of a Rough paper. The natural brightness of the paper surface corresponded with what I wished to capture.

Avoiding overworking

In watercolour, it is crucial not to overwork and when we notice this happening, it is often too late. Making an effort to simplify your painting will help to avoid overworking, so here are a few starting points for you to try:

Think in stages Limit yourself to working in this order – lights and underpainting; mid-tones; darks and simplified details (see pages 105–107 for more on the order of painting).

Use the right tools An effective way of simplifying is to use the right size of brush for the job needed: use the smaller brushes only for details, not larger areas of wash. The larger the brush we use, the less detail it is possible to paint with it. We can use this practical limitation to help with simplification.

Work small Working on a small scale will help you bring the subject, no matter how large, down to its simplest forms and features. Practise simplifying by painting on a small scale of about 28 × 18cm (11 × 7in) – big enough to count, too small to be fussy.

Time yourself In watercolour it can be difficult to set a time limit – a well-established exercise in simplification – because so much depends on drying time, how the subject can be divided up, and if we need to avoid wet against wet areas. As a rule of thumb, however, aim for less than three hours to complete a small painting of about 28 × 19cm (11 × 7½in).

Building skills

- Look for counterchange. This is where a light object is contrasted with a darker object behind it (or vice versa) revealing form.

- Look for where green can be used with effect. Green is an invasive colour, so if we paint as seen, it can take over a painting and create difficulties with balance. Paint in any greens last as it is easier to balance and pick out shapes as needed.

- Because green contrasts with everything else, it can be used to break up blocks of uniform shape. Look for green areas or details when painting rooftop townscapes, as it can be used to paint around elements to create form.

- Watercolour works best used efficiently. Express what you want in the simplest terms – anything more is a distraction. Overworking will quickly obliterate a potentially good watercolour.

- Aim to simplify without losing interesting content or the subject's identity.

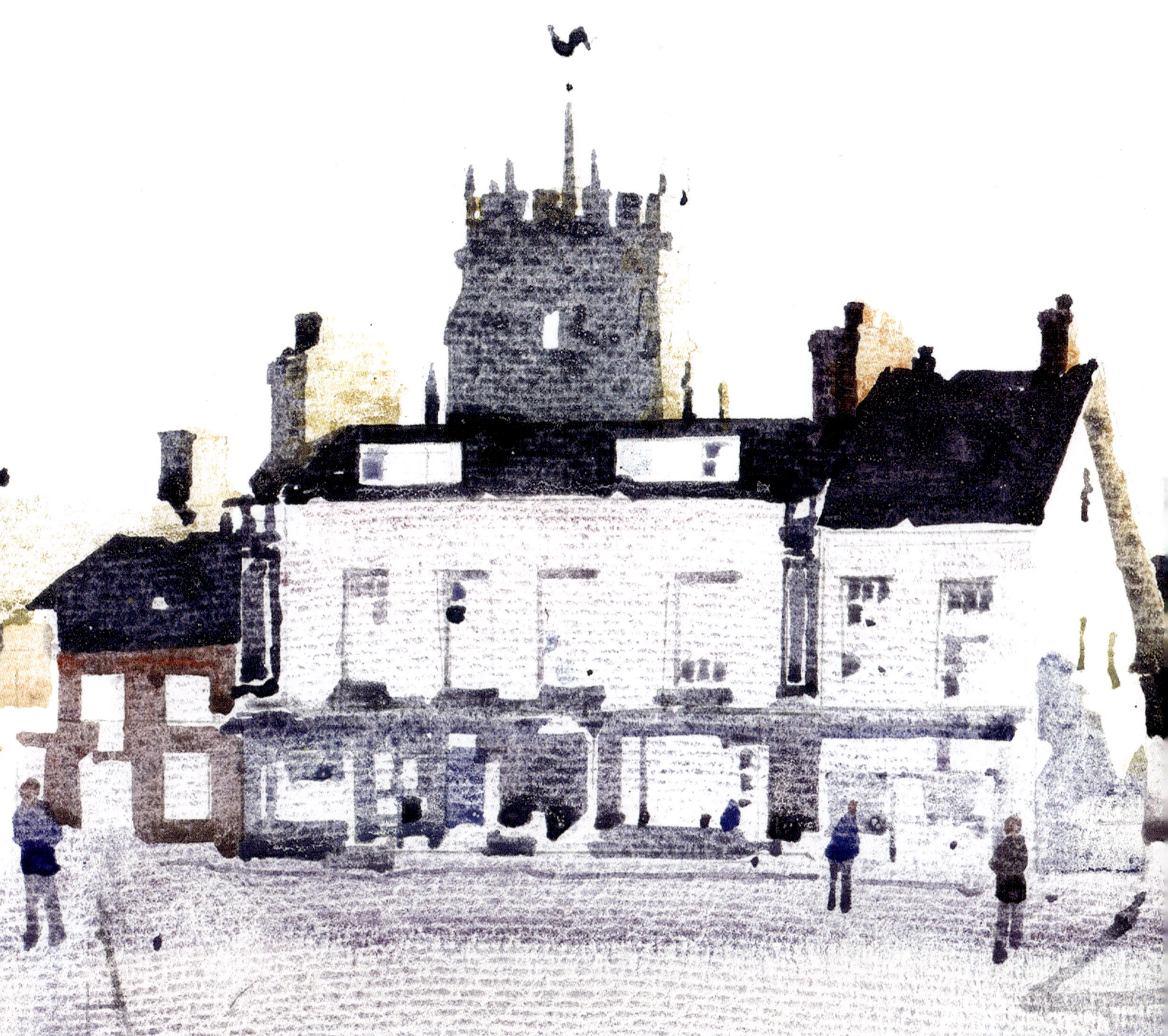

Colyton, Devon

28 × 18cm (11 × 7in) Saunders Waterford 300gsm (140lb) Rough surface paper

Early morning light is always fascinating. Here, the early morning light is coming low from the right, casting long shadows and throwing much of the subject into shade – not least the roofs, which helped to simplify their form. You'll see that they are treated almost as one solid mass – quick and efficient at this scale.

Cathar Bridge

Balance and simplification

This is a great subject because it had many appealing elements – the monumental architecture with contrasting shapes and styles, the ancient Cathar bridge and its reflections as well as the contrasting colour and forms of the trees.

Rather than having a single key element as the focus, this complicated subject lends itself to an 'all-over' type of composition, where balance and simplification are important factors in making it a success. Ensuring the finished piece retains the drama and impact of the scene is key.

Setting up

The scene presented many possible compositions, so the first decision was where to place the cathedral. I opted to place it on the top left of the paper, as this would allow me to simplify it effectively, while maintaining its presence as a major part of the design.

Wanting to include the bridge, I found a place where this beautiful piece of ancient architecture would lead the eye into the scene.

Dealing with the heat

It was a sweltering day, so I took the following precautions:

- I picked a shaded place to paint – more comfortable for me, and it ensured that the paper surface would not reflect too much glare.
- I added a little gum arabic into the water to increase drying time.

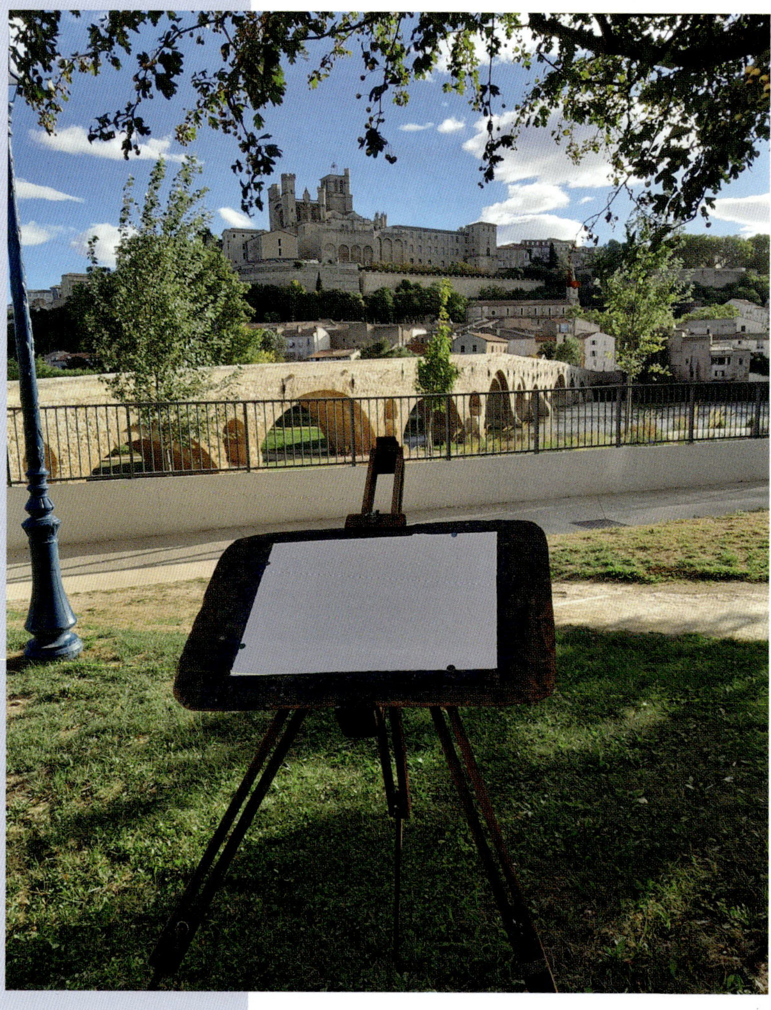

YOU WILL NEED

Watercolour paints: potters pink, cadmium red, cadmium yellow, viridian, light red, raw sienna, brown madder, Naples yellow, cobalt blue deep, ivory black, French ultramarine, cobalt blue

Brushes: one large round, size 8 round, size 6 round

Paper: 38 × 28cm (15 × 11in) 300gsm (140lb) Rough surface watercolour paper

Soft eraser and gum arabic

The finished painting

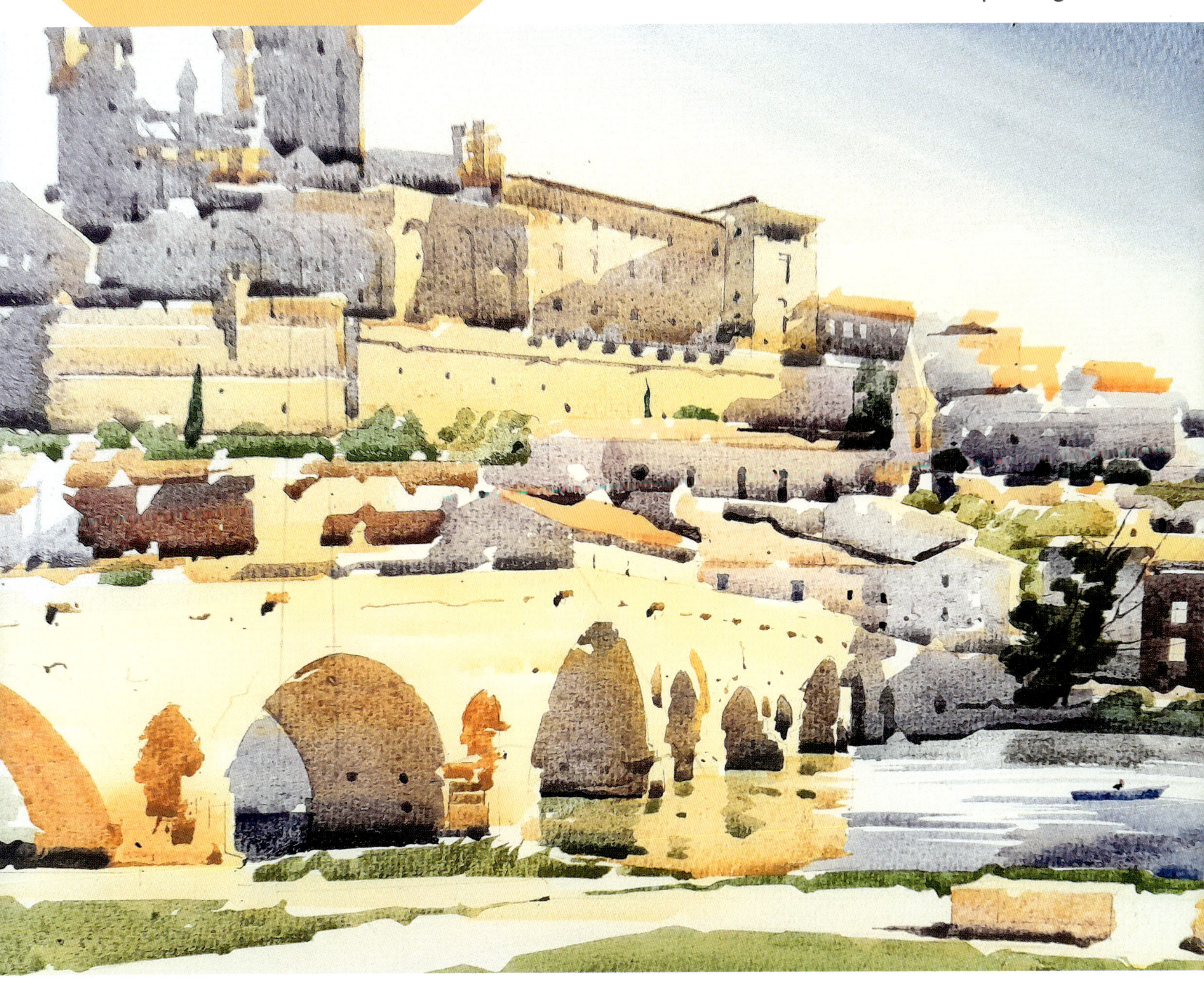

Stage 1

Having decided to place the cathedral at the top left, I drew in just the main masses of the buildings and shapes. I was quite careful to draw accurately as problems could easily arise.

When you come to making your sketch, be aware of a potential problem with putting the composition out of balance – it is easy for the cathedral to draw the eye too much. To avoid this, be careful where you put in detail, and aim to shift the weight to the right of centre of the picture. This will help to create a balanced composition.

Building skills

- To avoid fussiness, use the largest brush you can control for a given area. This will also help achieve pure washes.
- The lightest tones in a watercolour are made up of the white of the paper. The next brightest tones are those where sunlight touches the subject and other highlights: I call these 'off lights'.
- 'Off lights' are one tone off the lightest, so for example if pure Naples yellow is the lightest, an off light would be Naples yellow mixed with a touch of (for example) cobalt blue.

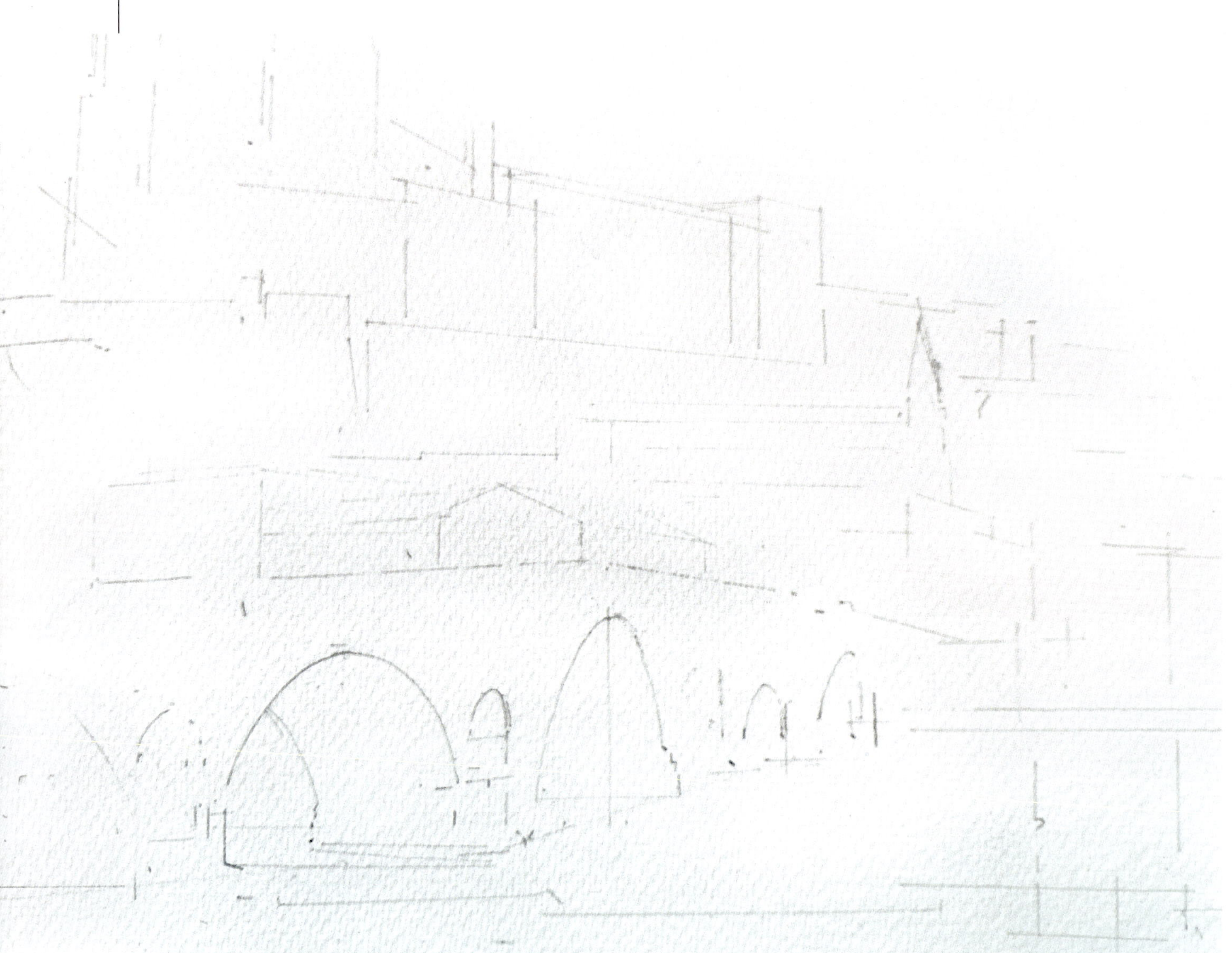

The preparatory sketch. Note that I have avoided putting too much detail into the cathedral early on. As it is so complicated, I knew I would return to the drawing at a later step, so at this stage, only the main shapes are in place.

Stage 2

Throughout this stage, use a size 8 round brush – this brush is good for both broader areas and some more detailed work.

Start to paint in the lights with a mix of Naples yellow, potters pink and a touch of cobalt blue where off lights appeared.

To ensure the bridge appears a little brighter than the church, use a mix of Naples yellow with cadmium yellow to paint it in. Towards the bottom of the bridge, bleed in a mix of raw sienna and potters pink.

Pick out some of the lighter roof tones at this stage using a size 8 round brush with a mix of cadmium red and raw sienna for the warmer roof colours, and a mix of Naples yellow and cadmium red for the cooler tones.

Adapting on the spot

At these early stages, you can change the painting quite considerably to better reflect the scene as it develops. Keep an open mind to possible improvements.

Here, the light was changing, and the scene was improving so I decided to go with those changes and put in more lights. Some of the lights were right next to each other so I had to wait for the first layer of paint to dry to avoid the areas bleeding into one and other.

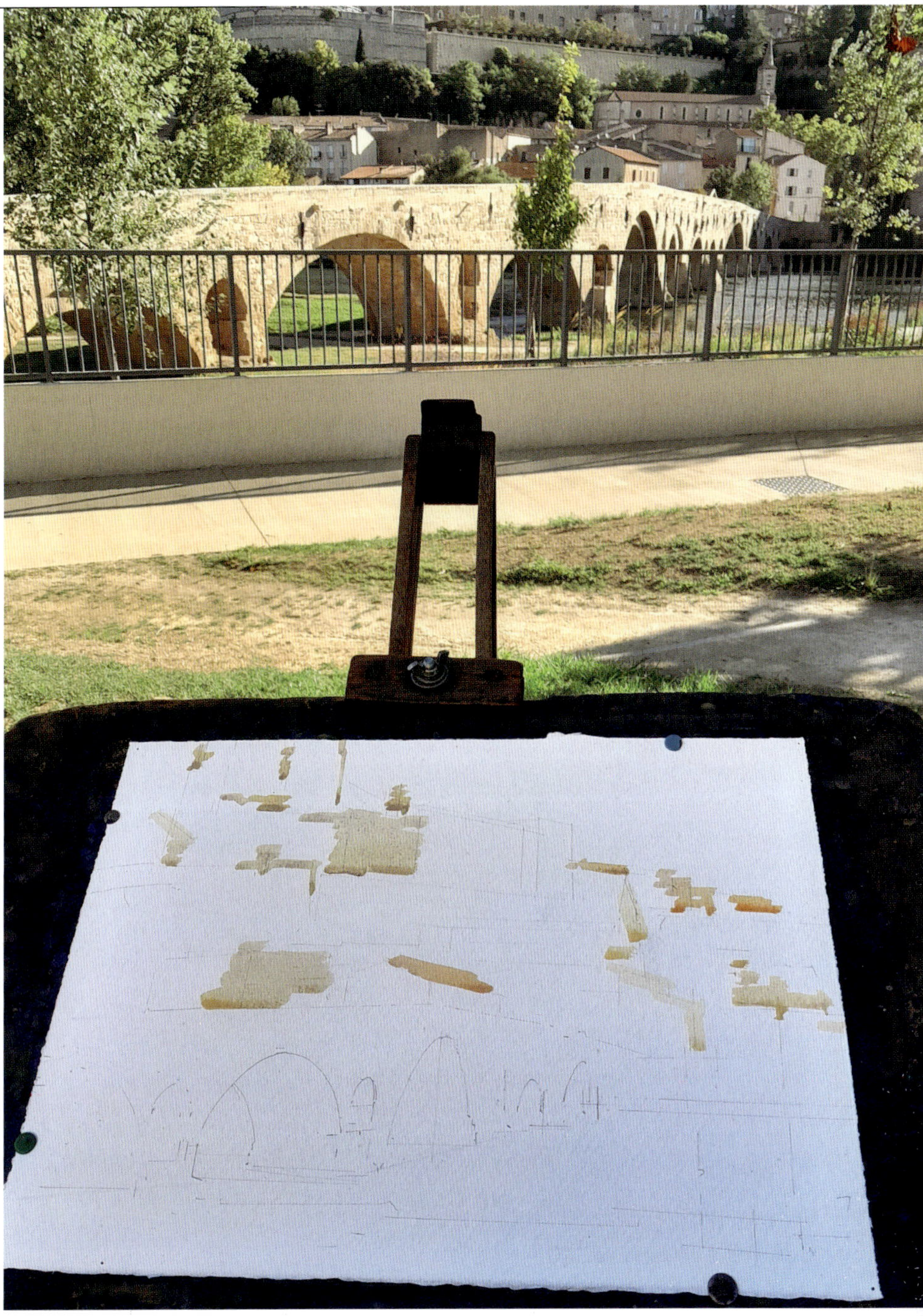

I decided to leave the sky blank for the moment as I was still considering what to do with it. Since skies change a great deal, they can be used to balance a piece relatively late on in the painting process if necessary and I was thinking of how to do that – either with a simple wash or a sky with clouds.

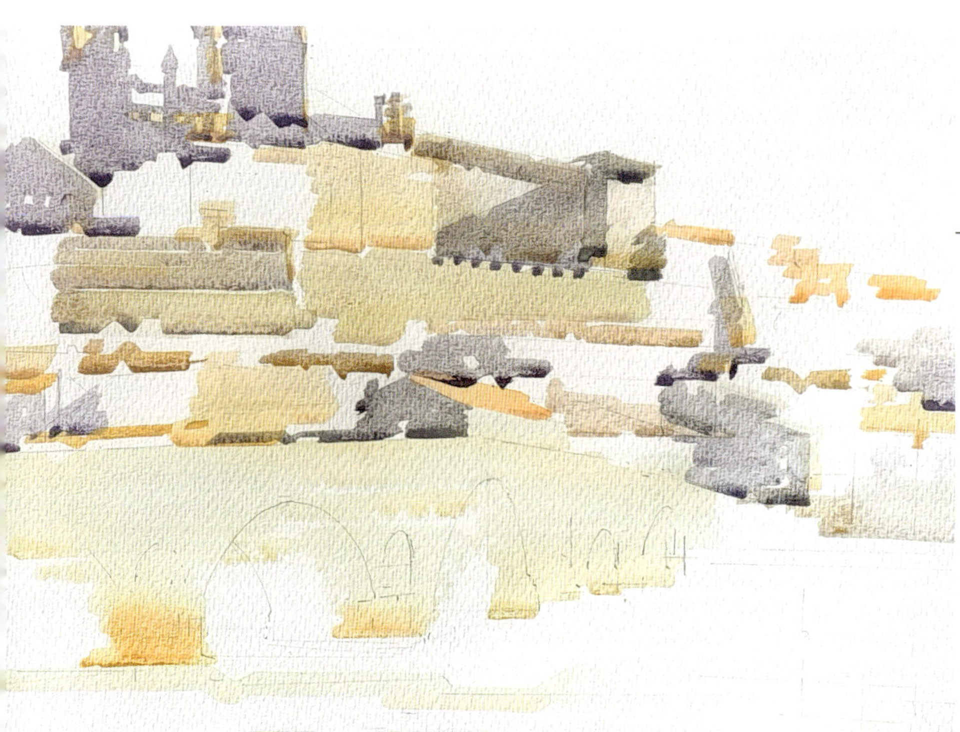

Stage 3

Start to add some of the shaded areas using a mix of cobalt blue deep with varying amounts of potters pink and raw sienna. Light is a major aspect to this scene, so look for reflected colour in the shaded areas, too.

Draw in some of the shadows and then use a size 8 brush to paint them in with mid-toned mixes of cobalt blue deep, potters pink and brown madder.

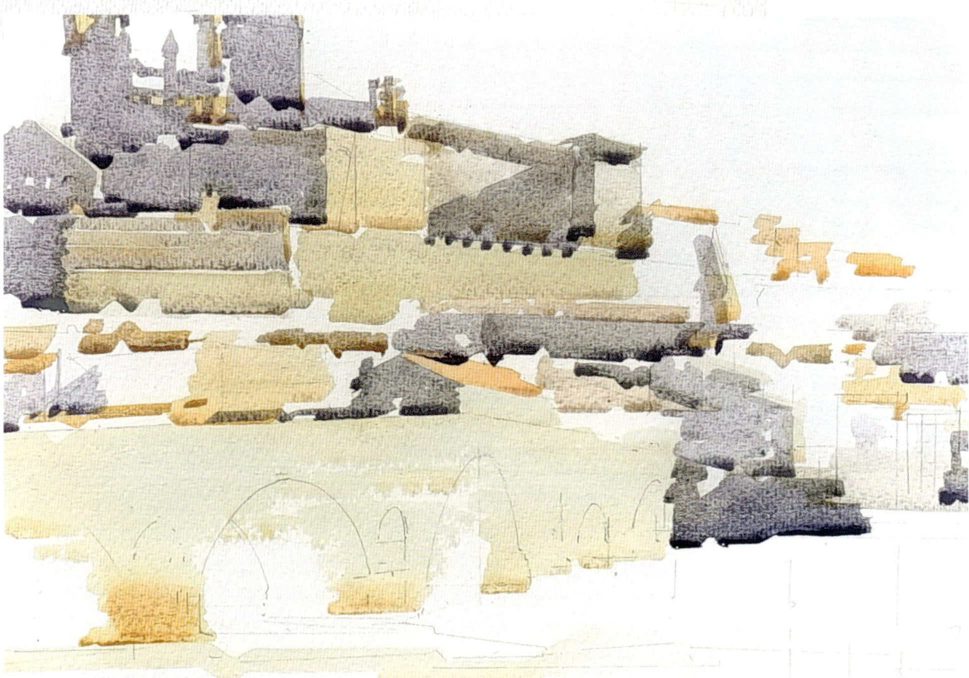

One eye on detail, the other on the overall

Because of the nature of the subject, it is necessary to 'pick away' at it through this stage by working gradually. Be aware, however, that this approach risks the painting becoming fragmented.

To avoid this, aim to paint in broad terms rather than getting fixated on details, and unify what is in shade by using similar tones for all of these areas.

Stage 4

With the shadows largely in place across the scene, it's now time to concentrate on creating form and starting to identify where some details might go on. Be careful not to over-detail the cathedral at this stage. Try to keep the details to the right of centre and on the bridge, as shown to the right.

Using the same brush and mix as in stage 3, vary the amount of water to control the tonal value. Raw sienna can also be added to the mix, to increase the sense of reflected light – as seen in the arches of the bridge. Put down a graduated wash here, adding more cobalt blue deep at the bottom of the wash. Swap to a size 6 round brush for the smaller, more defined areas of wash.

Next, add details to the foreground: suggesting the arches of the bridge with shadows, and using some of the stronger tones to create contrast.

Foliage and greenery

With the bridge in place, develop the greenery to create more contrast and help define the forms of some of the buildings. All the greens were put down with a size 8 round brush. Use viridian as a basis for all the green mixes, and mix in yellows to create a range of cool and warm colours: for the warm green in the foreground, for example, use a mix of raw sienna and viridian. For an intense green, mix viridian and cadmium yellow.

For cooler greens further away, mix Naples yellow and cobalt blue deep. Other pigments can be added to alter the green, for example for a grey-green, add potters pink. For stronger, deeper tones of green, mix viridian, ultramarine blue, and brown madder.

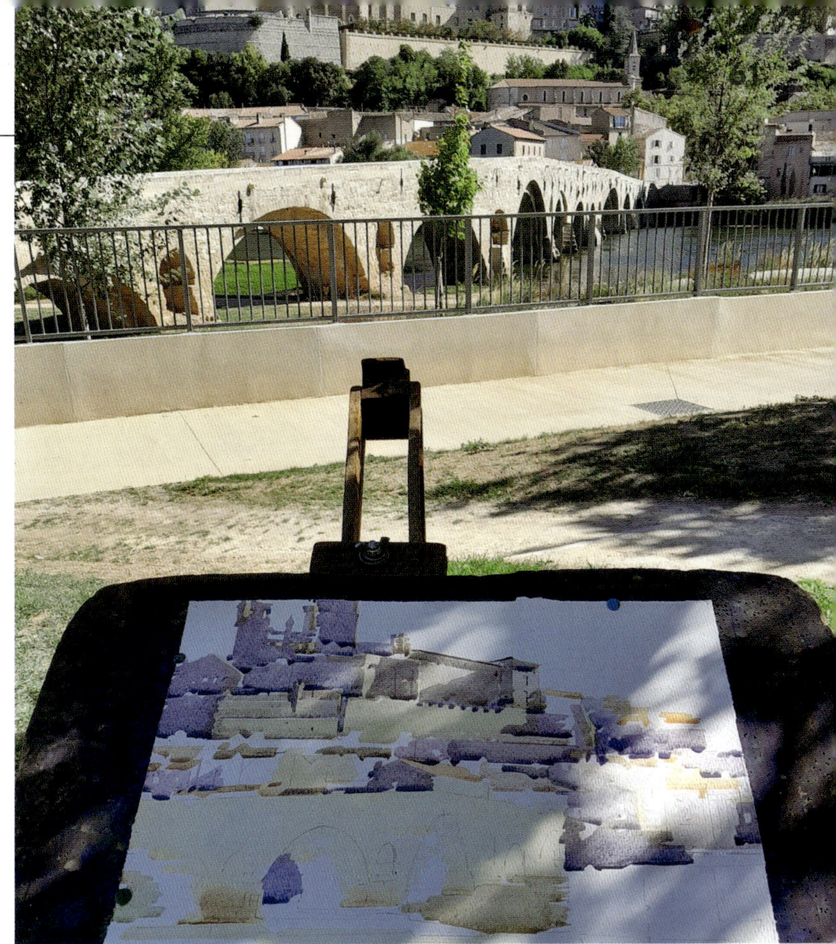

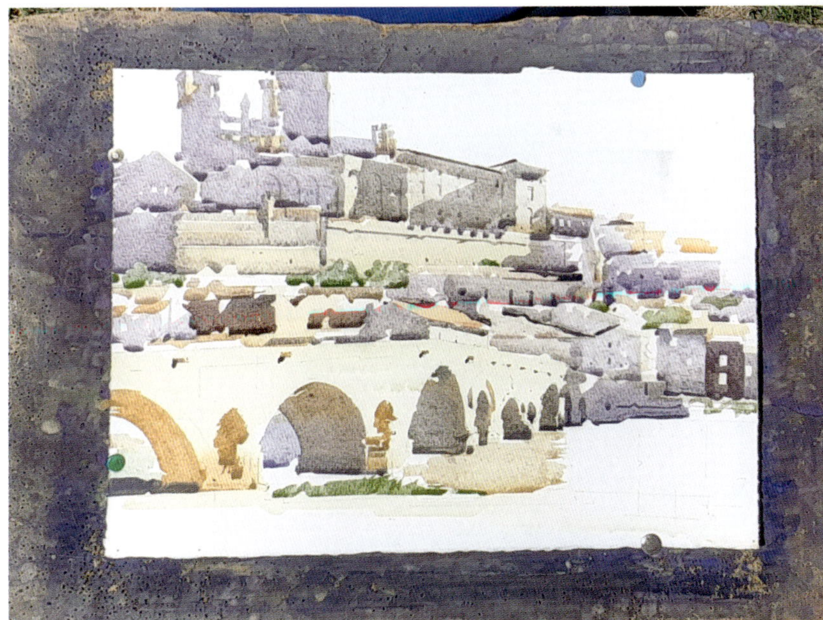

Details

Step back and assess the painting. Add some of the finer details, such as windows and arches, where they will help to balance the composition.

Any underpainting shining through subsequent washes will affect the resulting colour as seen on the surfaces of the buildings to the right of the cathedral.

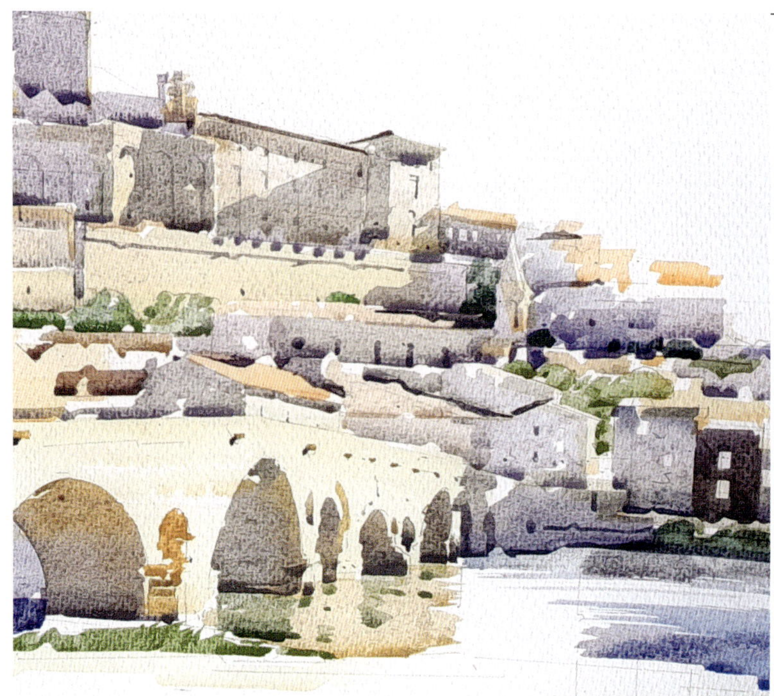

Stage 5

In keeping with the theme of simplicity, paint just a simple wash of French ultramarine for the sky, using a large round brush. Anything more complex risks the painting becoming too busy. Although the background should be simple, make sure there is a stronger tone of blue in the top right-hand corner – this is in order to balance the strength of the cathedral on the left and also to tie in with the reflected blue in the water.

Use simple blocks of colour to describe these reflections – a mix of raw sienna, light red and cobalt blue deep for the reflection of the lighter surface of the bridge and a mix of viridian, Naples yellow, and cobalt blue for the reflected arches. The lighter parts of the water reflect the sky, so use a mix of cobalt blue deep and potters pink here, putting them down with a size 8 round brush. Swap to a size 6 round brush to add details such as the boat on the river and the tree on the far bank.

Building skills

• It is rare to see reflected colours in the same tone as the object. Usually with reflections in water, light surfaces are reflected darker and dark surfaces are reflected lighter.

Once the paint had dried, unwanted pencil lines were rubbed out with a soft eraser. You can see the finished painting on page 57.

Another approach

While you're on location, why not try painting a follow-up picture to practise further? Working on a small scale pushes us to reduce and edit our subject. As before, the first step involves identifying the blocks of shapes and therefore areas of paint – but with less space, we're forced to make big compositional decisions early on.

Here, the shape of the cathedral and structures underneath could be painted in one (the lights and underpainting) or two washes (shadow plus detail).

Beneath the cathedral, the mass of buildings across the water needed a little more resolution, but were in effect another block. The greenery is used to help define those blocks and bring contrast.

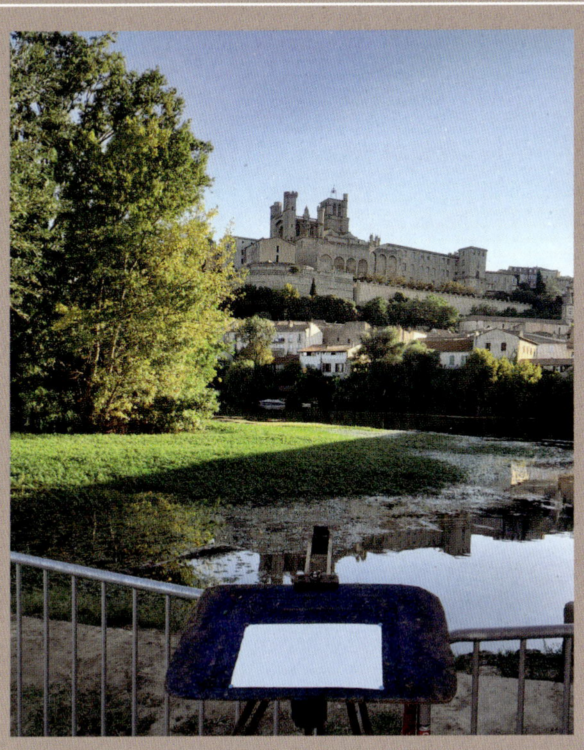

Béziers
28 × 19cm (11 × 7½in), 300gm (140lb) Saunders Waterford Rough surface paper
A different view of the same subject. At just half the size of the project painting, this is a great example of how simply working on a small sheet of paper can be used to help simplify a scene.

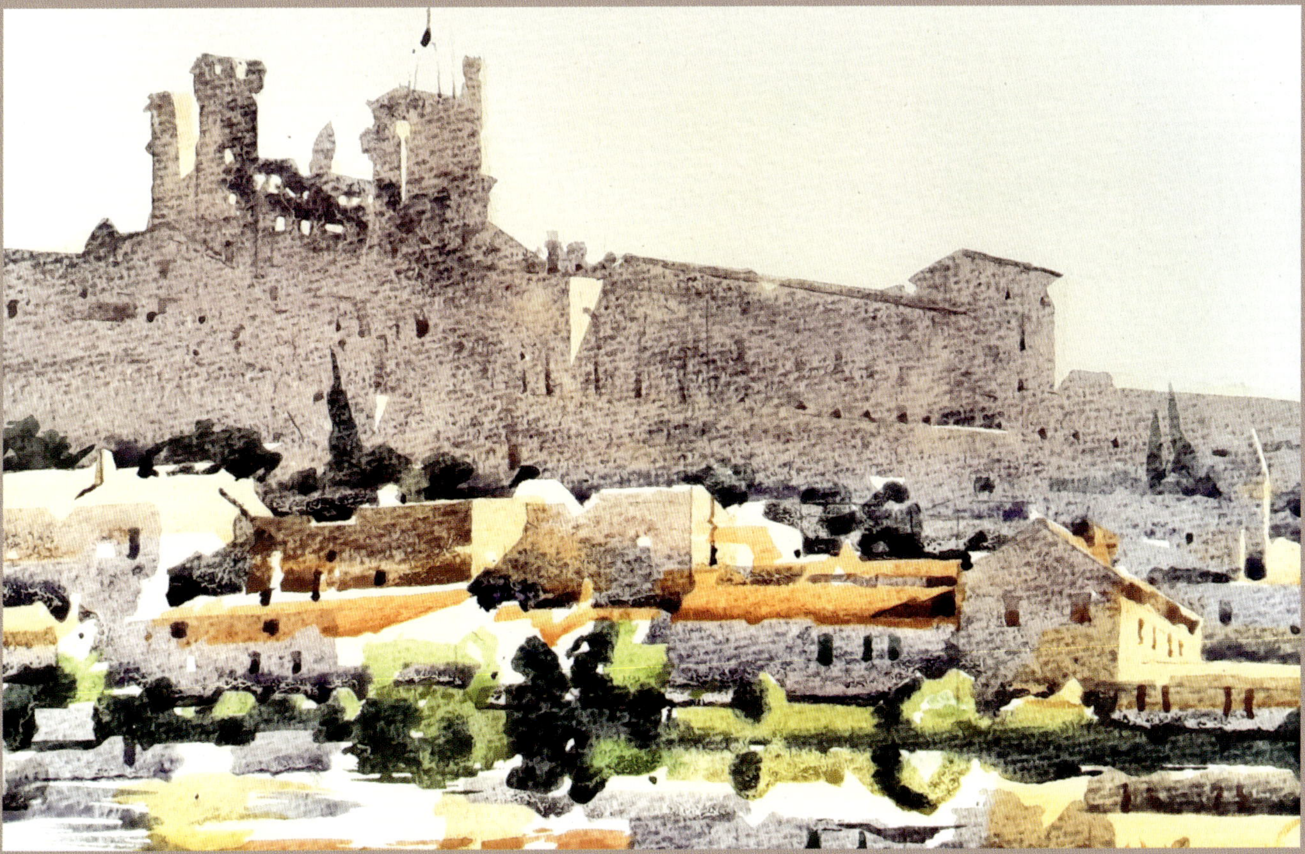

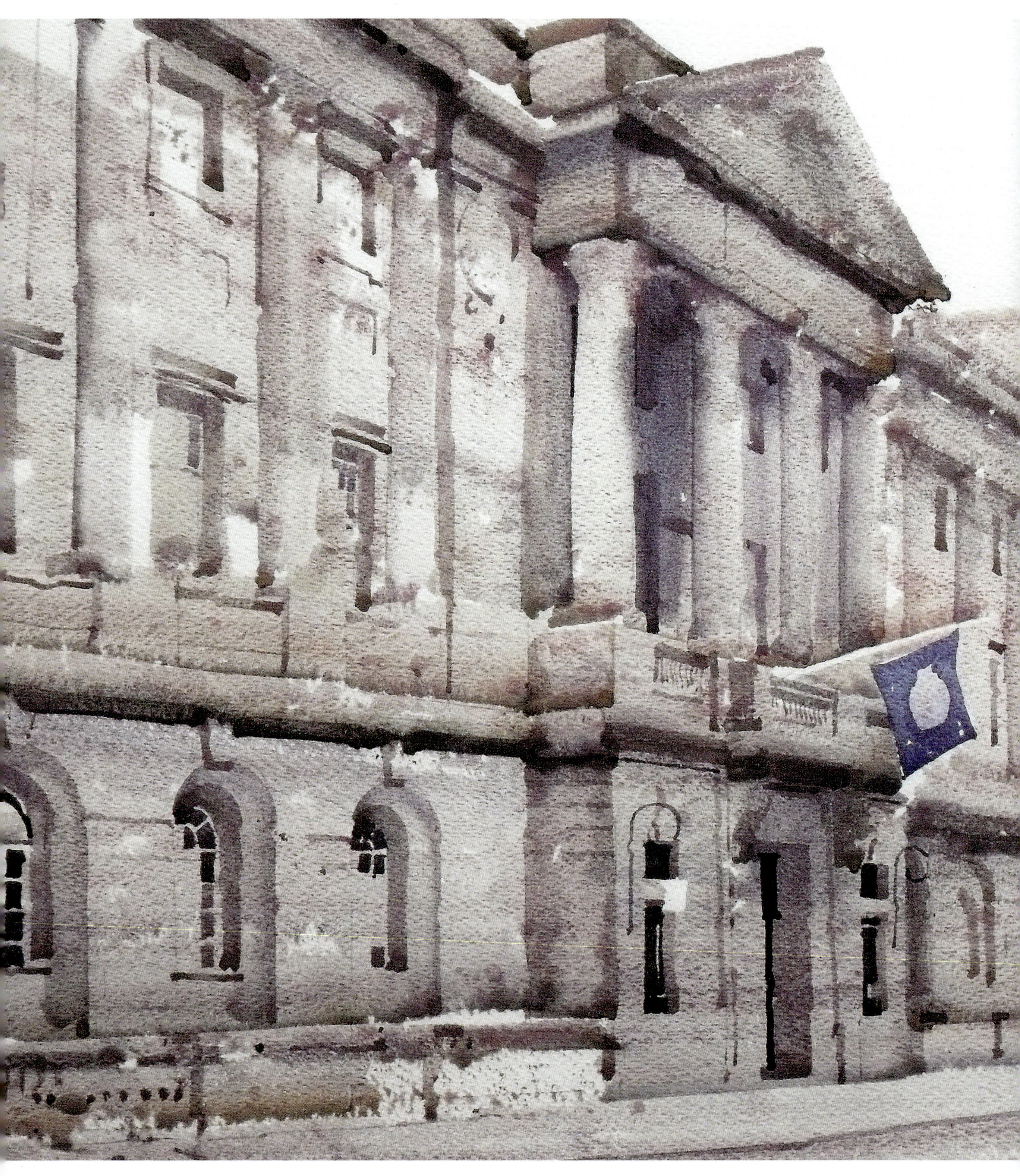

Drawing and perspective

Perspective can be a thorny challenge. When a subject is drawn correctly, the drawing goes unnoticed – but when wrong, the errors stick out like a sore thumb and can easily ruin a painting.

Rest assured that however complex and intimidating perspective may seem, we must understand it only in simple terms to use it effectively in our paintings. Developing your drawing and observational skills is crucial to accomplishing this and for this reason practising is important – and preferably directly from life.

Painting a picture is not just putting brush to paper but the result of a culmination of decisions and experiences – so in this chapter we explore perspective with a particular view to improving our observational skills and achieving accuracy in our drawing.

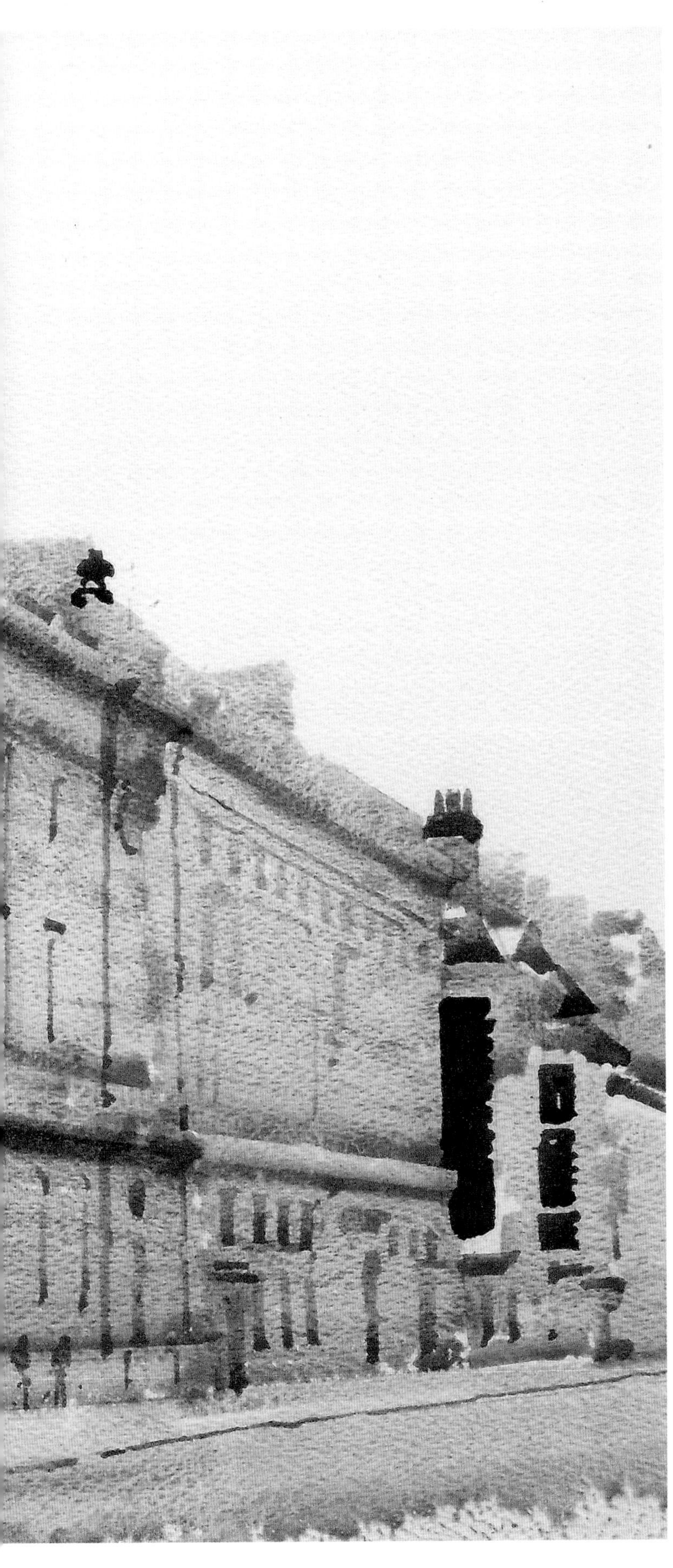

The Royal Automobile Club, Pall Mall

56 × 38cm (22 × 15in) Millford 300gsm (140lb) Rough surface paper

This view of the RAC clubhouse throws it into dramatic perspective because the building is high, and the street is not wide enough to get any further back.

The architecture includes various forms such as triangles, arches, rectangles and cylinders in the columns. You need a firm plan; and using a straight edge to draw up against can be useful where accuracy is needed.

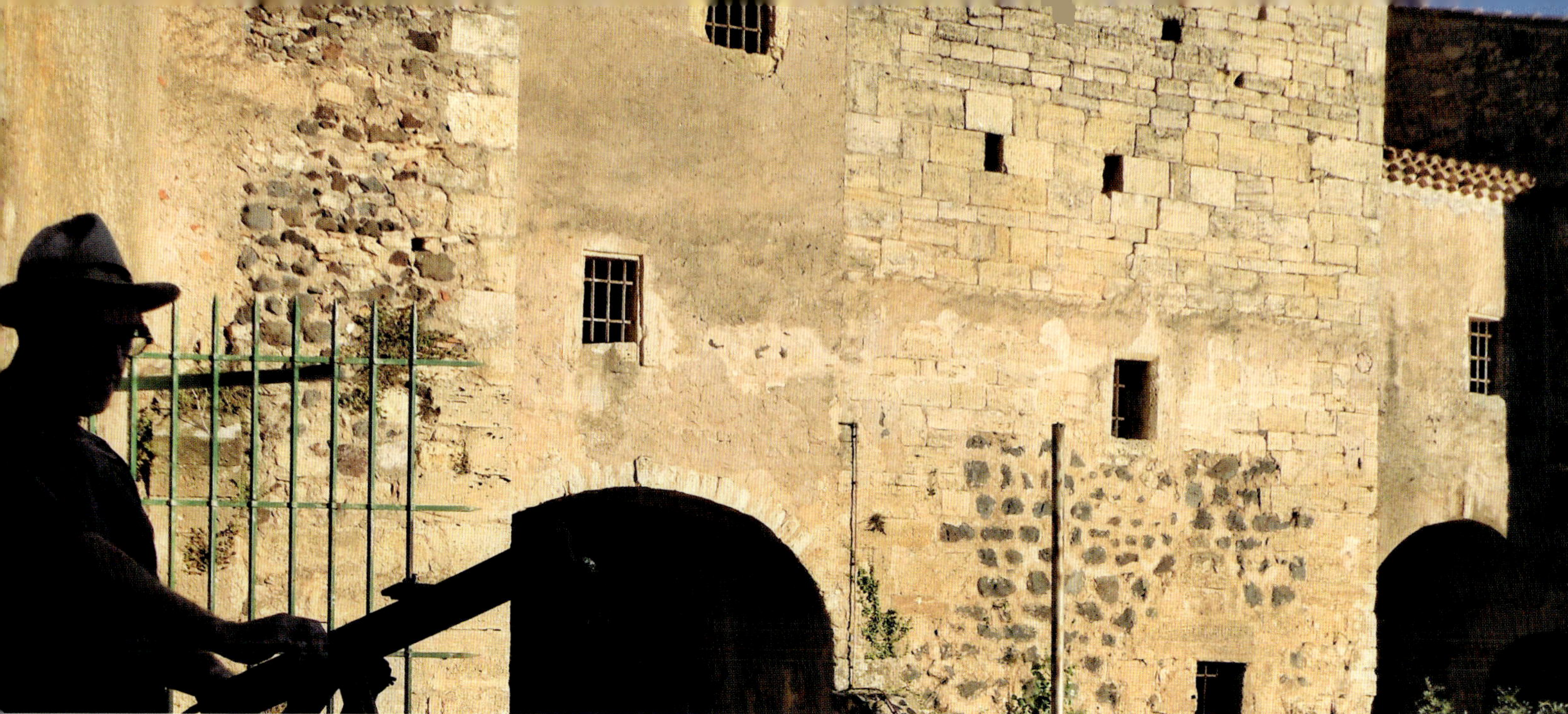

The importance of drawing

Drawing is a vital tool. It goes hand in hand with observation – and both your drawing and observation will improve in line with each other as you practise. In a watercolour, drawing establishes the composition and the structure, as we saw earlier (see pages 46). Drawing is therefore the first stage of selecting what we wish to say about our subject.

Practising our drawing will help us to evaluate the shapes in front of us, and to understand our subject and our position in relation to it. Part of this process is evaluating a subject in terms of tonal values, and this is also crucial to the way we put down watercolour.

I use drawing in a purely functional sense, so the marks made in my initial drawing do not form part of the finished image (as they might in pen and wash, for example).

Drawing buildings

Figure drawing is an effective way to learn because you can see immediately if something is wrong, but I feel that you can learn to draw by drawing anything. As the artist and illustrator Rowland Hilder (1905–1993) put it, we learn to draw by drawing.

You have likely tried drawing in the studio way: focused on a single object. Studio practice drawing is valuable because it teaches us how to analyse a subject. When tackling buildings, architecture and landscape, however, it is best to draw the *plein-air* way. To learn how to draw architecture and the shapes we find in buildings and street scenes we should draw them directly.

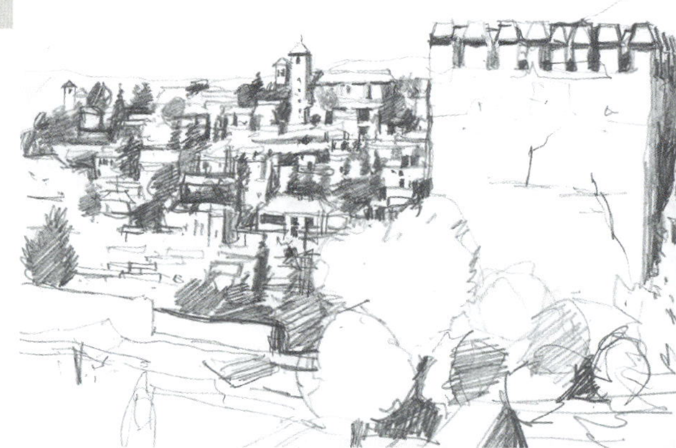

I use drawing to help me with defining details as well as the general forms. It also helps me to understand particular parts of the subject a little better.

Timed studio sketches

Drawing is all about the evaluation of shapes, so let's start by using the objects you find around you: chairs, easels – anything can be your subject matter.

For this exercise, you need just a soft pencil such as a 2B, an eraser, and a piece of paper – 30.5 × 25.5cm (12 × 10in) is ideal, as the size will help you in reducing the subject to its crucial components. The objective is to learn rather than create a finished work of art.

- Start by spending twenty minutes to make a first drawing. When drawing, hold the pencil between your thumb and forefinger and let the whole arm move. Don't worry if it seems a little 'tight' – making this first sketch will allow you to loosen up a bit.

- The next step is to change the position of the subject and repeat the process, allowing less and less time for each subsequent drawing, until you are spending no more than five minutes from start to finish. This will develop your sense of what elements are important to the subject.

- After this process, start again at twenty minutes, this time including what is behind the subject in the studio and how this relates to the object of the drawing. This encourages you to explore depth, space and the relationship between objects – crucial for portraying buildings.

Foundations

- It does not matter where you start a drawing. Just choose an easily seen and measured feature and relate other features to that dimension. For a figure, this might be their head. For architecture, you could use one edge of a building.

- Avoid adding details until the main features are established – after that, draw in as much detail as you wish. If we start with details it is easy to lose sight of general proportions.

- Use photography with care. It can be useful for information and detail, but it has limitations.

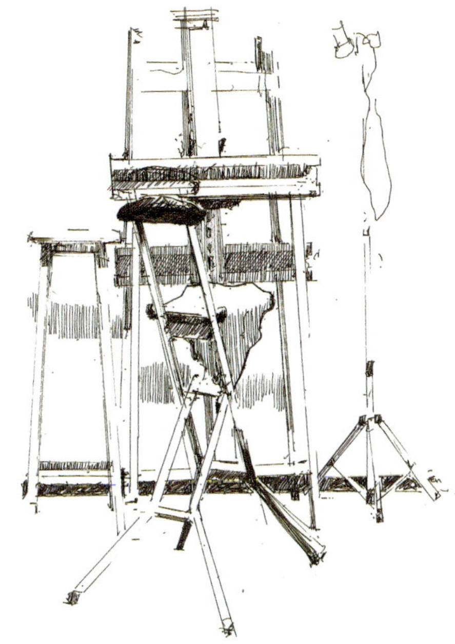

First sketch: subject only

This ink drawing was done in twenty minutes with the objective of seeing how various objects interacted.

I recommend using a pencil for the exercise when you start out; but once you are more confident, using ink can be an excellent exercise, as it will help reveal and improve faults as you reinstate corrected lines instead of erasing and starting again.

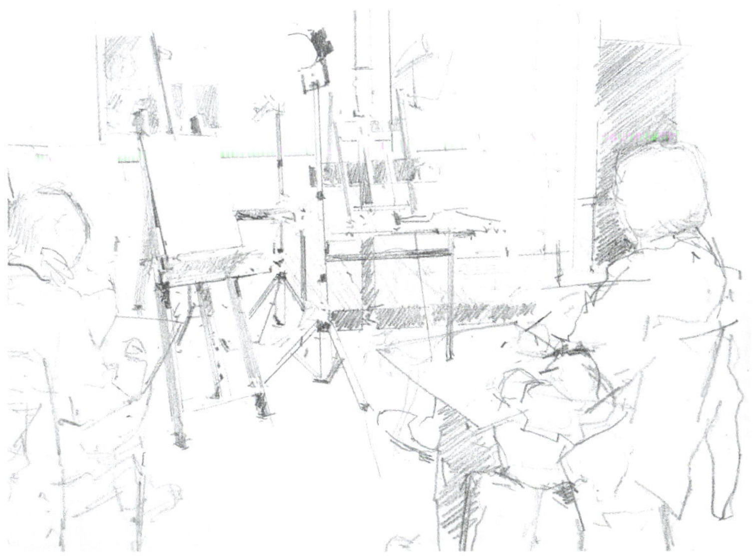

The subject in context

This drawing of one of the groups I teach was an exercise in capturing context. One step on from the drawing of objects in the studio is to draw them in their setting. In the controlled environment of the studio, it's easier to grasp the idea of how separate objects interact in a drawing: an important lesson.

Drawing from life

Once you have some practice in drawing inside, move outdoors. Drawing outside will help with understanding perspective and, crucially, with editing the scene. There are advantages both practical and in terms of enjoyment for exploring a subject *in situ* – it is a great experience to paint on the spot and an exciting way to produce art.

For our purposes, as well as defining the subject the drawing gives us the structure of the painting and establishes the composition and how we use the drawing in this sense is described in the demonstration.

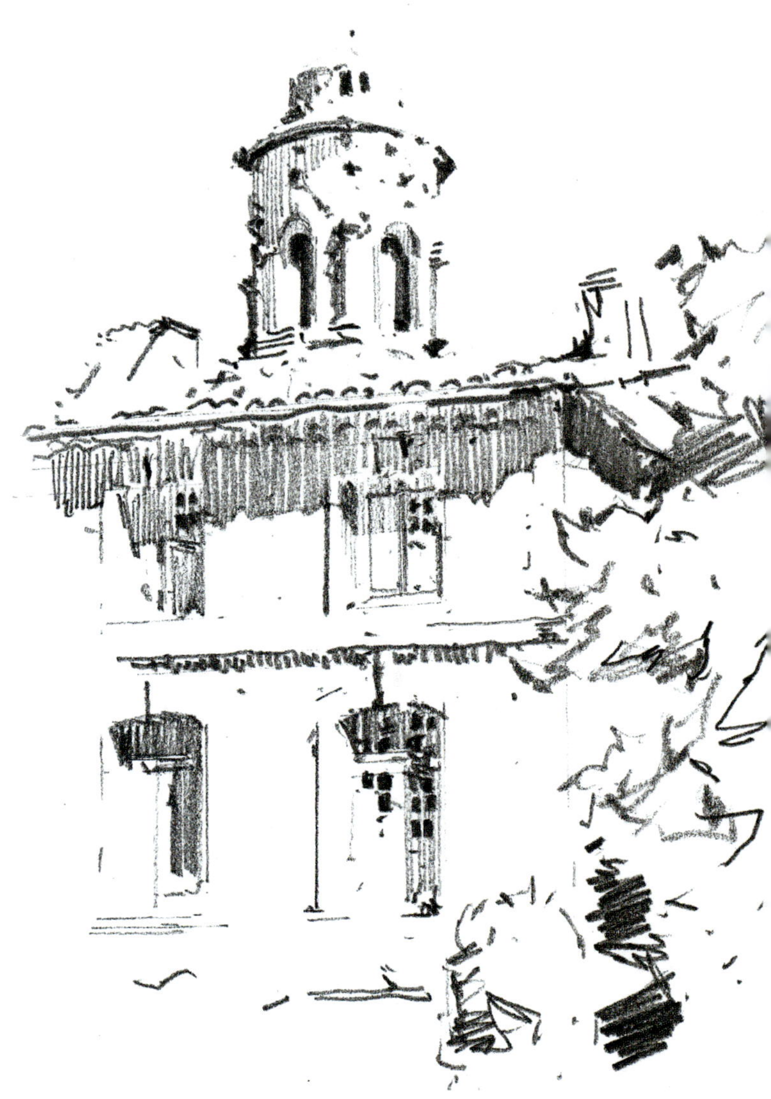

Cassan pencil

Sketching from life with a time limit will really help identify and focus your attention on the essentials of a scene and see how large objects relate to each other. This quick 10 × 12cm (4 × 4¾in) drawing, of a lantern tower at Chateau Cassan, concentrated on light and form. It took just five minutes.

Building skills

- Sketch as often as you can. Any object will do.
- Draw one part of your subject and relate other parts to it – this will help you get the proportions right.
- Concentrate on the general larger forms of an object before adding any detail.
- While measuring against a pencil, use an outstretched arm and close one eye – this flattens the view and makes it easier to judge relative sizes.
- For speed, keep detail minimal – you can always add it later if you need a better understanding. If this is done during painting, it is important to wait for the paper to be completely dry to avoid scoring or creating marks that cannot then be removed.
- Any unwanted pencil marks should be rubbed out at the end, once the painting is finished and properly dry. Erasing lines can damage the surface of some papers or affect how the paint sits on it.

Evaluating tone

Judging tonal value allows us to recreate light, shade, and depth in our painting. In practical terms it is the relative strength of objects, shapes and surfaces.

Crucially, we can use drawing to learn how to evaluate a subject in terms of tone. What becomes useful for watercolour, where we work from light to dark, is to evaluate a subject in three tonal strengths. The first is to identify the lightest areas and that is left as an outlined white paper (in the watercolour this would be lightest wash or white paper). The second, using cross-hatching, is the mid-tone; while the third tonal strength is expressed using closer cross-hatching and is used for the areas of darker tone. In a further stage, marks can be used to create detail and define form.

There are obviously many tonal values seen in our subjects, but this is a straightforward way, in the context of using watercolour, with which we can learn how to evaluate a subject.

Darkest tones
Cross-hatching worked with thicker lines.

Mid-tones
Hatching (closely spaced parallel lines) creates tone.

Lightest tones
Clean white paper.

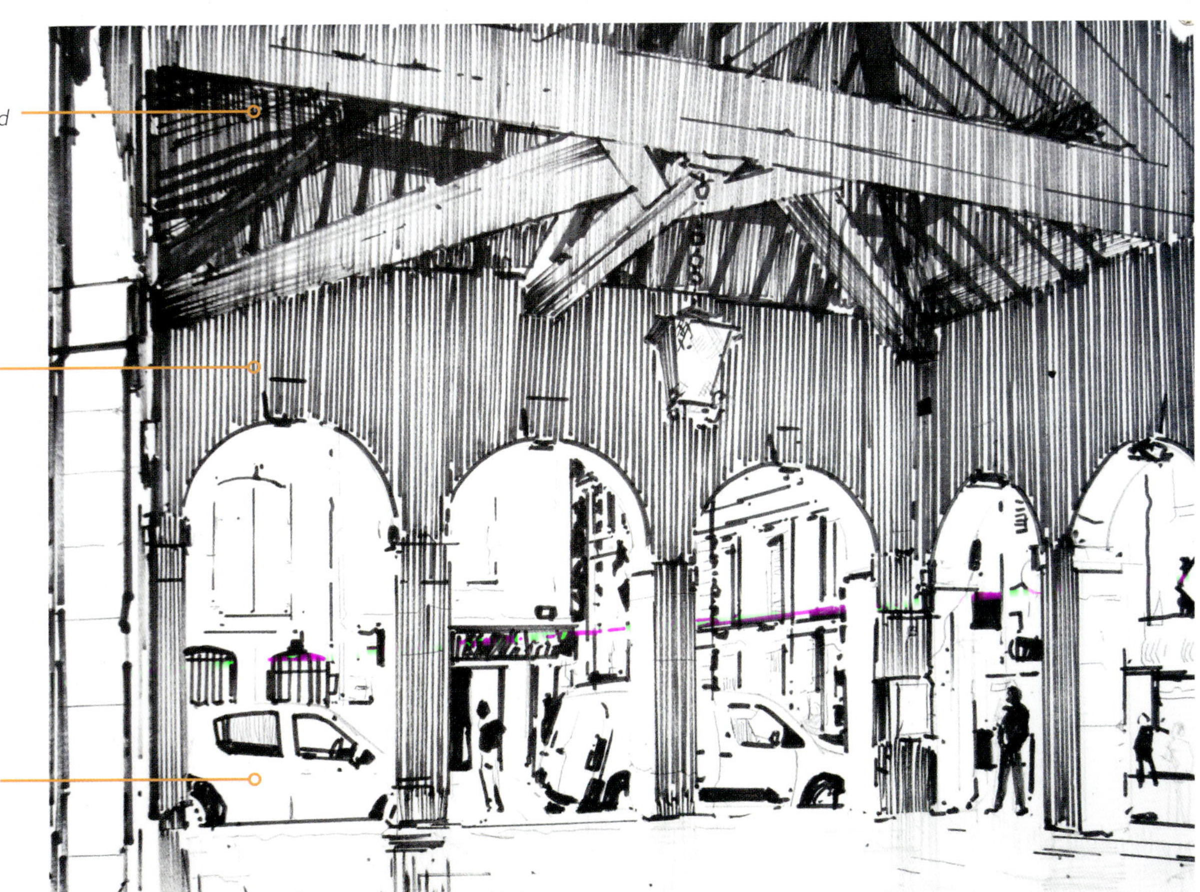

Marseillan Covered Market, tonal drawing

This drawing, done for the purpose of a tonal study lesson for my students, made use of lines, in three tones with lines of varying thickness and gaps between. The purpose was to use the drawing to help evaluate the scene in terms of tone.

Watermill

Tone and perspective

The basics of drawing perspective and tonal evaluation provide vital foundations for any watercolour. By developing these skills in combination with subject selection and composition we can dramatically improve our chances.

This watermill, near where I live, has numerous surfaces and shapes, both regular geometric forms and irregular. We'll start with a working drawing in pencil that includes directional arrows on the drawing to show how perspective works in practice.

For the purpose of this drawing demonstration, I have used heavier lines that can be seen more easily. If you are intending to produce a watercolour like the example on page 77, draw fewer shapes and use a lighter touch.

YOU WILL NEED

Two 2B pencils

Eraser

Easel, board and pins

**Paper: cartridge paper,
27 × 24cm (10¾ × 9½in)**

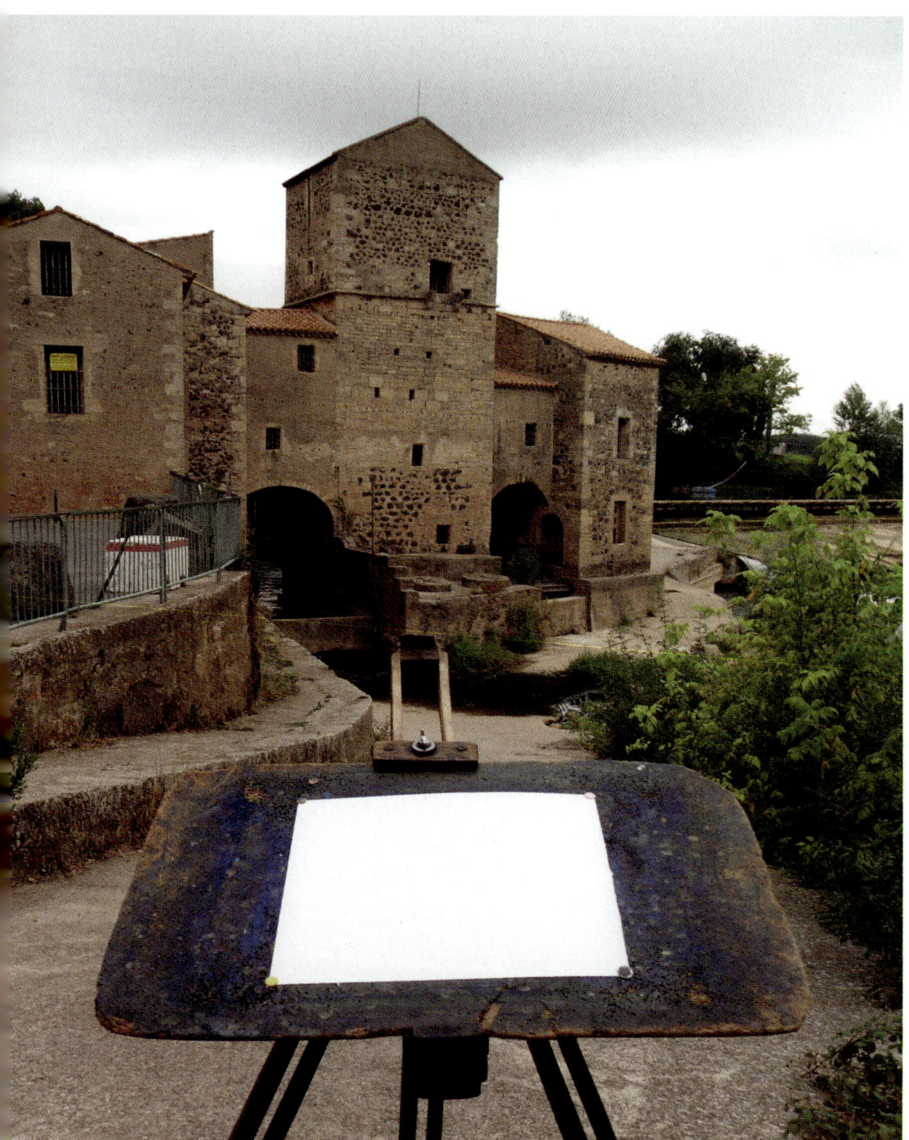

Setting up

Scaling up by zooming in can create problems, particularly with depth. I find it easier to draw at 'sight size' – that is, the subject is drawn on the paper at the same size as it appears before you.

Position yourself directly in front of the subject, so that you are not drawing off to one side. If the content you wish to include of the subject is high up, it is easier if you have sufficient distance from it, so you do not have to strain to see it all.

Perspective can become a little over-dramatic or contrived if done from a sitting position, so I decided to stand for this painting. The sort of easel seen in the images is crucial.

Importantly, while we are drawing, we are also observing and many of those observations don't make it onto the paper at this point but are key to gaining an understanding of the subject.

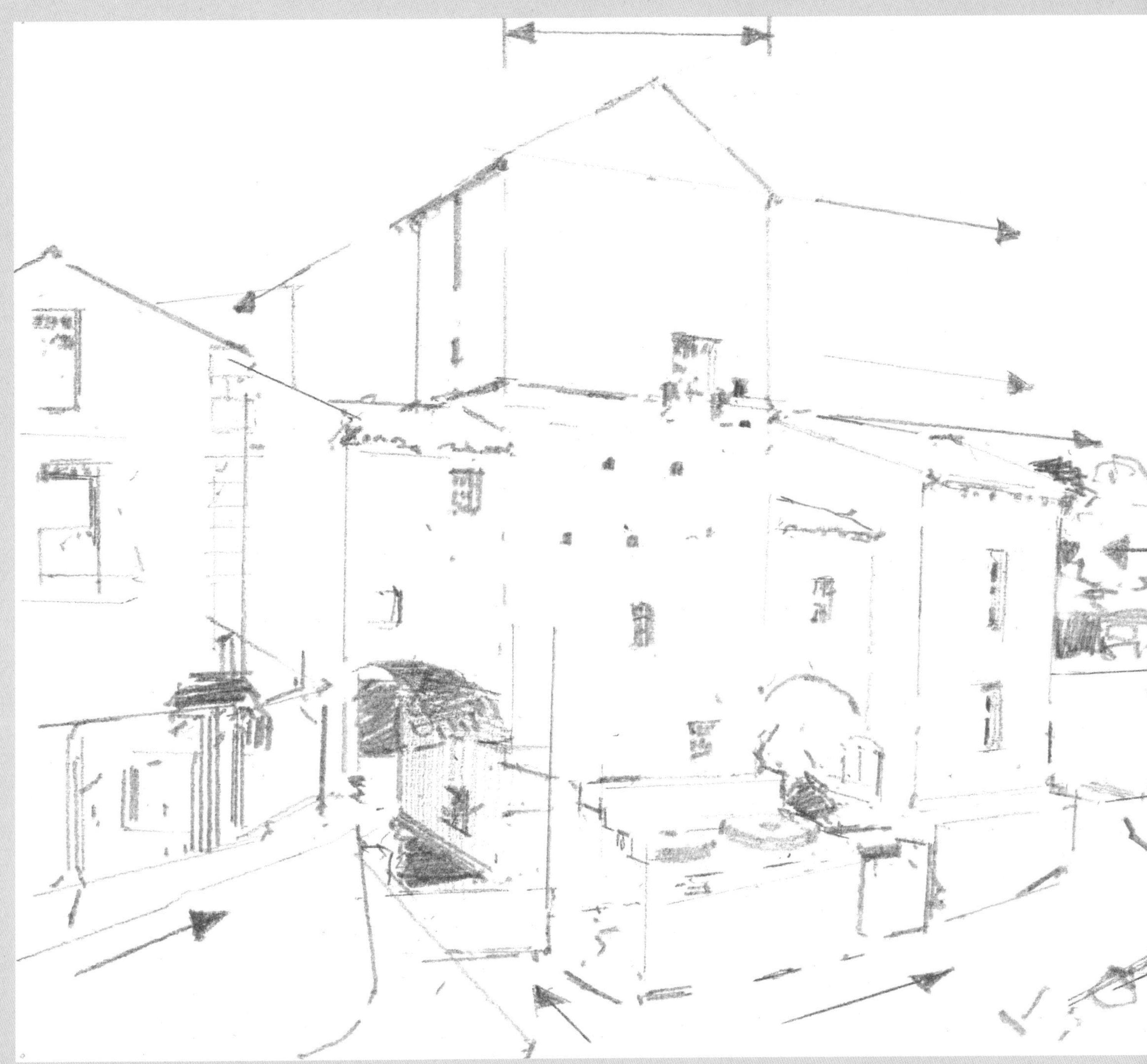

The finished perspective drawing

Stage 1

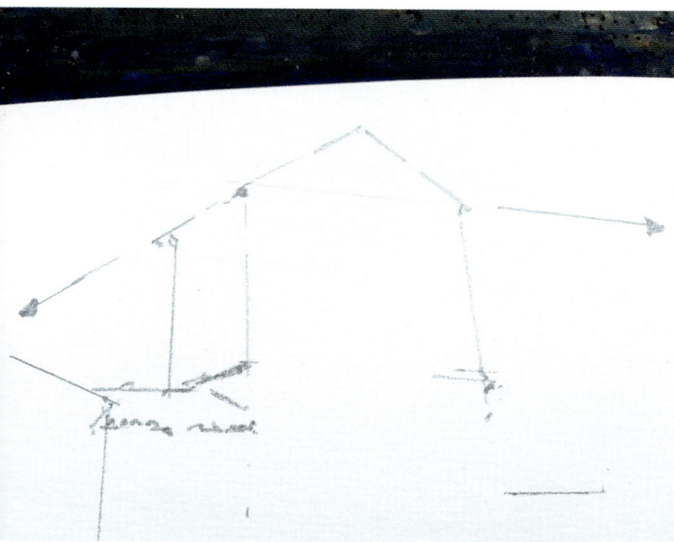

Think in terms of simple shapes when evaluating a structure. Here I thought of the central tower as a triangle on top of a rectangle.

The arrows indicate the lines of perspective.

In painting and drawing architecture we are mostly dealing with geometric shapes and our relation to them – this applies to all architecture and so it is helpful to be able to evaluate shapes and at what angle we see them.

In the context of a watercolour, the drawing provides the structure of the painting. In theory you can start in any place on the paper and with any part of the subject, but I find it helps to start with and place the principal object or feature – in this instance the tower.

Placing it slightly off-centre, start by establishing the height of the central tower on the paper. You can work out its proportions by measuring with a pencil and outstretched arm, as shown below.

Before putting pencil to paper, work out the placement. Areas of interest should be placed well within the frame of the paper, and you should avoid placing objects near the bottom edge, as this can affect how the eye leads into the painting. Depending on the subject, it is less crucial if the top of an object leaves the picture. In this instance, however, the top of the mill provides an interesting shape and including it allows us to see more of the structure.

Using the pencils both to check lengths and as straight edges to draw against, build up the shapes of the central tower.

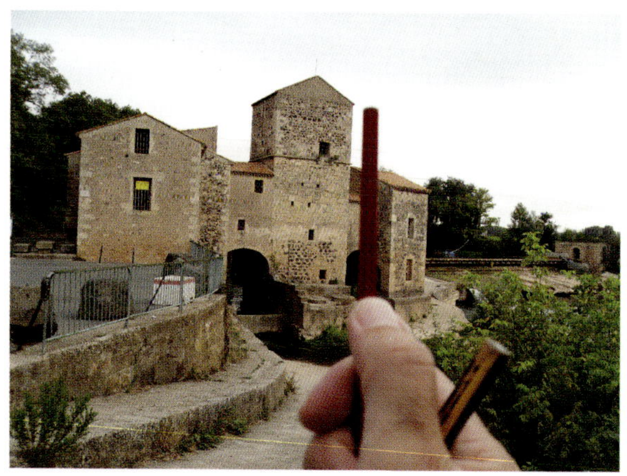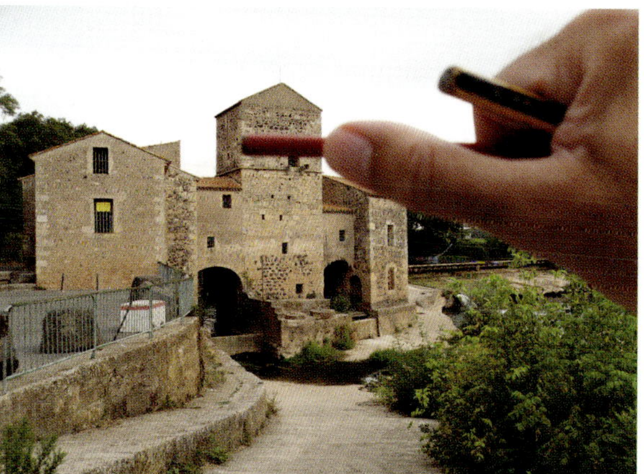

Ready reckoning

When measuring we hold a pencil with an outstretched arm so that the measurement remains constant. Keep one eye closed to flatten the image.

I find it useful to use two pencils that can help with drawing verticals, measuring, and checking angles or direction of line.

Stage 2

Once the principal form of the tower is established, start to draw in the surrounding architectural features, working down and outwards from the tower. It is important that we understand the forms – but we do not need to be architects to achieve this, just good observational skills.

You can use a pencil aligned with the edge you wish to draw to understand the angle (see below left). To judge the angle between points in the drawing – such as at the top point of the middle tower and the point on top of the roof on the right – you can hold a pencil outstretched touching each point (see below right).

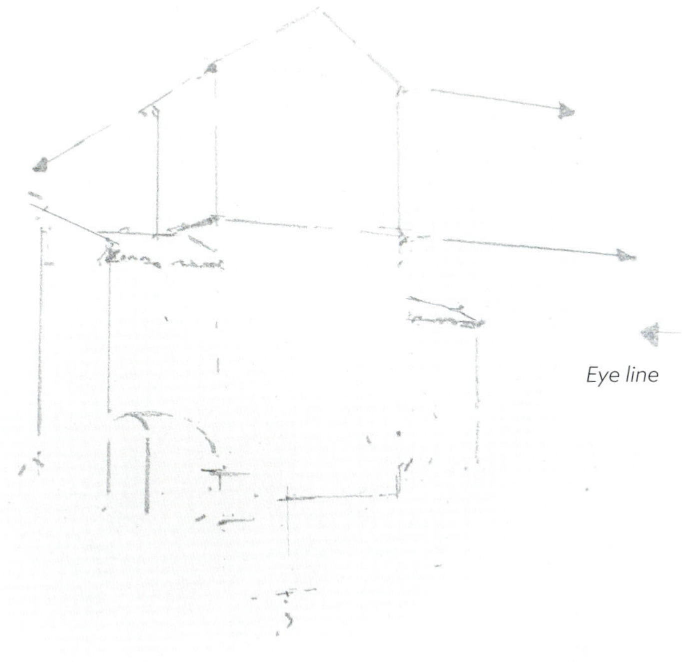

Use the lines of perspective to help with placing subsequent developments. Note the arrow that appears on the right of the image. This is the level of the eye line, which lines of perspective head towards. Adding it in at this stage will prove useful.

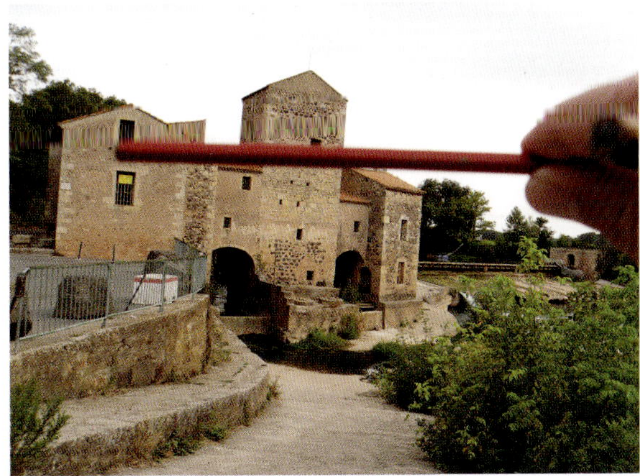

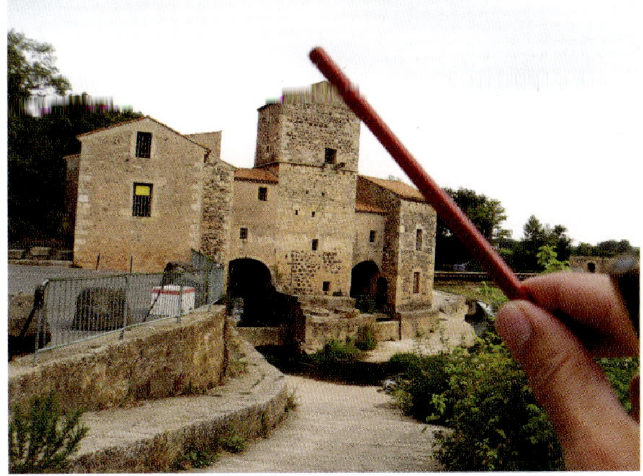

Comparing position of features

Hold a pencil horizontally to compare relative positions and heights of various features (above left). Align a pencil between points of reference to check the relative position and angle between them (above right). These quick reference measurements will help you to ensure one part of the drawing correctly relates to another.

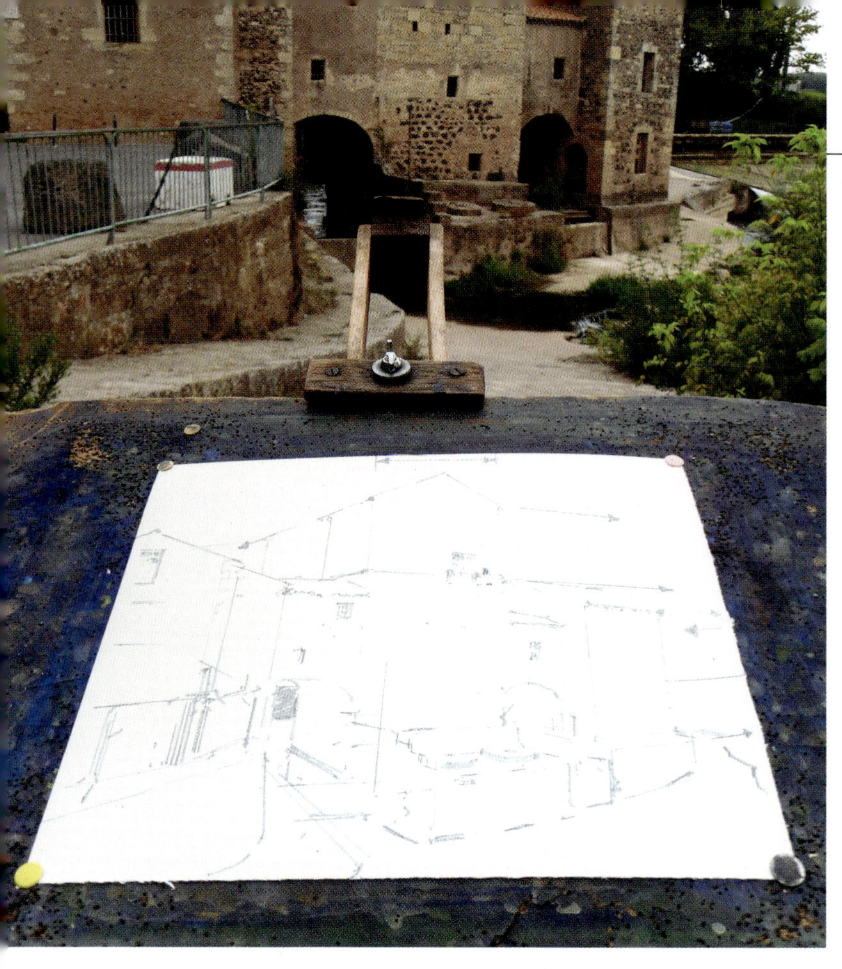

Working outwards from the tower, continue to place in the forms using the techniques described on the previous pages. Be careful to stay consistent, and keep referring to the subject rather than making assumptions based on what's on your paper.

The structure of parts of this mill are unusual because of their function, and this can make you second-guess your observations. For example, the structure on the right is trapezoid, so the angles on the roof appear a little strange.

Architecture can often throw up unexpected surprises like this. One great advantage of working from life is that we can walk around our subject to evaluate the angle of various surfaces and shape of structures – just stay true to what you actually see, rather than what you expect to see.

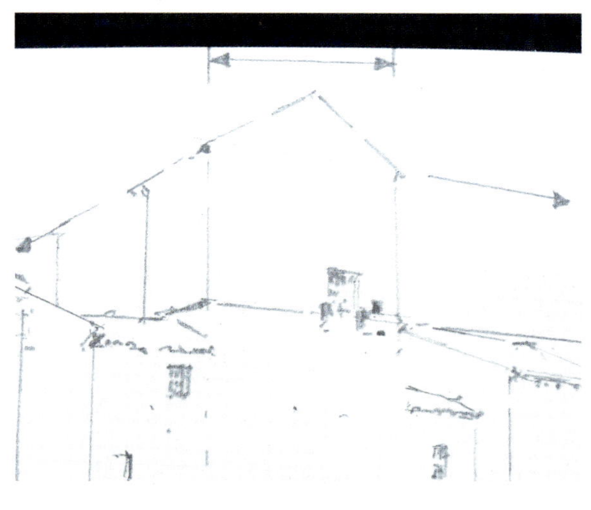

Making a key reference

Above the central tower you can see I added a measurement. Taken from the central feature – in this case the width of the tower – this is useful to measure other elements against.

To use this measurement, hold the pencil up at arm's length so the end aligns with one side of the tower (or other reference point). Place your thumb in line with the other side. Without moving your thumb, and keeping your arm outstretched, you can now move the pencil to compare with other shapes – the tower, for example, is two 'widths' from the water level to the start of the roof.

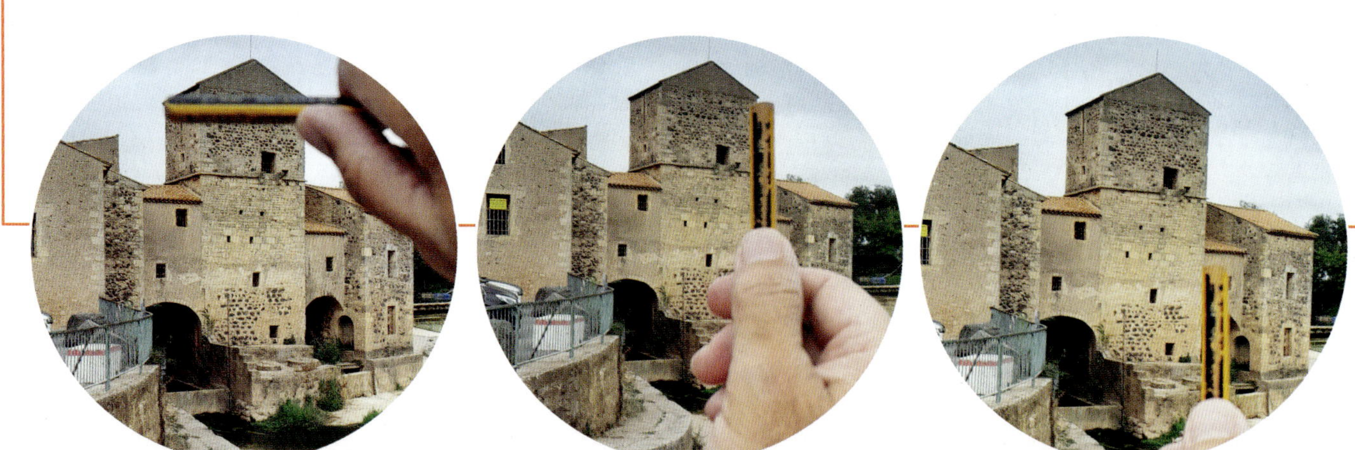

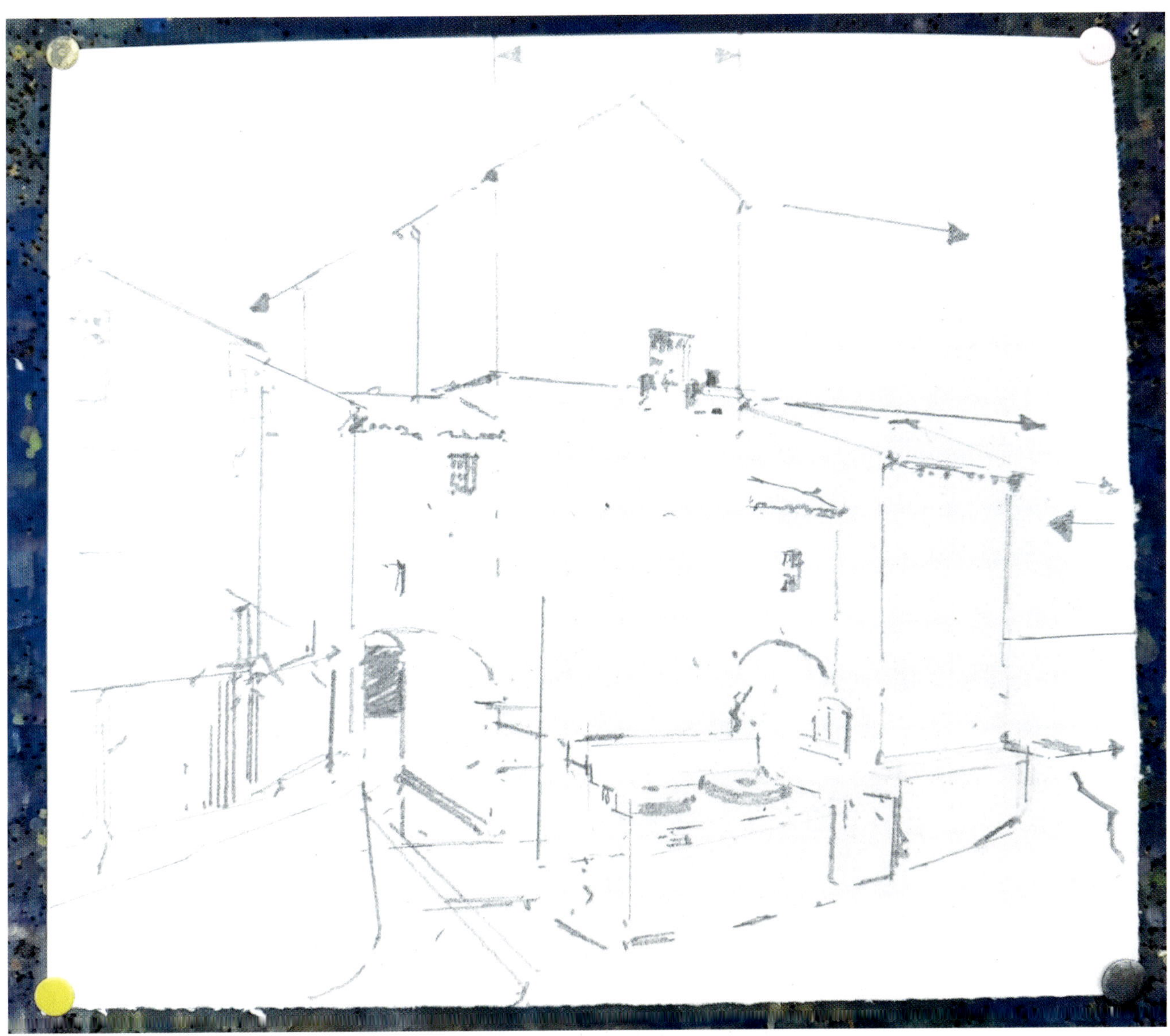

Finishing touches: adding details

Details are the last stage. In features such as windows, all lines follow the rules of perspective, so make use of the angles and lines established earlier.

If there are shadows, they too will follow the lines of perspective. I try to choose details that add something in terms of interest or defining content – not just because they are there.

The finished drawing can be seen on page 71.

Building skills

- Watercolourists are often concerned about 'tightness' in their paintings. Tightness and accuracy should not be confused. Tightness looks incongruous and affects how we relate to and read the painting. It can be minimized by carefully choosing drawing materials.

- Avoid using rulers that create sharp-edged drawings.

- An accurate drawing should go by unnoticed, instead allowing the painting to shine.

Using the drawing

The Mill at Saint-Thibéry is near where I live in France, and I have drawn and painted this mill a number of times. The same place can offer a number of different opportunities for the artist, so it's worth exploring and trying different approaches if you find an inspiring scene.

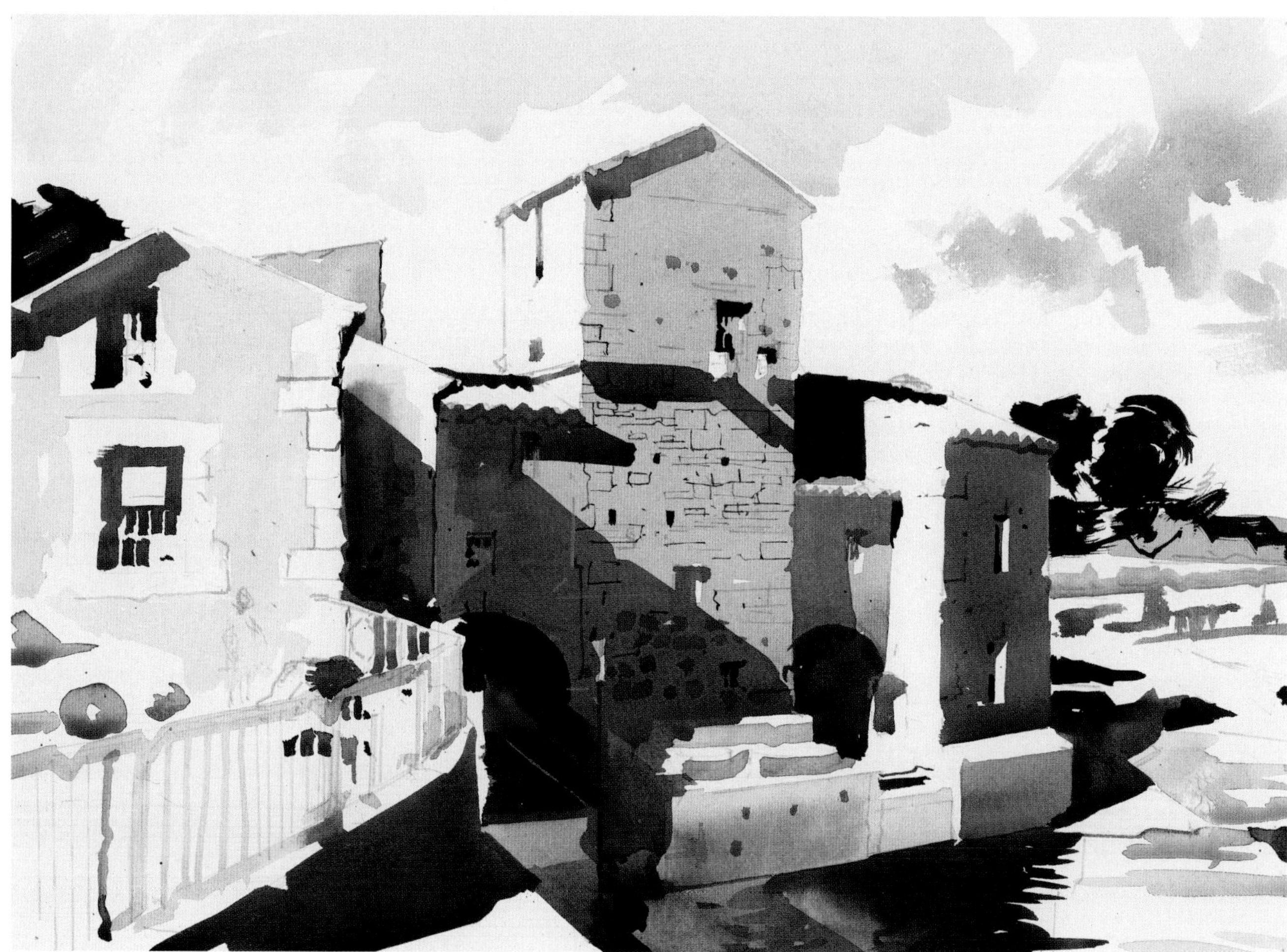

Tonal sketch on grey card

For this tonal sketch, I followed the same process as described in the project with regards to the drawing. Progressively stronger shades of a grey mix were then added to create form.

For this sort of sketch, I work in three tonal stages: starting with lights, moving on to mid-tones and darks. This helps me evaluate comparative tonal values and corresponds with the order of painting needed in watercolour.

Tonal sketch of Le Moulin de Saint-Thibéry
38 × 28cm (15 × 11in)

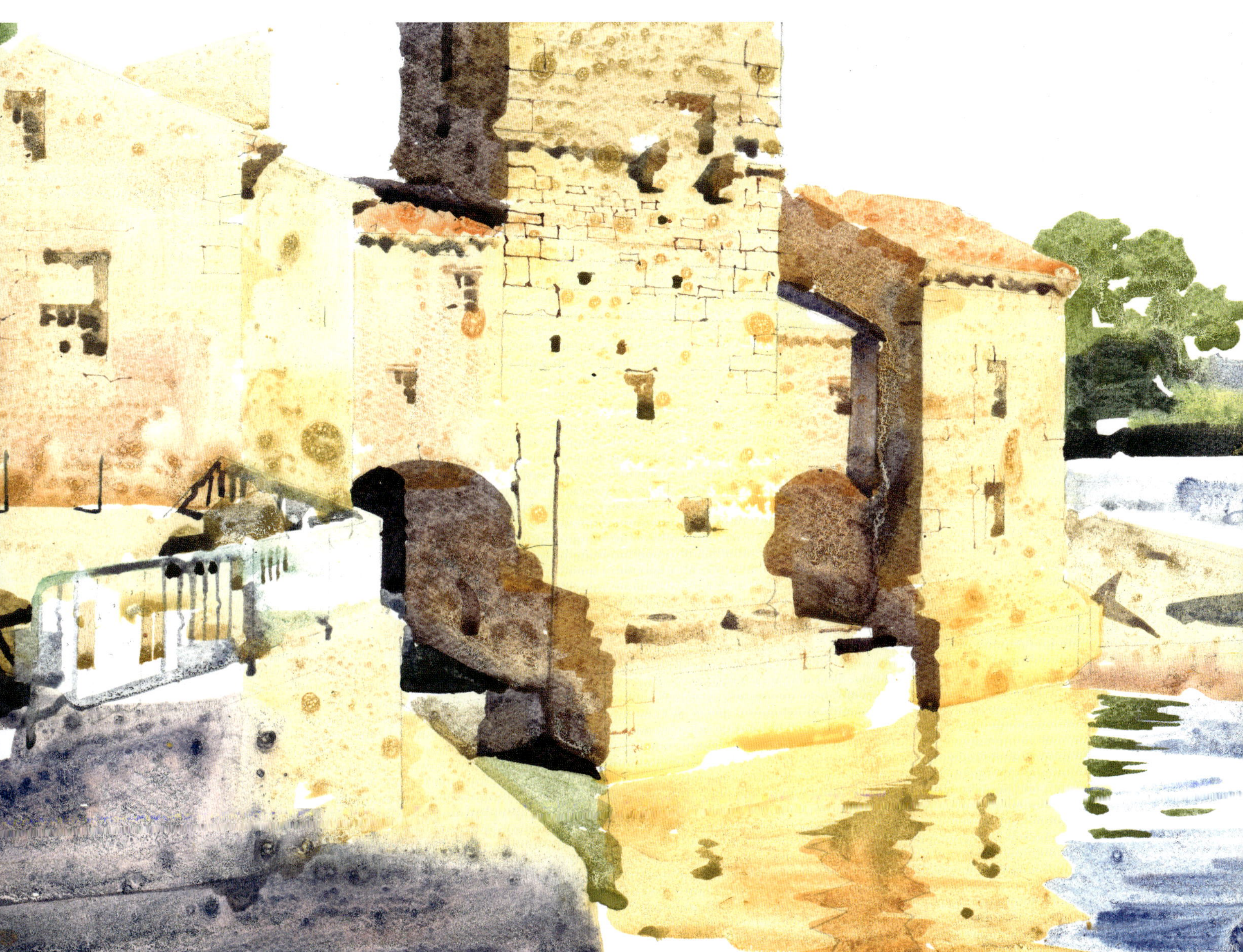

Watercolour

In this version, painted on 300gsm (140lb) Saunders
Waterford Not surface paper, I focused on the lower parts of
the structure and the water.

As mentioned at the start of the project, I used much lighter
– and fewer – lines for the underlying drawing here than in the
dedicated pencil drawing version.

Le Moulin de Saint-Thibéry
38 × 28cm (15 × 11in)

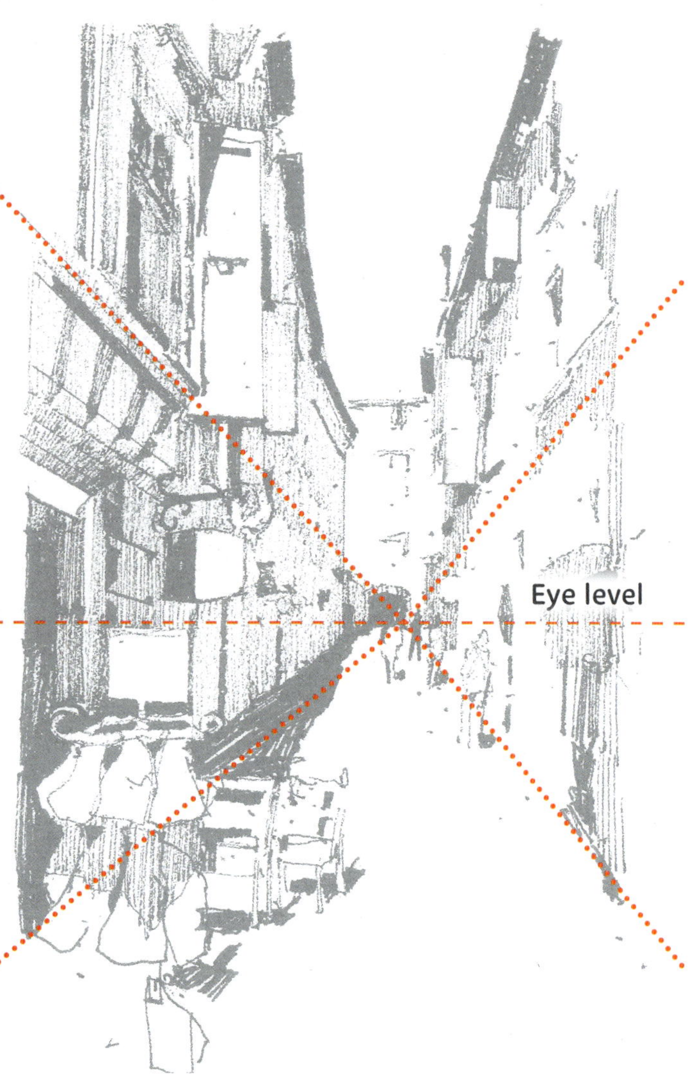

Perspective: theory and practice

You have probably heard the same lessons in perspective over and over again, but if problems in your paintings persist, the origin is likely not in your understanding of perspective, but in how to judge the various angles and proportions we find in physical subjects.

When painting or drawing architecture from life, it is key to remember that we are simply dealing with a small range of geometric shapes and our relation to their lines. If you can identify those shapes and lines, things will naturally fall into place.

It is crucial to establish our eye level: the horizon line where the vanishing points will sit, and all converging lines will head. Any lines above our eyeline will slope down towards the horizon, while any below will slope upwards to the horizon – as shown in the drawing to the left. Here, this view is uphill and so the eye level is closer to the level of the bottom of the head of the figure on the right.

The rules of perspective are easy to grasp, but it is crucial to see how these rules actually apply to the observed world. Go outside and roam around looking at geometric shapes in buildings, in windows, in arches and so forth. Observe how the principles apply to what you observe – and you will find how these abstract ideas apply in reality.

Common perspective traps

Slopes If a building is on a slope and we are looking uphill, the line where the building meets the ground will slope uphill towards the horizon at a steeper angle than if on a flat surface. Conversely if sloping down, the line will slope at a less steep angle towards the horizon.

Foreshortening Another point to understand is that we see more of the side of an object nearest to us than that further away: the side of the wall marked A needs to be longer than the more distant B, even though they are the same height.

Curves Circles and arches can be a little more difficult to understand as they form ellipses (C), but the same principles apply as in any other shape. They still follow the same principle that we see more of the open side of the arch nearer to us.

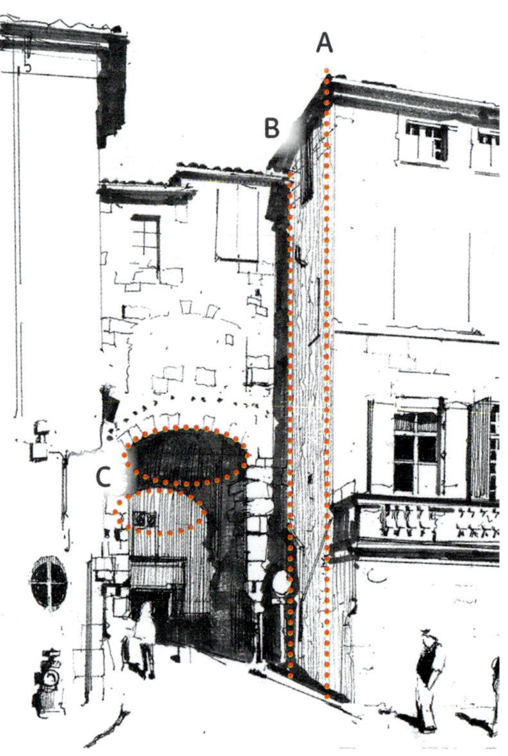

Help with judging perspective

In architecture, many drawing errors relate to direction of line and proportions and there are a number of simple methods to help us establish the direction a line follows or the shape and size of a form.

The measuring method Well-known and easy to follow, this involves measuring a shape against a pencil held out at arm's length and then comparing with other measurements. The incline or descent of a line can also be judged by using the edge of a pencil held up to the line you are judging, and this will help understand what angle the line is at. There are other similar methods such as using two pieces of card held at one end, with one placed on the vertical and the other on the line you are judging. This will give a perfectly accurate measurement that can then be used in your painting.

Lines of reference Constantly draw lines of direction from whatever straight-edged object happens to be nearby. This can be done on any spare piece of paper and with any pencil or pen at hand and it helps to train the eye.

Trust your eye Always use whatever you can to help you to judge an angle, but be aware that photography, particularly of architecture, changes and bends perspective – in fact, so much so, that it is easy to tell when an artist has used it as a basis. When we work from life and need a better view to evaluate a form, all we need to do is move slightly to one side or take a closer look – we cannot do this with a photograph and for this reason we cannot learn to draw by working purely from photographs.

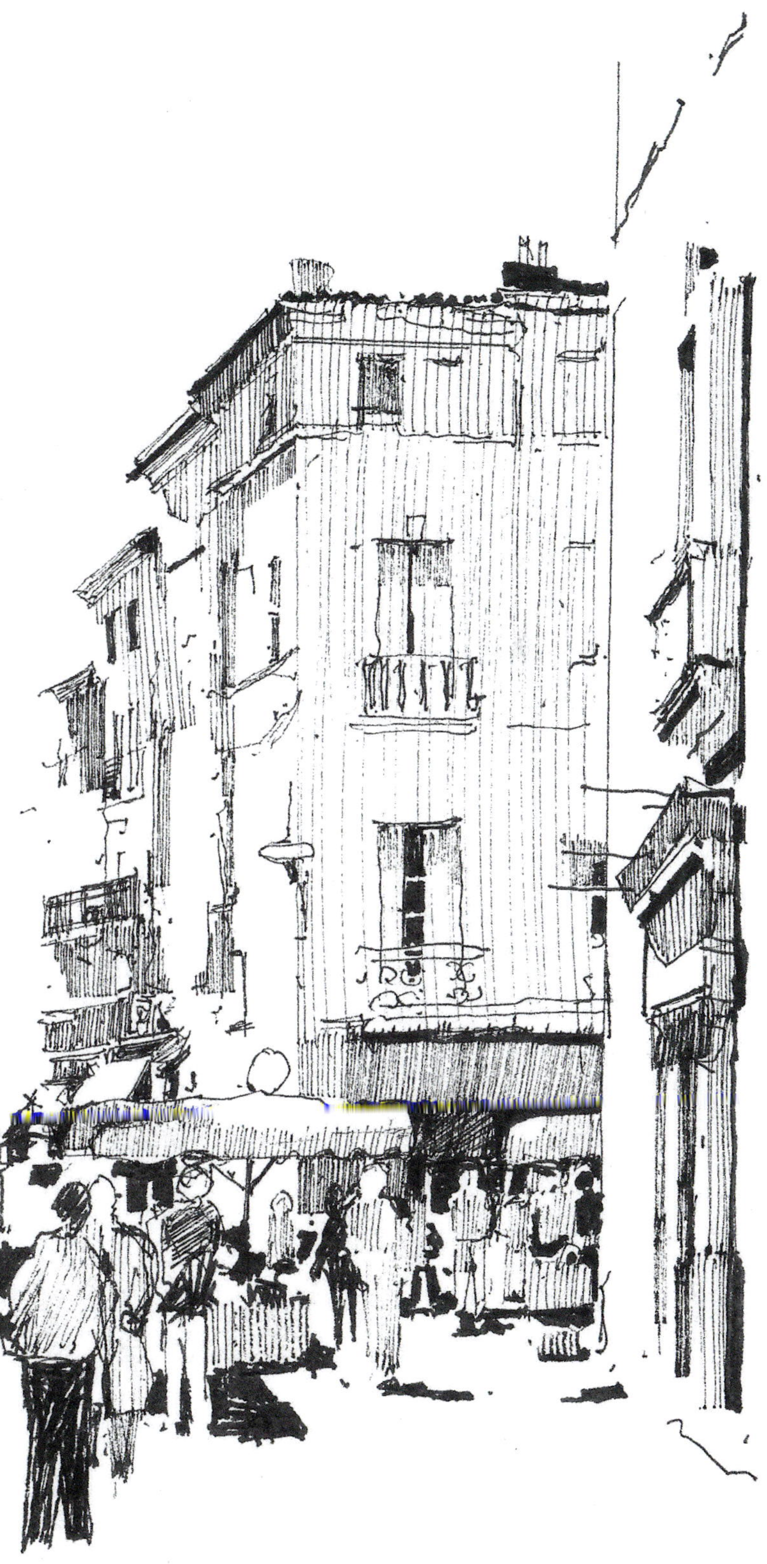

Improving your drawing

To improve your drawing, you must be strict with yourself and never accept something that looks wrong. We must remain focused on measuring and judging angles and shapes.

Pencil drawing can be worked on – rubbed out, adjusted and so forth, but it is also useful to learn drawing as a discipline. When I started to learn drawing architecture, I worked on half-imperial sized 56 × 38cm (22 × 15in) paper and drew directly on the paper with Indian ink. As a learning process, this was excellent – all errors were seen and problems in judgement were revealed and so could be identified and worked on. Because every mark was permanent there was no room for complacency – which is often why errors are made.

Poullis Gallery sketch

This is a detailed ink drawing of my gallery. It measures 38 × 28cm (15 × 11in), and took about an hour. Using a fine nib allowed for a studied and detailed approach of the view, particularly of the forms of the ceiling.

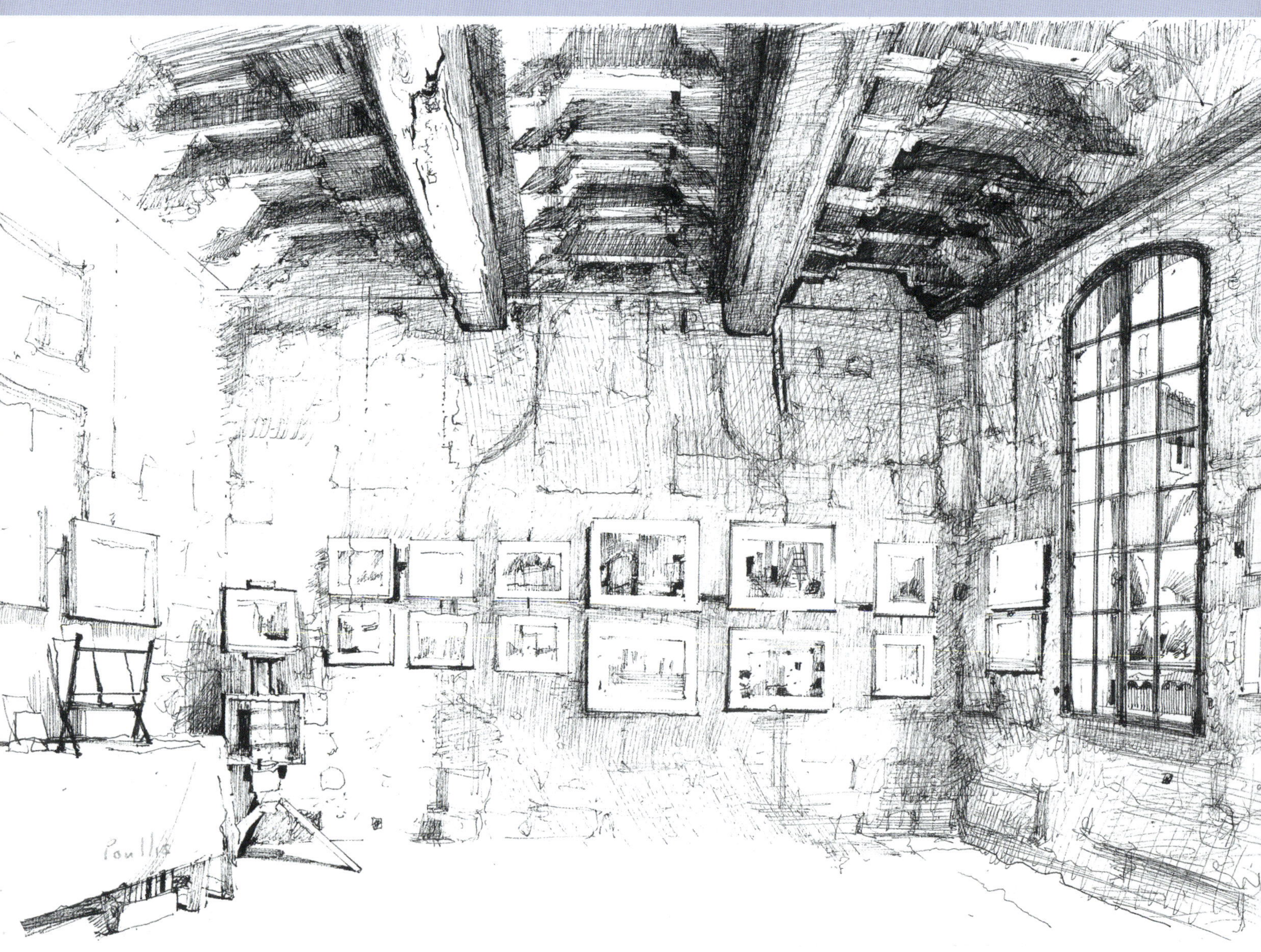

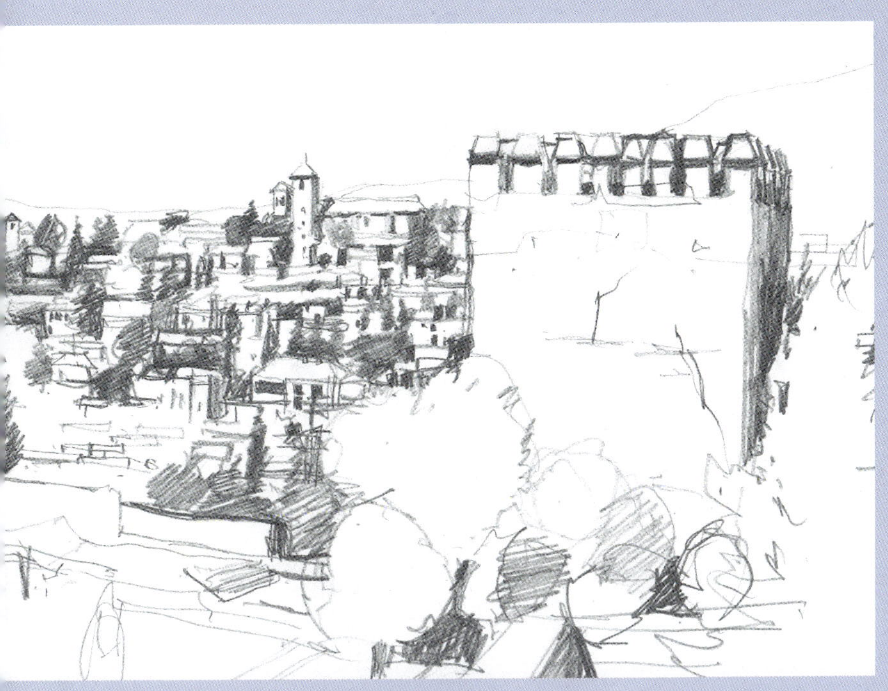

Alhambra Palace in pencil

Drawn in around twenty minutes, this sketch allowed an exploration of this complicated subject. This gave me a firm grip of the view before I started to paint.

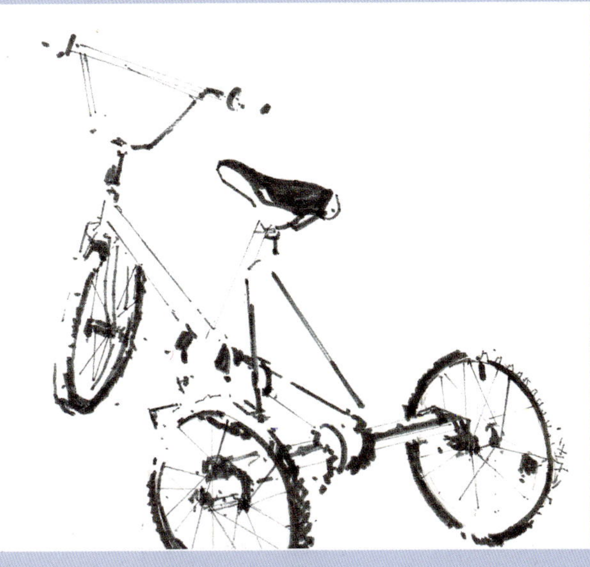

Tricycle in ink pen

This was a terrific subject for practising drawing circles, which become ellipses when seen in perspective.

Building skills

- Try not to place your subject too close to the edge of the paper as this can look cramped.
- Avoid placing shapes (the top of a chimney, for example) just on the paper edge – it looks better either completely in or completely out.
- Position yourself and the easel directly in front of the subject, not to one side, as this will make drawing easier.
- When you start your drawing, try and draw one part right and then relate other objects to it, making sure that the eye level is consistent throughout.
- Avoid concentrating on drawing one object to the exclusion of its context – it's all too easy to then find it does not properly relate to the rest of the picture.
- Editing the scene to say just what you want to say will give the painting focus. I personally draw in the main structure then draw further features only as needed – usually if I need a deeper understanding of some feature – as the painting progresses.
- Look for perspectives that interest you rather than obvious 'full face' views, this can help create compositions that are more personal.

Creating drama and interest with perspective

When we look for subject matter, we should always consider how perspective will affect the structure of the painting. The closer we get to a structure, the more dramatic the perspective will be.

Our viewpoint determines and affects the composition, so perspective can be used to significant effect to create drama in painting architecture. It can also be used as a device to lead us into a subject.

Another way of heightening drama is to use a lower eye level and an elevated position to place the horizon extremely high up on the paper or even off the paper so we don't see it. In the painting of *Sète* on pages 48–49, the subject is viewed from high up. By placing the horizon high on the paper, a dramatic view is established.

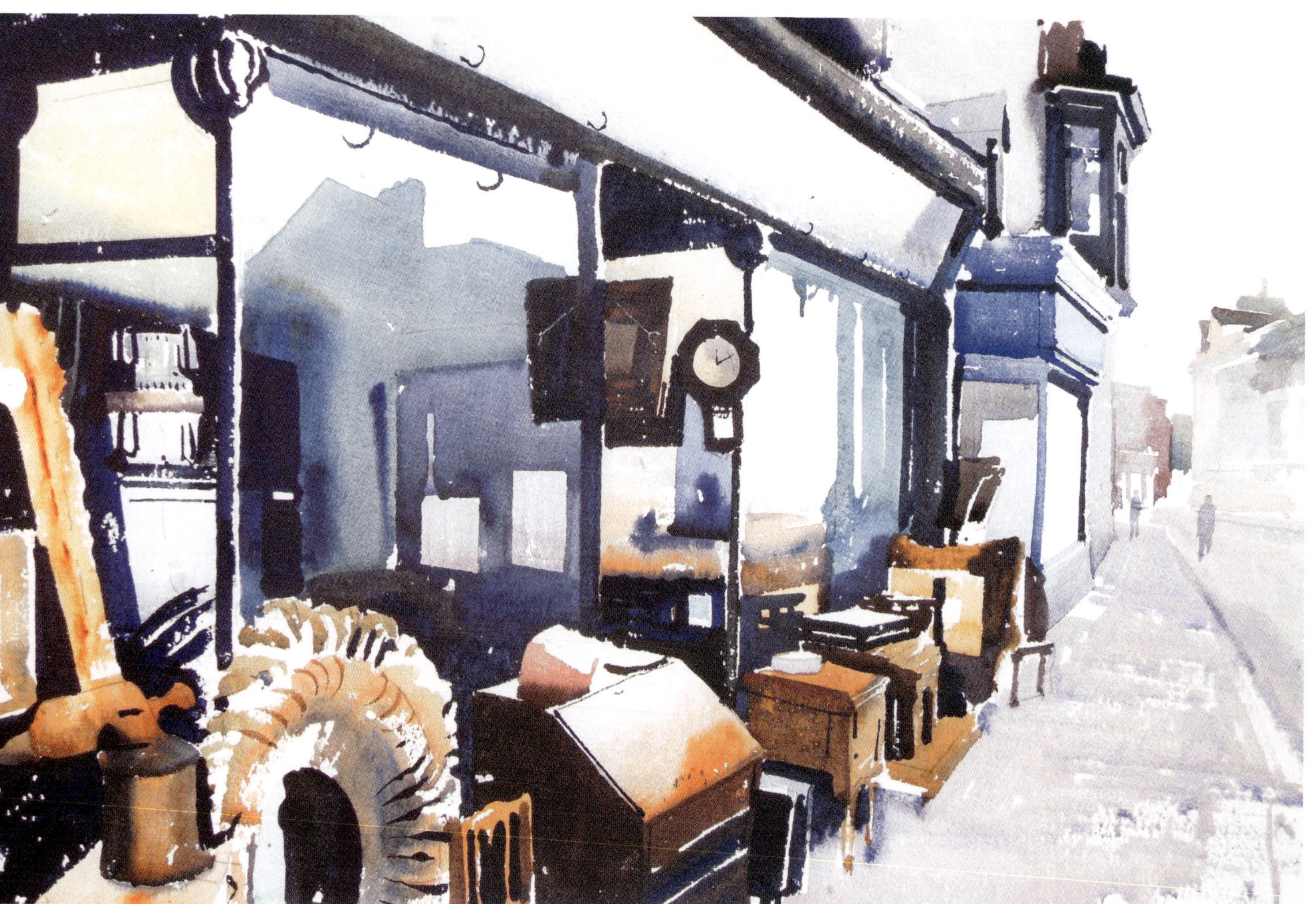

Monmouth

56 × 38cm (22 × 15in) Saunders Waterford 300gsm (140lb) Rough surface paper

This subject provided an opportunity to explore reflections and atmosphere as well as the various forms of the objects in the shop. The viewpoint is key in leading the eye along the street, while the unusual perspective makes the painting feel dynamic and arresting.

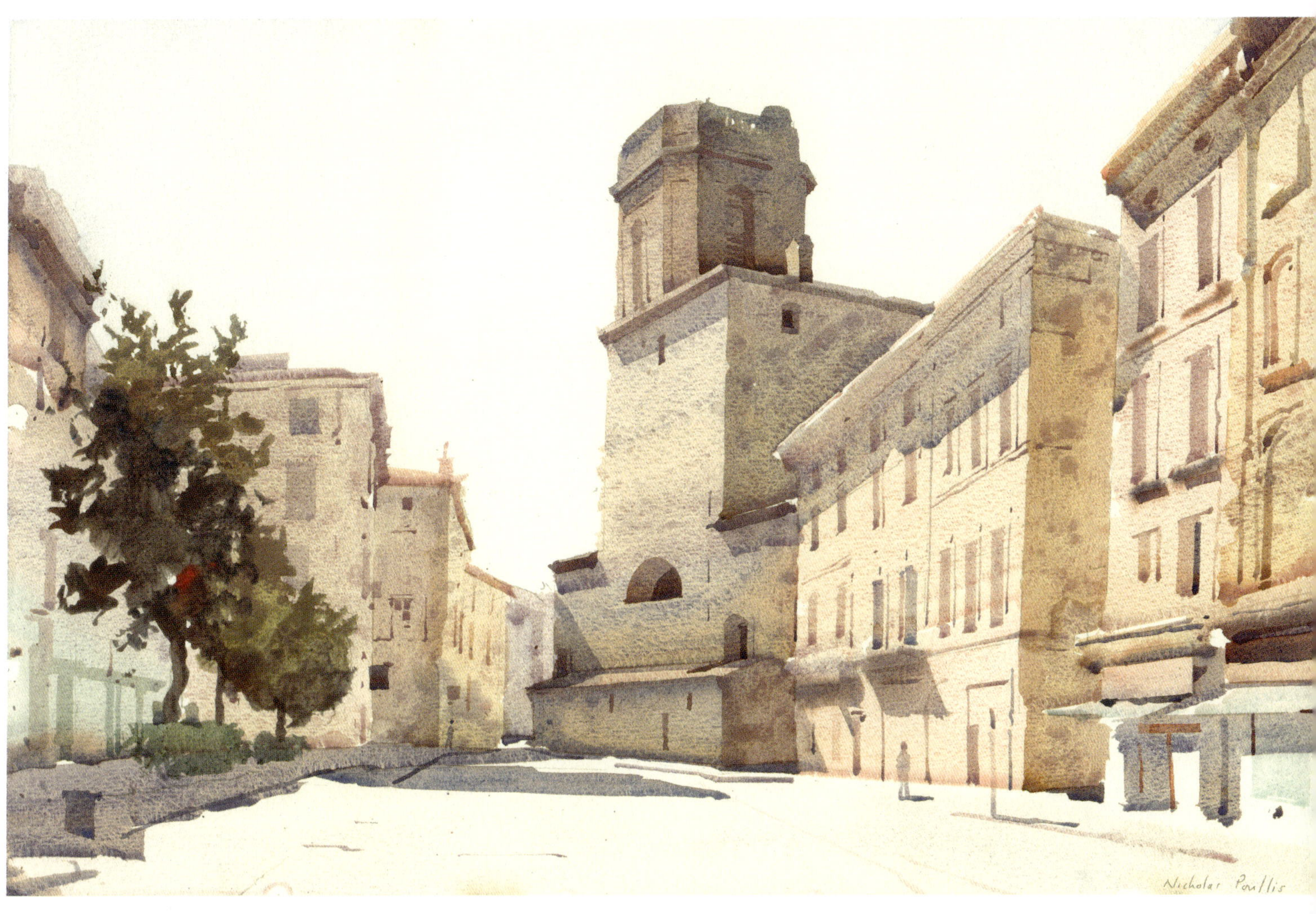

Place Marché des Trois Six, Pézenas

56 × 38cm (22 × 15in) Saunders Waterford 300gsm (140lb) Rough surface paper

We mostly use perspective when painting architecture or in a view where there is a line such as a road and it is always referring to geometric shapes we find in the subject and our position relative to them. It is worth noting that, as well as solid objects, shadows will also follow the lines of perspective.

Shady Corner

When painting atmospheric buildings we are often trying to represent light and shade while simultaneously using light and shade to create volume and form. While it is important to choose a subject that appeals to us, it is important that we select in other, more analytical, terms too. For example, one crucial question to ask oneself is does this subject have sufficient content to use as a basis for a picture?

This street scene in Pézenas has various aspects that makes it a great subject: the forms of the contrasting architecture create aesthetic appeal; it includes plenty of attractive features that add content and interest, like the shop front, shutters and windows; and the street in the centre recedes into the picture, creating an unusual design as there is a central vanishing point.

YOU WILL NEED

Watercolour paints: cobalt blue, cobalt blue deep, French ultramarine, Naples yellow, raw sienna, viridian, cadmium red, light red, potters pink

Brushes: size 5 and 8 round, large round, size 4 rigger

Paper: 30.5 × 25.5cm (12 × 10in) Hahnemühle 300gsm (140lb) Rough surface watercolour paper

2B pencil

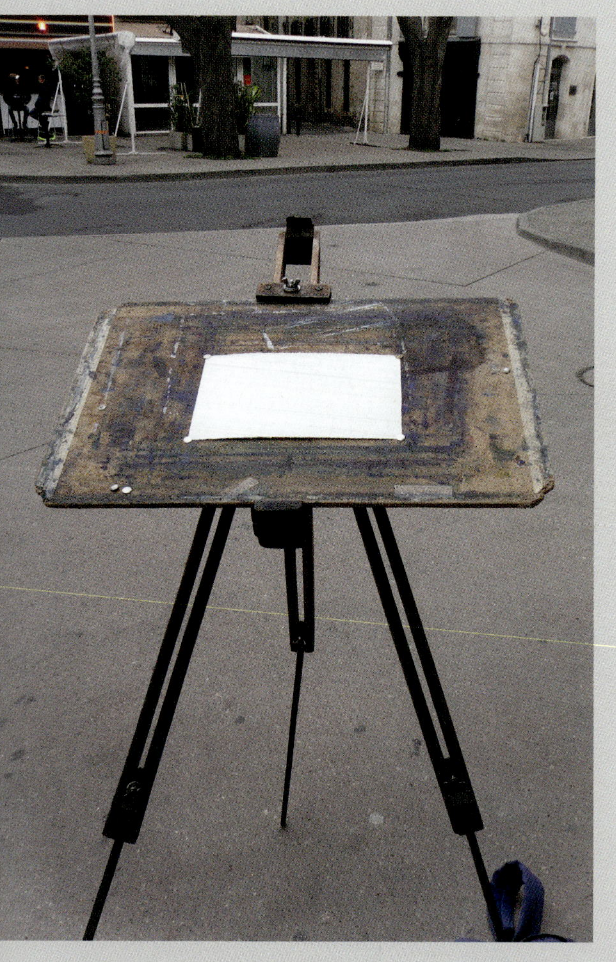

Setting up

For this subject, where the perspective and depth are key, it's particularly important to set up your easel at the right height and at the right incline. Double-check that you are positioned directly in front of the subject at the right distance from it. This will ensure you are neither 'zooming in', nor so close that you struggle to evaluate extreme angles. Importantly, do not move position once you have started, as this will cause confusion.

Equally important is speed for capturing light and shade. Even when working at a quick pace the lighting will change, if not in intensity, then certainly in direction over the painting session. For the finished picture to make sense we need to fix the lighting direction early on and this is easier over a shorter working period. Once you find a good potential subject, do not waste time pondering: just make a start.

A final point for setting up for this painting: I used the 'wrong side' of the paper – the back side of Rough paper is less textural, and the machining marks are clearer. I felt this would better serve the subject.

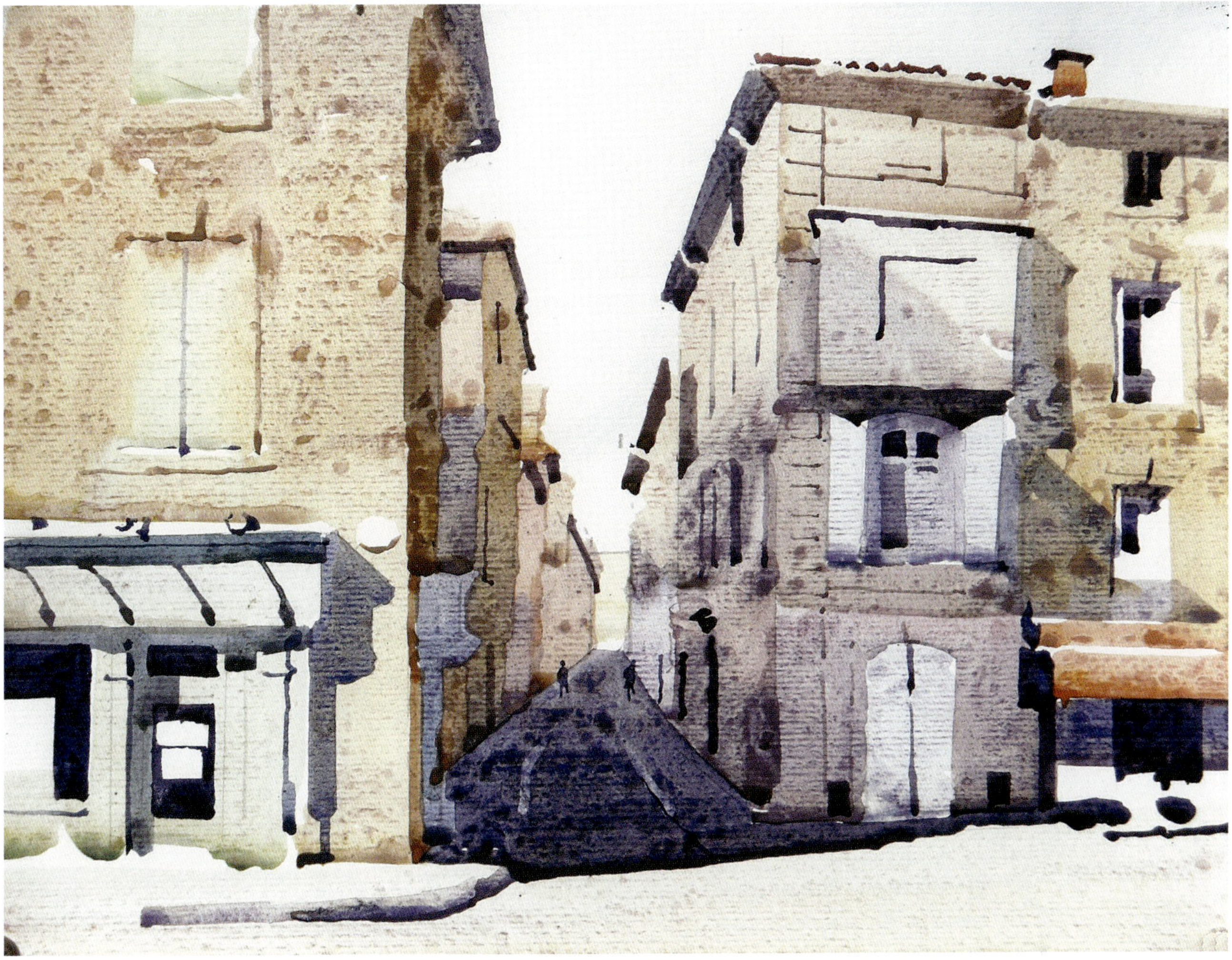

The finished painting

Stage 1

The drawing will define the structure of the finished painting – you can compare the two here. Simplicity, speed and accuracy are our aims: the initial drawing is purely to help us in the painting stage and differs from the more studied drawing of the mill (see page 71).

Using a 2B pencil, spend a few minutes establishing crucial forms and features such as the shutters on the right and the shop front on the left. Add edges that follow the lines of perspective such as eaves, where the roof meets the walls and sticks out from the plane of the wall, and lines where the buildings meet the pavement.

You can draw in architectural features such as windows more fully, or simply indicate their position. For speed, I suggest keeping the drawing basic. If you need a better understanding of a particular shape at a later stage, it can be added then.

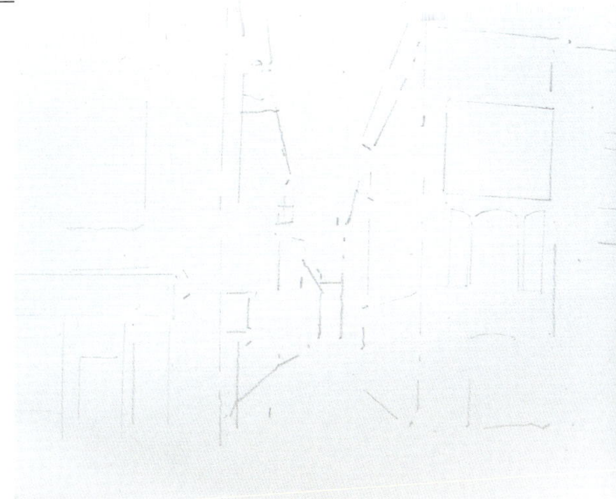

The initial drawing.

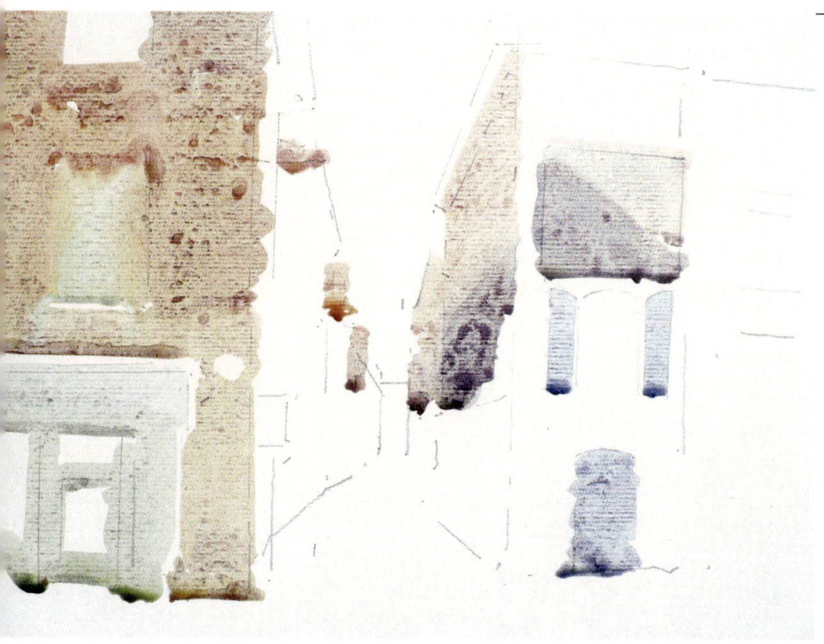

Naples yellow and potters pink feature in almost all the mixes – note how this helps to unify the different areas.

These washes must dry completely before subsequent washes are put down to keep the edges crisp and to avoid bleeding.

Stage 2

Working from light to dark, use a size 8 round brush and graduated washes to establish the lightest tones.

Paint the surface on the right of the central street with a graduated wash Naples yellow and potters pink, adding cobalt blue deep and potters pink for the soft-edged shadow. On the building on the left, use a mix of raw sienna and a little cobalt blue with some potters pink – note the granulation that results. Use a mix of viridian and Naples yellow and work wet in wet for the shuttered window.

Paint the shop front using potters pink, Naples yellow, cobalt blue deep and viridian in various combinations. Leave a gap of clean paper around the shop front to keep the edges crisp. Finally, add the shuttered door and shutters on the right with a mix of cobalt blue deep with light red.

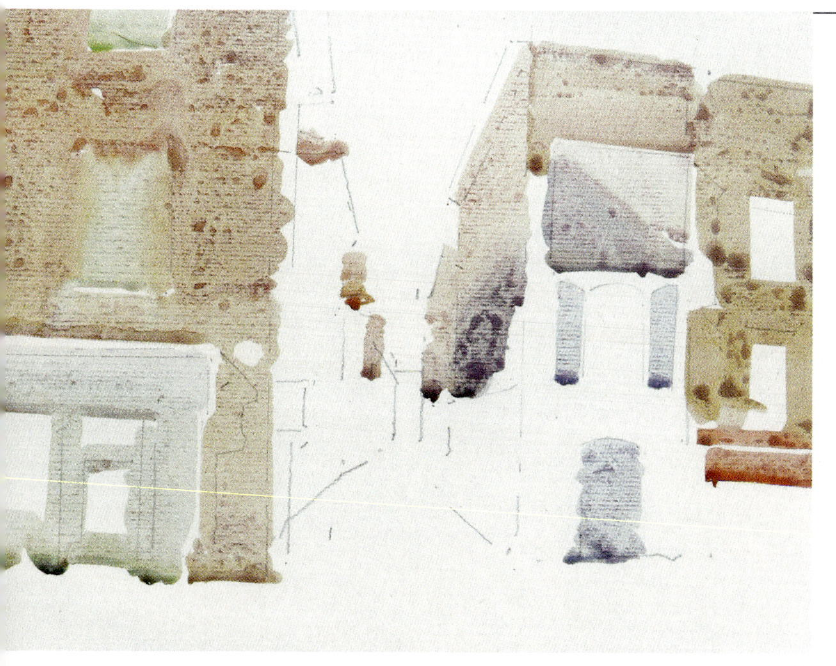

Stage 3

Still using the size 8 brush, start to define the various forms in the subject using slightly stronger tones of the mixes used in stage 2. For warmer tones, such as in the building on the right, use more raw sienna in the mix; and for cooler tones, such as at the top of the building to the right of centre, facing us, add a little more Naples yellow and cobalt blue deep in the mix. Use a cadmium red and raw sienna mix for the awning on the building on the right-hand side, and leave gaps in the flat and graduated washes for the windows.

The sky is a graduated wash with cobalt blue at the top descending into the white of the paper put down with a large round brush with plenty of water. This extremely pale wash ensures the sky contrasts tonally with the buildings, and keeps the focus on the light on the buildings.

Stage 4

Paint the sides of the buildings in shade with a graduated wash, starting at the top with a mix of cobalt blue deep and light red then descending into a mix of cobalt blue deep, raw sienna and potters pink. Don't go too dark: there is a lot of reflected light here, so even shadows are painted in a relatively light tone.

Still using the size 8 brush, prepare a mix of Naples yellow, cobalt blue and a little cadmium red and apply a wash for the foreground. Use plenty of water to keep the wash light and retain contrast. Swap to the size 5 round for architectural details.

Change to the size 4 rigger and use a mix of cobalt blue deep and potters pink to pick out some of the stone shapes and window surrounds on the building on the right of centre. Add smaller stronger shapes, such as window panes, with the size 5 round and a strong mix of French ultramarine and light red.

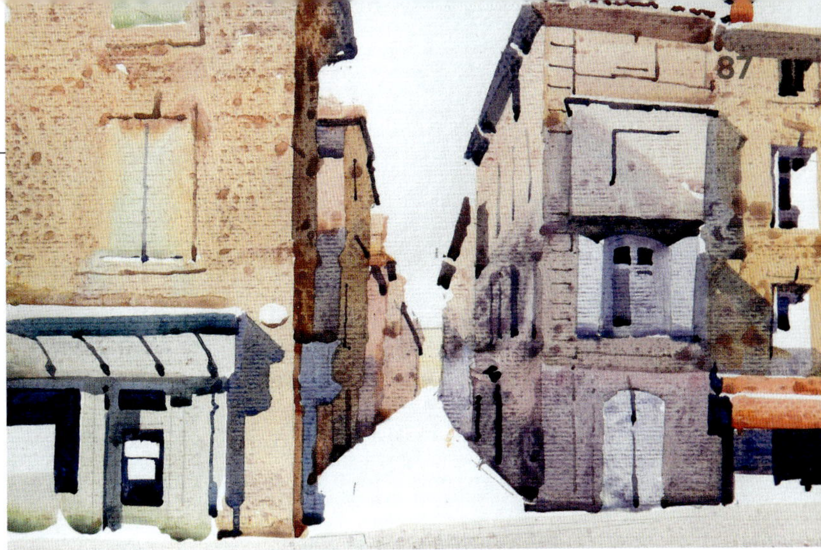

Some lines we observe in reality will complicate the form we are depicting; so edit the scene carefully to avoid confusion.

Forms are revealed by the lighting, so details like windows can be created quite simply by painting their shadows, and the shapes of posters in the shop window are simply areas of white paper that have been painted around.

Stage 5

This stage is about balancing the composition. There are no firm rules for this, so we must do what we think looks right – and be prepared to learn from mistakes.

For darker tones, use a mix of cobalt blue deep and varying amounts of potters pink with a size 5 round, as a little more control is needed. Raw sienna can be added for warmer areas. Finer lines can be added using a size 4 rigger.

For the strong shadow on the ground, use the size 8 round to apply a graduated wash, starting at the far end of the street with the cobalt blue deep and potters pink mix. Introduce a mix of French ultramarine with a little light red – this mix has more tonal depth – as you advance. Keep most of the contrast at the bottom of the shadow to help bring it forward. Once the wash is dry, gently lift out highlights and reflections on the curbs using the size 4 rigger. The shape of the shadow of the curb leading into that shadow was added with a size 5 round with a mix of cobalt blue and potters pink running into a mix of French ultramarine and light red.

It is important that any additions such as figures do not distract from the architectural focus of the painting. The positioning and scale of figures was chosen with care; it was a quiet day and so I added just a couple of figures to give scale to the buildings and a little life to accurately capture the scene.

The degree to which we can simplify can depend on the size of the painting. Because of the small scale of this painting, some areas such as the buildings up the street could be reduced to their simplest forms. If the painting had been larger these areas would have looked empty.

The finished painting can be seen on page 85.

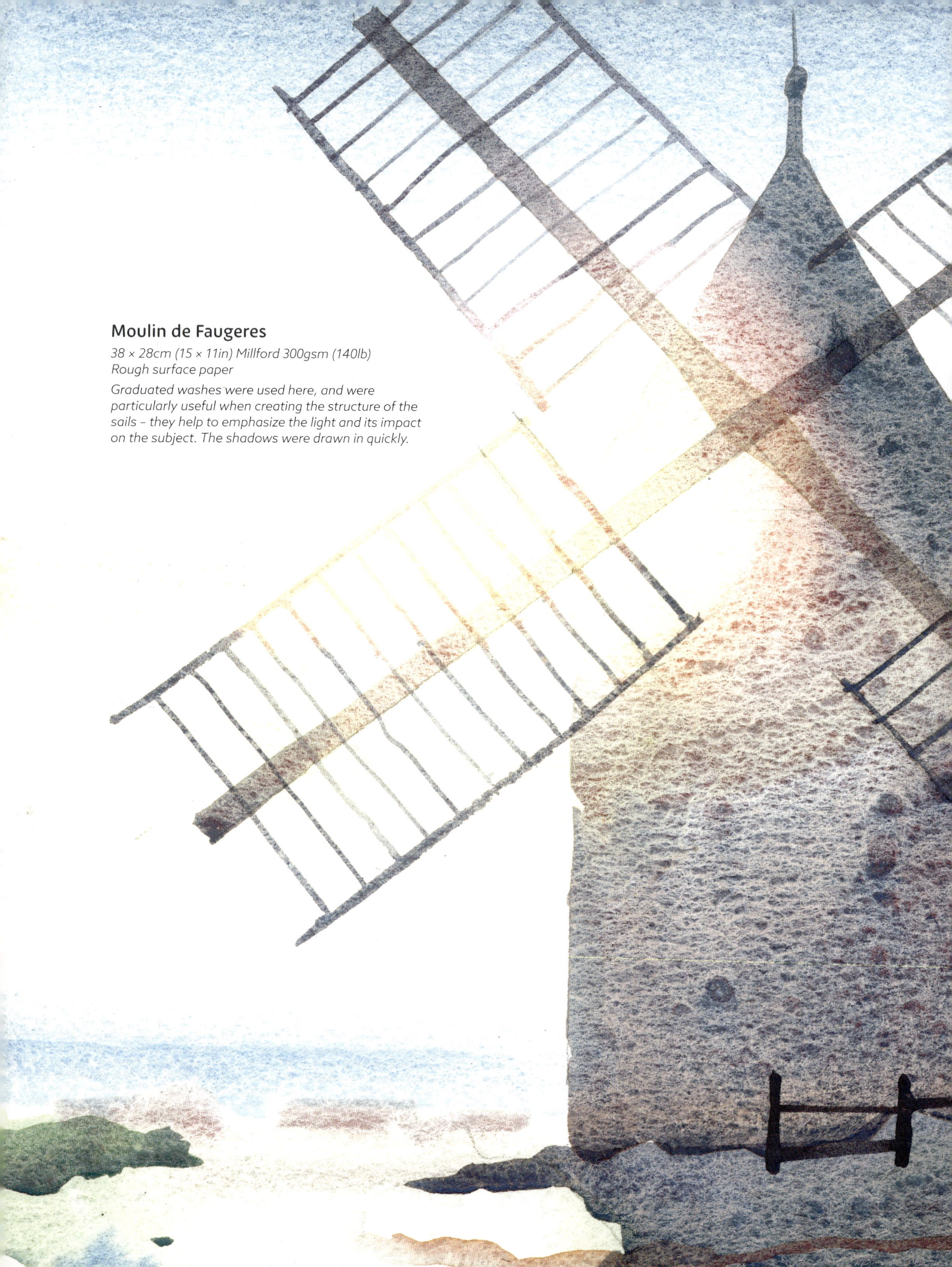

Moulin de Faugeres

*38 × 28cm (15 × 11in) Millford 300gsm (140lb)
Rough surface paper*

*Graduated washes were used here, and were
particularly useful when creating the structure of the
sails – they help to emphasize the light and its impact
on the subject. The shadows were drawn in quickly.*

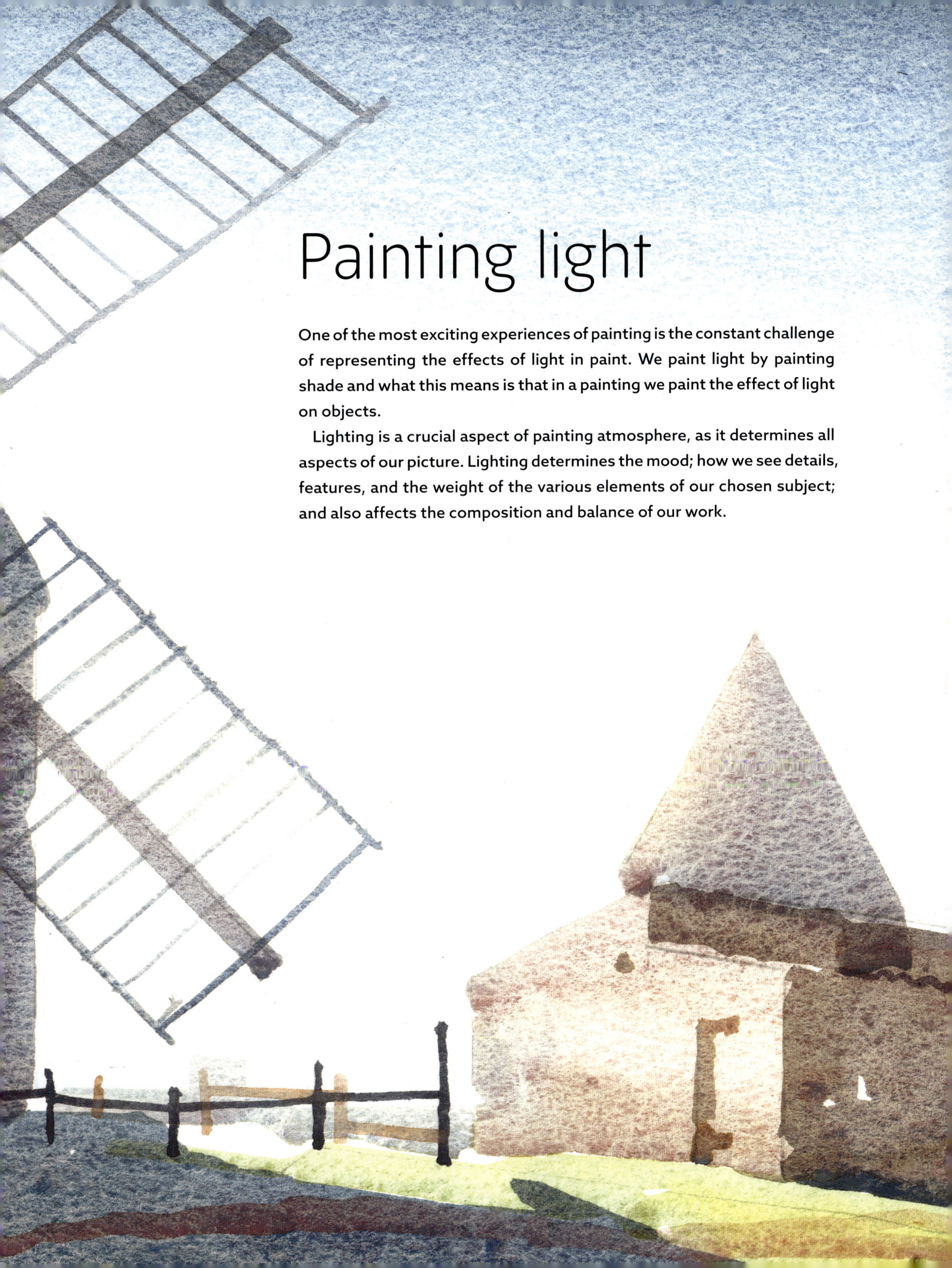

Painting light

One of the most exciting experiences of painting is the constant challenge of representing the effects of light in paint. We paint light by painting shade and what this means is that in a painting we paint the effect of light on objects.

Lighting is a crucial aspect of painting atmosphere, as it determines all aspects of our picture. Lighting determines the mood; how we see details, features, and the weight of the various elements of our chosen subject; and also affects the composition and balance of our work.

Light and time

Because the sun will move in relation to your chosen subject, it is crucial to work with a sense of urgency to capture a particular effect of the light. The change will be dramatic and, on some surfaces, rapid. If possible, get to know the setting beforehand, so you know where the sun will be at a certain time of day, and which direction it will move in relation to the subject.

Adapt the order of painting so you start painting those elements that will change fastest first. On buildings, the appearance will change the quickest where the sunlight scrapes along the surface at the same or a similar angle, and so these areas should be dealt with as a priority. Conversely, other areas of the painting will change less quickly – or hardly at all – and so the painting of these areas is less urgent and time-sensitive. Be aware of where shadows will develop, and of the potential use of those shapes in the design of your painting.

Foundations

- It is particularly important to work quickly in the early stages as you establish the lights.
- Draw in shadows in one stage – if you draw one shadow in the right place, then an hour later draw another shadow, you run the risk of confusion as the light stops making sense.

Speed, sunlight and water

In *Feeding Time*, the sun is reflected in the water and the shadows cast by the shape of the mill help to add interest to the reflections. These shadows are an important part of the composition and structure of the painting.

This scene had a lot of movement in it and those things had to be drawn in quickly in the desired place – so speed was of the essence. A few spare pieces of my lunch helped move the ducks into position.

Sunlight on water will lighten reflected shapes. In contrast to this, light shapes tend to be reflected slightly darker. While it is quite difficult to paint because of the discomfort factor, painting into the sun forces you to find solutions and discover ways to convey both what you experience and what you are trying to reveal about the subject.

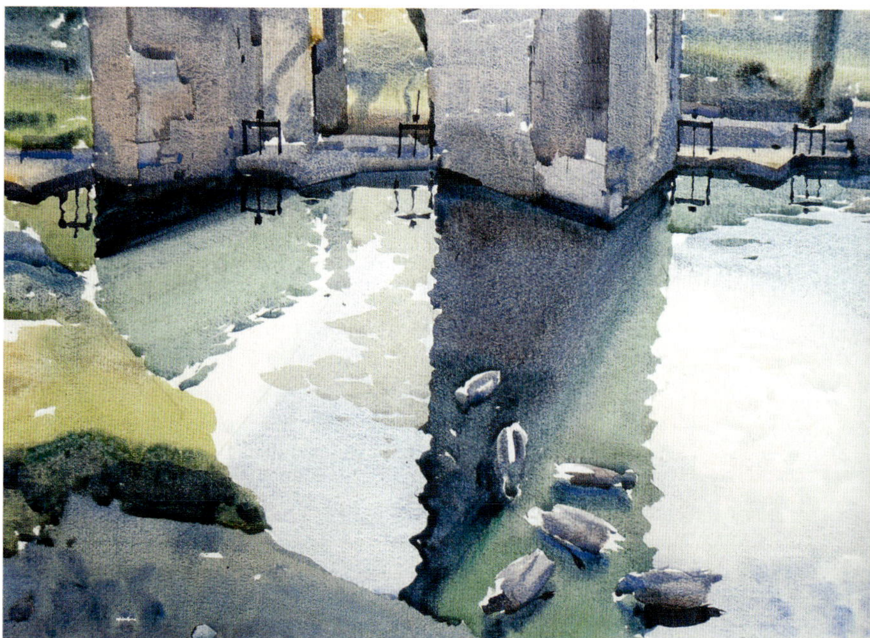

Feeding Time, Cordier
56 × 38cm (22 × 15in) Whatman 300gsm (140lb) Not surface paper
Sunlight on water can be an extremely attractive element in any subject but the painting must also have useful content. Interest is provided, in this instance, by the ducks and the reflection of the mill.

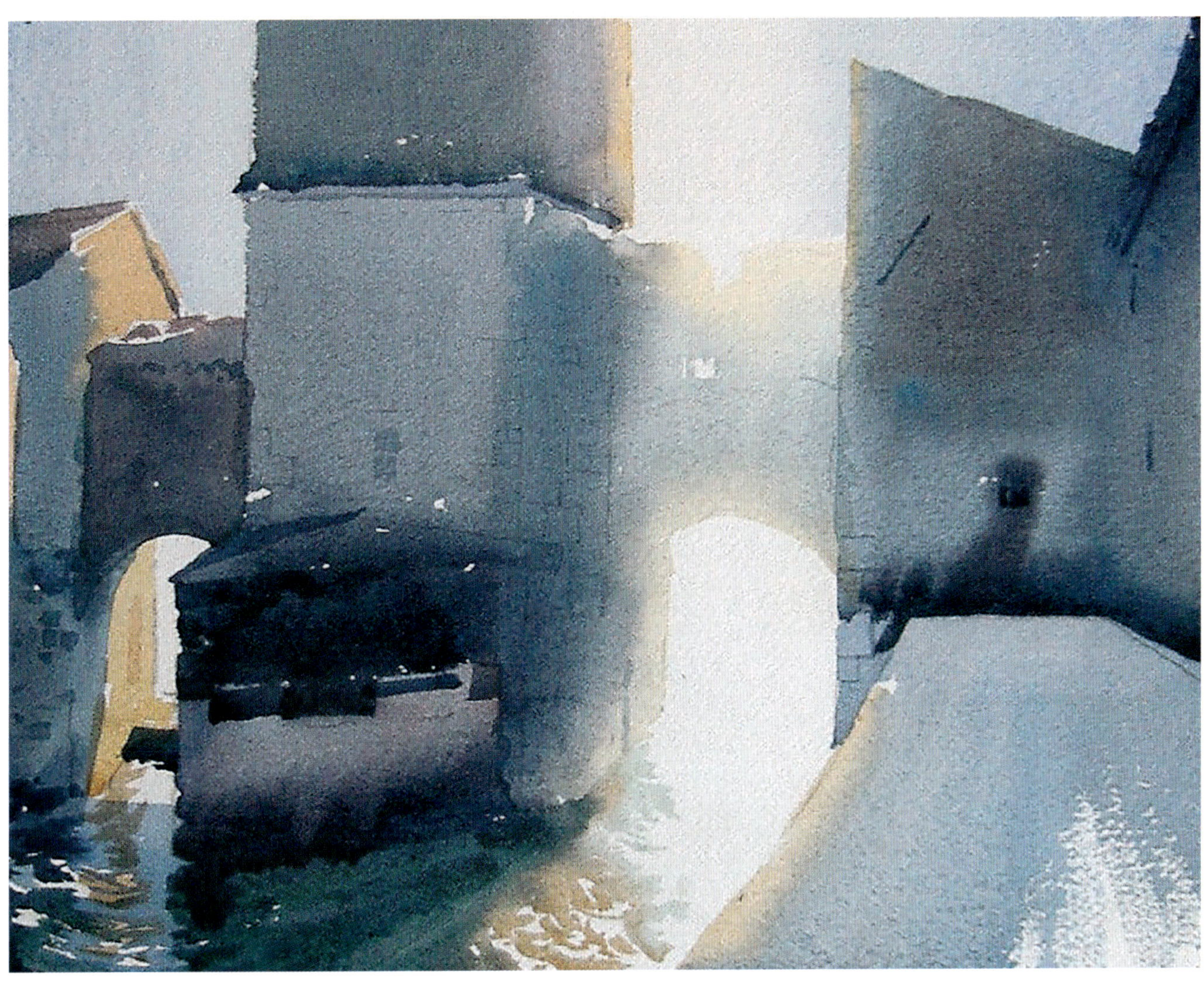

Strength of light

Stronger lighting can reveal details and texture particularly
when just striking the side of a building. In low level lighting,
with less detail and less defined features, mood becomes
more important, while contrast and colour range can become
more of a problem. When seeking a subject in this situation
I find it an advantage to find a natural strong design – as
in the painting here, which is far more about the effect of
strong sunlight on the overall structure than it is about any
identifying details of the mill.

Moulin Saint-Thibéry

30.5 x 25.5cm (12 x 10in) Millford
300gsm (140lb) Rough surface paper

*Natural compositions usually work the
best. Here, the position of the sun perfectly
suited this composition and subject. I used
graduated washes to try to express the effect
of the sunlight on the view of the mill.*

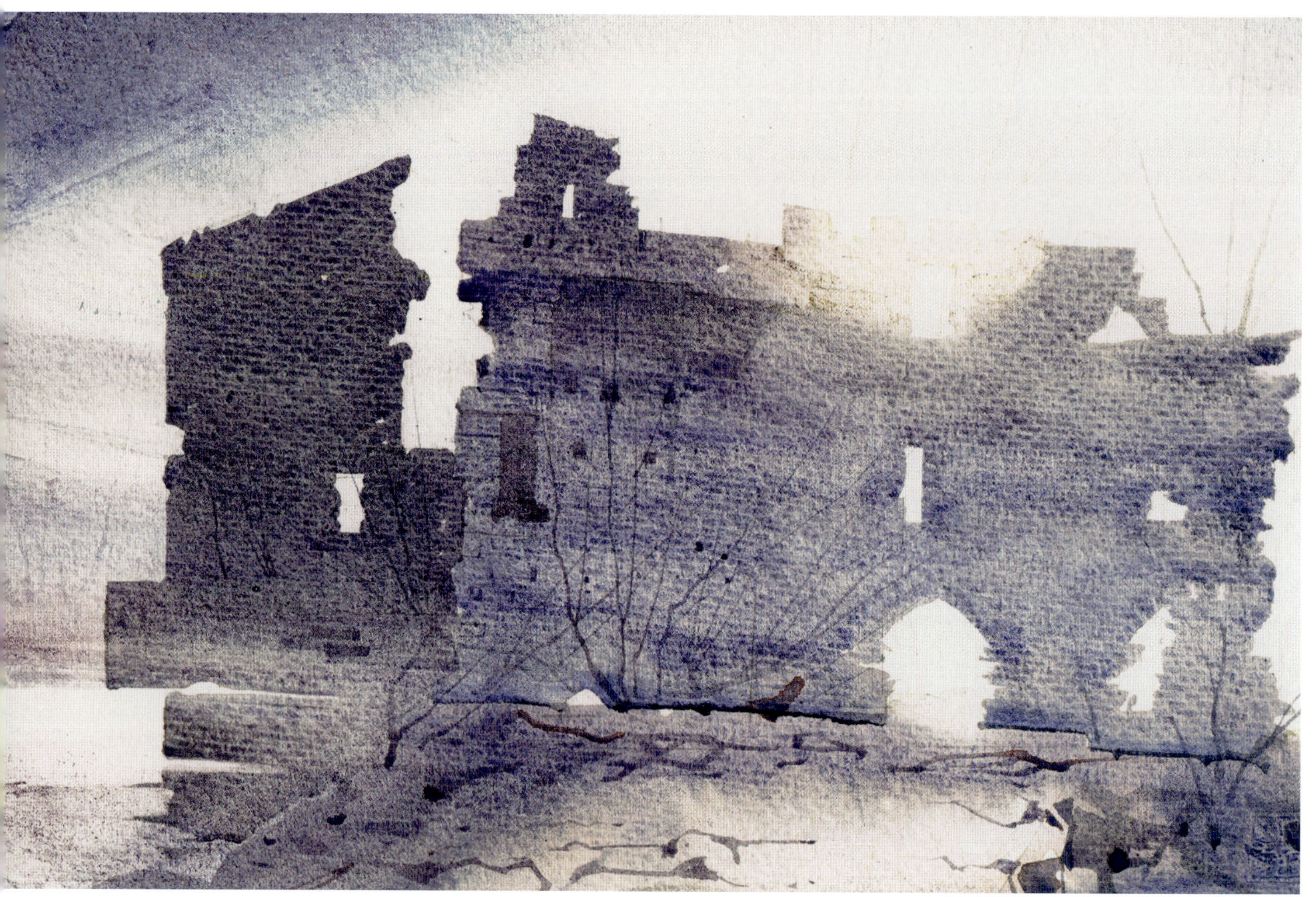

Moulin Sunrise

28 × 18cm (11 × 7in) Saunders Waterford 300gsm (140lb) Rough surface paper

In this early morning scene, there was a lot of vapour in the air and the effect of diffused lighting was an important aspect.

Angle of light

The direction and height of the light source is a key factor to consider. In the early morning or evening, the light is at a low angle. This, perhaps unexpectedly, throws roofs into shadow – only when the sun rises enough will they begin to catch the light, and details will be revealed.

The colour of the light is slightly different too at dawn and dusk and colours can become richer. The lighting can also be affected by water vapour seen sometimes when painting next to a river or a harbour. This will affect how light is diffused.

A pragmatic approach is needed to adapt to the movement of the sun at a low angle. For subjects where the atmospheric effect is fast-changing like this it is not merely important but crucial to work quickly – say what's important and move on.

If a subject is lit with the sun from behind us, lack of contrast can be a problem as the subject appears too flat, so I usually avoid this.

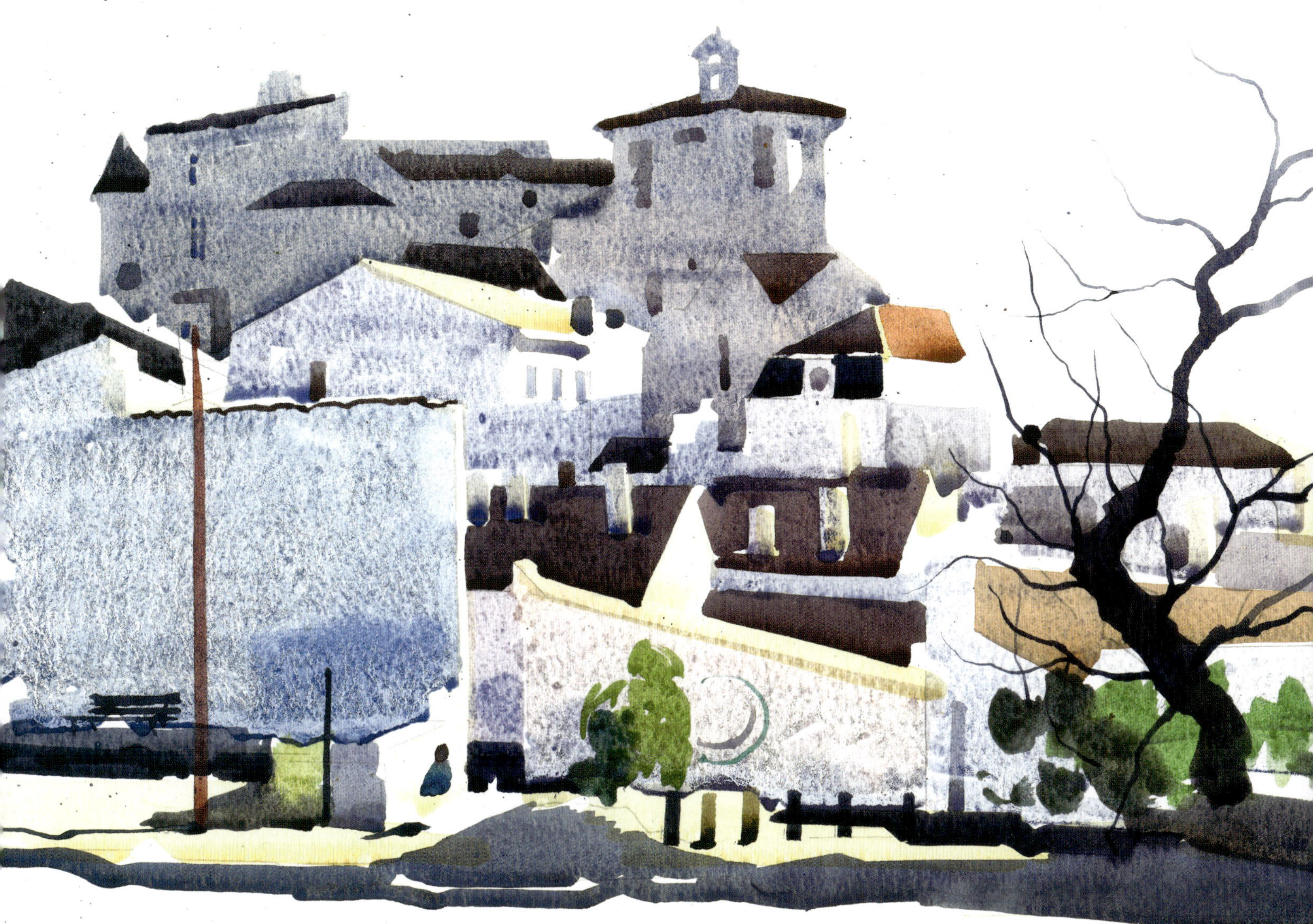

Contre-jour

Literally meaning 'against the light', *contre-jour* is a form of painting facing the sun (or other light source), and so the subject is mostly thrown into silhouette and shadow. Painting directly into the light creates an additional obstacle: how to see the subject and how to put that in a picture form that makes sense within a design.

In these instances, we are usually trying to give a sense of the experience, as well as giving the viewer an idea about the intense nature of the light source.

While learning and gaining confidence is very important, I suggest beginners tackle a less challenging lighting arrangement before trying to paint directly towards the sun. Not only is it much more difficult, it can also be quite uncomfortable looking into the light.

If you do decide to take the challenge, my advice is to work on a small scale – 18 × 12.5cm (7 × 5in) and get to know your subject well in terms of the direction the sun will move in. Work fast, use a minimum of drawing in the first stage and establish the volumes and lighting rapidly.

Puissalicon Contre-jour
[illegible]
300gsm (140lb) Rough surface paper

In this view, painted contre-jour, contrast between the various shapes was useful in creating the light effect and depth.

The painting on page 30 (and overleaf), Pinet, is another good example of this sort of approach.

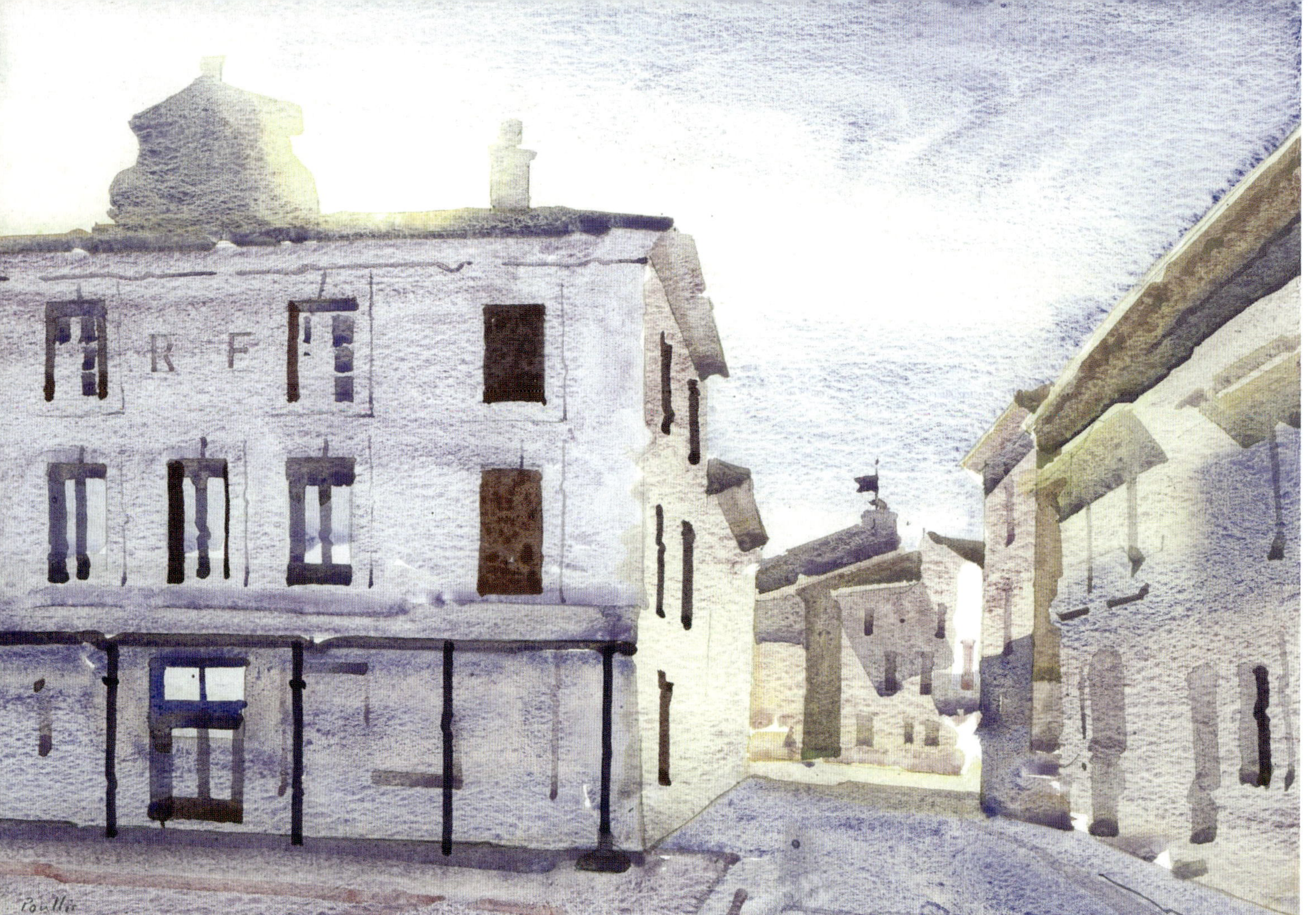

Lost and found edges

Intense light will profoundly affect the edges of objects. Lost and found edges – that is, where parts of objects disappear into the background – appear where things are lost in deep shadow, but they can also be highly effective when representing an edge affected by strong lighting.

Such lost and found edges can be created by placing a wash on paper that has wet patches on part of it, the 'lost' edge will appear on the wet surface and the 'found' on the dry.

An edge can be softened or made 'lost' by lifting out. You should choose materials that allow you to carry out the techniques you want to use, so if you prefer to lift out it is best to use a heavier paper. It depends on how vigorously this technique is applied but I find most decent quality 300gsm (140lb) papers will allow lifting.

Pinet

30.5 × 25.5cm (12 × 10in) Hahnemühle 300gsm (140lb) Rough surface paper

In this picture the sun is right on the edge of the building, the Mairie, where the edges were lost. Painting into the sun is always a technical challenge – but the rewards are often worth it.

Building skills

- Including the sun in a painting can create dramatic and exciting compositions and effects and is a challenging subject matter.

- If you include the sun, look for natural compositions where the sun fits nicely within the whole design.

- Use the sun as the lightest point in the painting.

- When strong sunlight shines on the palette or in our eyes, turn away or even step into the shade to judge better the colour you are mixing. Do not look directly into the sun!

- While looking at the work of watercolour masters will give examples of how they brilliantly deal with this difficult effect, it is important to find your own way of tackling it, so the picture is yours.

Indoor lighting

Interior lighting is a different ball game altogether as it is mostly shade or reflected light. One advantage of interior work is that lighting is consistent in strength and unchanging in direction – in effect like working in a studio.

When painting in an interior where the lighting is poor, choose a limited colour range – that way, even if you can not see the exact colour, you can still judge tone, which is more important to a successful painting.

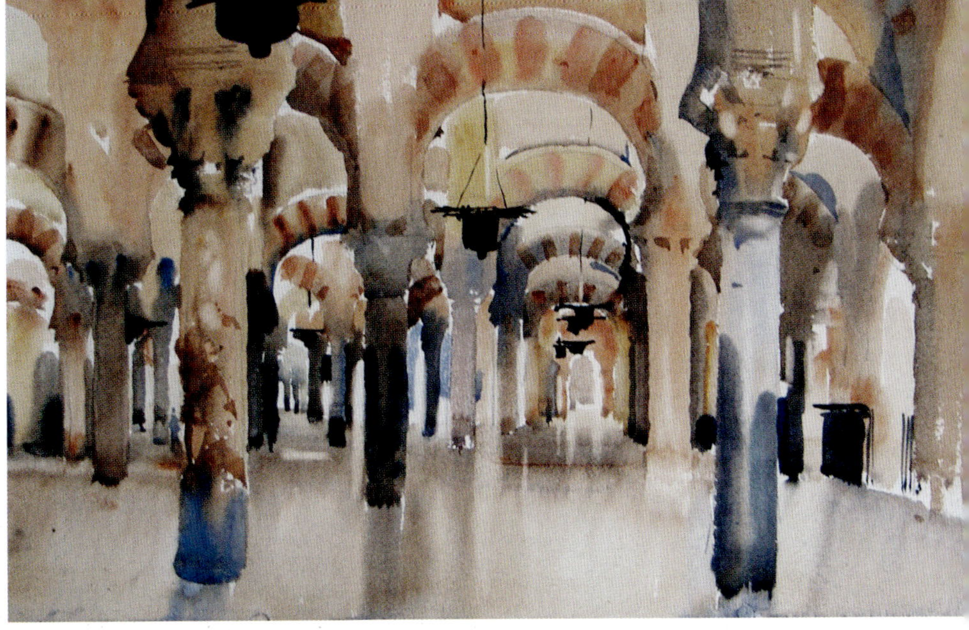

Mosque-Cathedral of Córdoba interior

56 × 38cm (22 × 15in) Arches 300gsm (140lb) Rough surface paper

In this low-lit setting, I had to allow my eyes time to adjust before starting work. When working I chose a limited colour palette but nevertheless had to repeatedly take my mixing palette into a light area of the Mosque to ensure the paint mixes were correct.

Strong contrasts

Contrasts are extremely useful in expressing something about the lighting. The shaded sides of buildings provide a great opportunity to pick out colours and amplify natural contrasts to create interesting shapes and effects. In painting the shaded side of a building, we are often painting reflected light.

Surfaces in shadow can appear to be more reflective than lit sides and will often pick up tints from facing buildings or the sky or other objects.

The building materials will dramatically affect this effect and reflected colours are particularly evident in buildings that have light stone or rendered surfaces or sometimes a wet surface. It helps to look for warm colours within the shaded areas: these can be extremely useful in portraying a lighting effect.

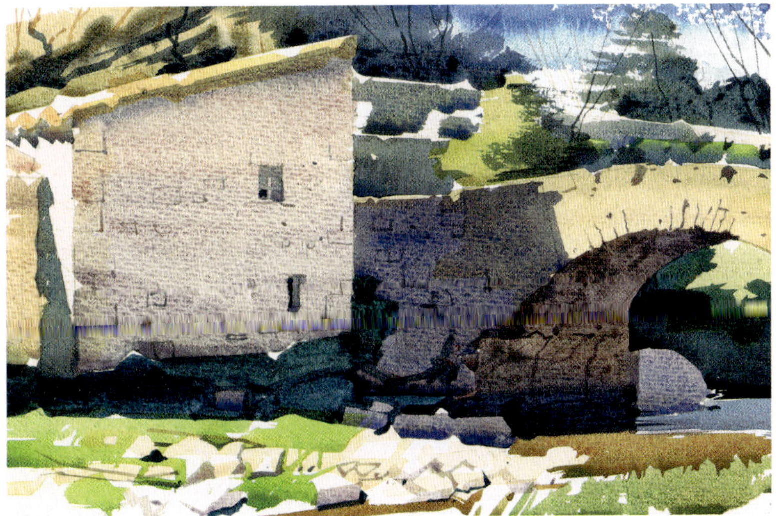

Moulin de Julien, Neffiès

28 × 18cm (11 × 7in) Saunders Waterford 300gsm (140lb) Rough surface paper

Painted in the spring, the lighting created quite a rich colour scheme in this subject. In more extreme lighting – in the South of France, during the height of summer, for example – the subject can take on a stark look. Contrary to what we might expect, in strong lighting colour becomes bleached out from lit sides and shaded areas are thrown into very deep shadow.

Market Hall, Early Morning

The market hall in Old Amersham was lit by dramatic lighting. This picture was painted in the very early morning when long shadows had the effect of amplifying the light falling on the buildings and also helped create form and depth. Because of the low angle of lighting, early morning light changes quickly and this is seen mostly on the movement of shadows falling on the surface of buildings, in this instance the market hall. I wanted to concentrate on the market hall and the buildings immediately around it.

YOU WILL NEED

Watercolour paints: potters pink, cadmium red, cadmium yellow, light red, raw sienna, brown madder, cobalt blue deep, French ultramarine, ivory black, cobalt blue

Brushes: size 6 round, size 8 round, large round

Paper: 28 × 19cm (11 × 7½in) 300gsm (140lb) Saunders Waterford Rough surface watercolour paper

2B pencil, soft eraser, gum arabic

Setting up

This is a natural composition with all lines leading to the market hall. This central structure is key, but as I knew the shadows would be important in the balance of the painting, I placed the hall slightly off-centre – this helped to ensure the finished piece would be visually balanced.

Despite this intentionally off-centre aim, I positioned myself directly in front of the subject for the drawing.

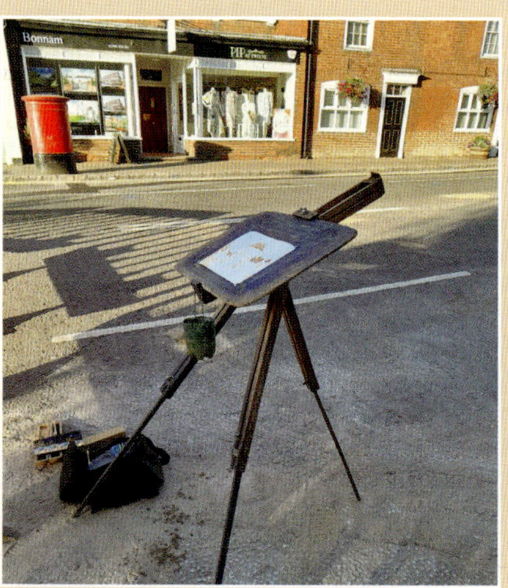

This photograph of my easel from the side shows the long shadows and warm light of the setting.

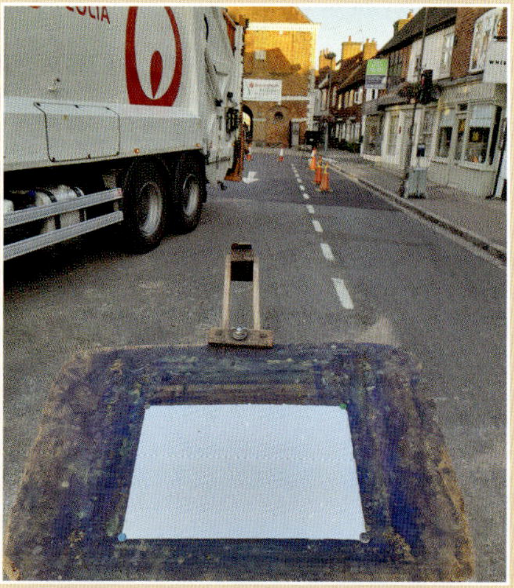

One of the inevitabilities of painting in situ is that life goes on around you. Often this is invaluable, but as you can see, sometimes it is not so desirable!

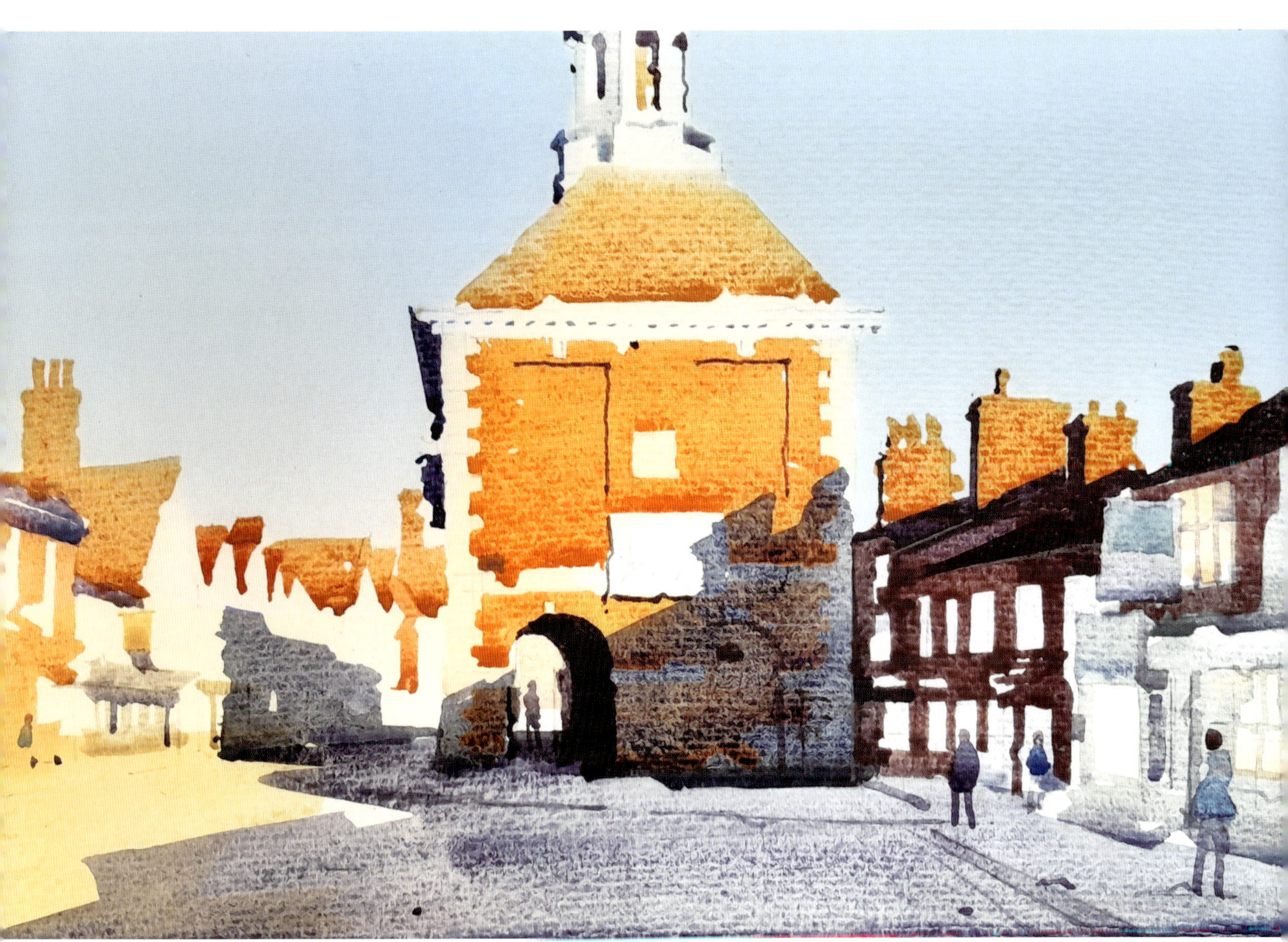

The finished painting

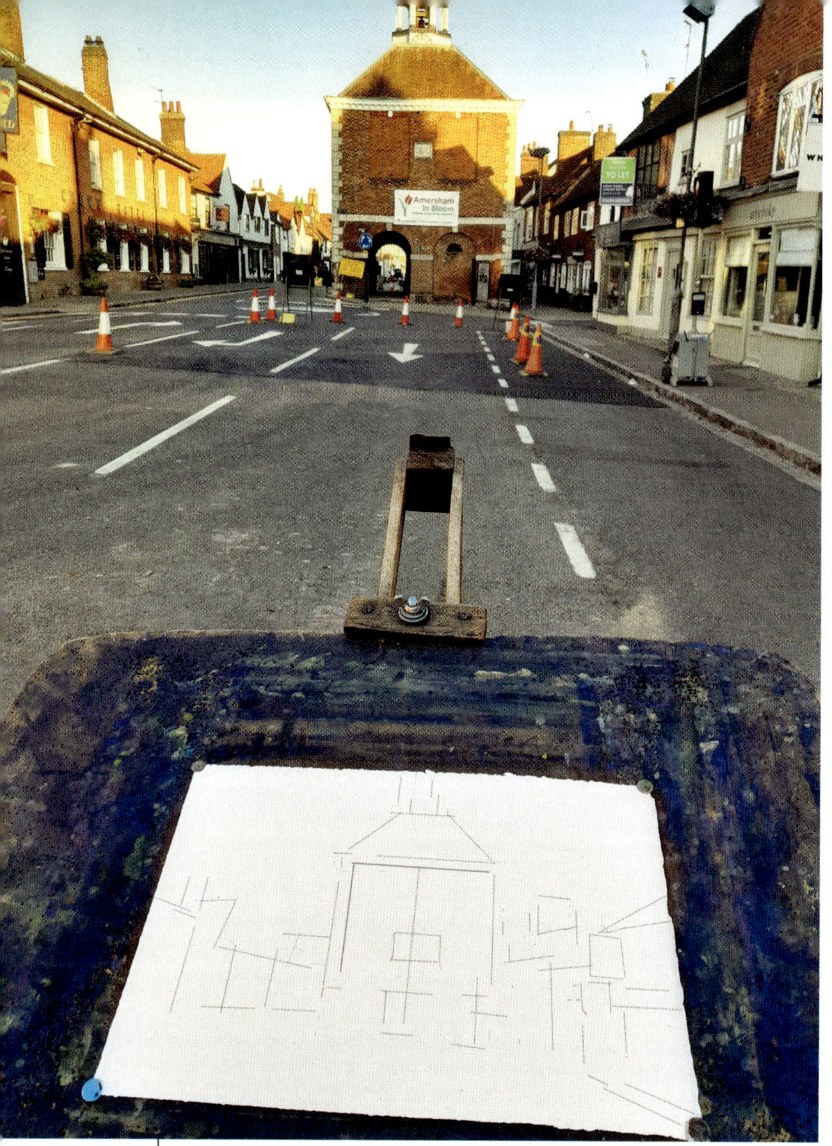

Stage 1

I knew the shadow falling across the front of the market hall would disappear but to show the light on the surface I wanted to include it, so I drew it in when they were in the position I wanted.

I kept the drawing extremely simple as I wanted to focus in on the lighting and not so much on the details – I also knew I had to work fast to capture this particular light effect.

Stage 2

Once the drawing is in place, put down a simple graduated wash of French ultramarine on the sky – the lit part of the painting should be of a high tonal key to emphasize the strong lighting.

The sky needs to recede to help create a little depth and allow the buildings to be more prominent or to come forward. Use a simple flat wash of French ultramarine for this area to ensure it does not draw the eye too much.

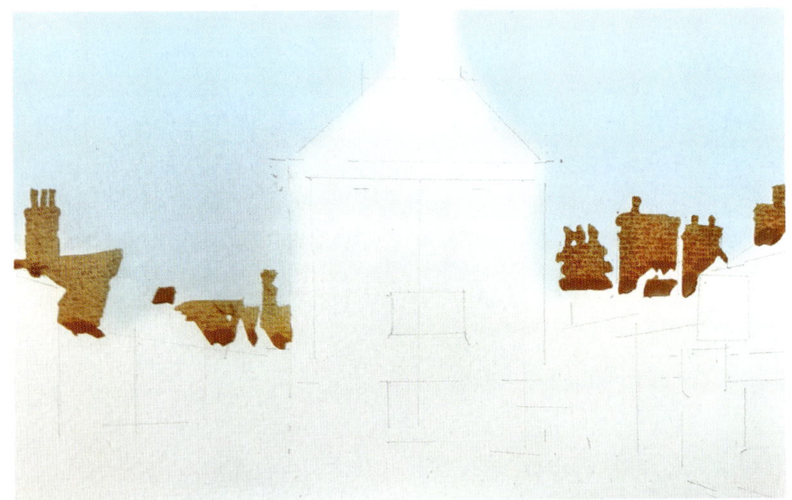

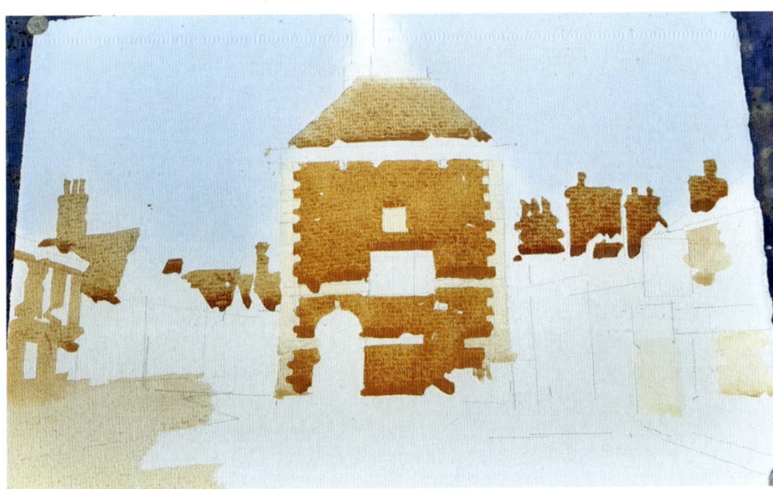

Stage 3

Once the sky is dry, place in little washes to establish the shapes of some of the buildings. The lit up bricks and roofs are quite bright, so use a mix of light red, cadmium red and raw sienna for the reds, and where they are a touch more vivid, mix in a little cadmium yellow.

Do the same for the lighter areas, including the road and reflected light in the windows on the right.

Allow the underpainting of the corner stones of the market hall to dry completely, then paint in the surface facing you using a mix of raw sienna, cadmium yellow and cadmium red. Once this is done, the lights are complete.

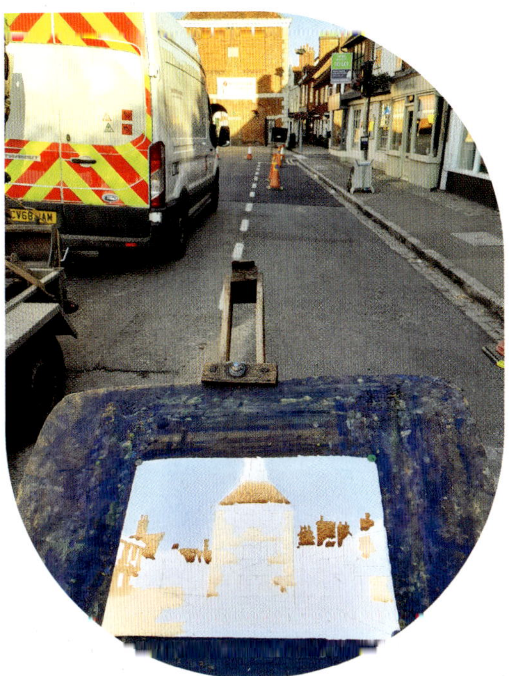

Midway through this stage, another large van parked in front of me so I had to move the easel about a bit in order to see what I was painting – if your initial drawing is solid, this should give you no problems.

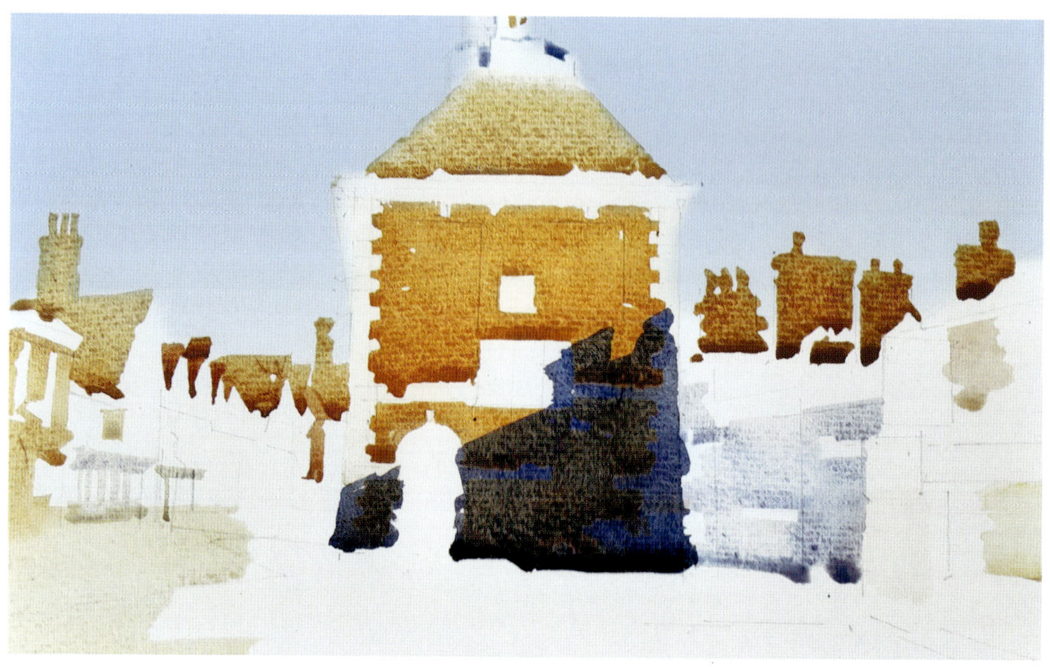

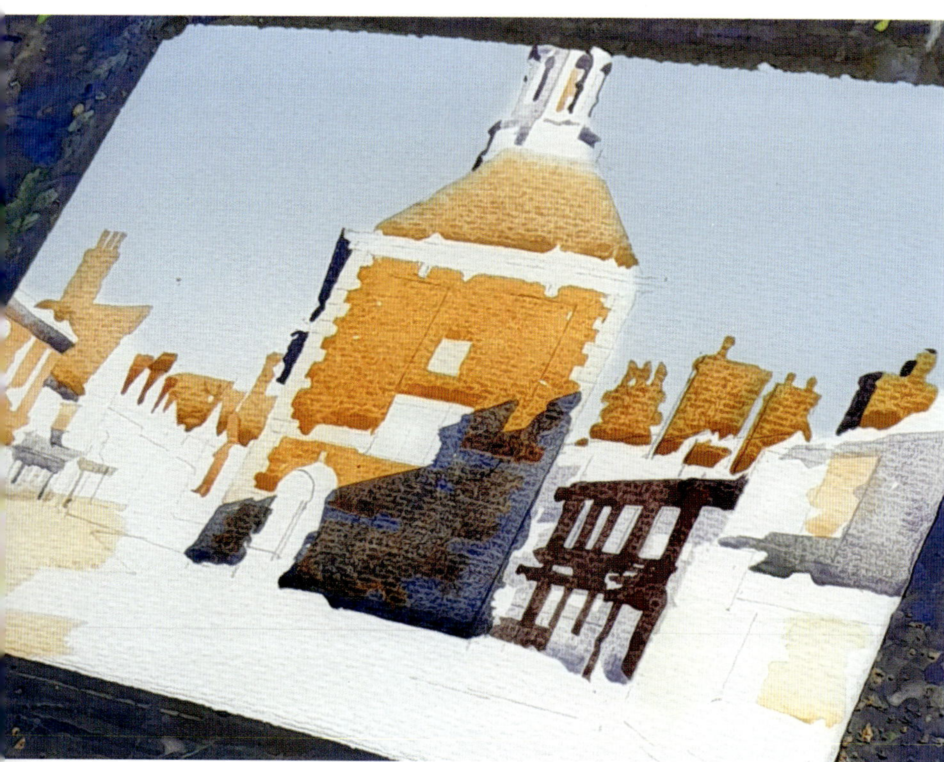

Stage 4

With the lights in place, you can now concentrate on what is in shade and start to add contrast – without the dark contrast of the shade, there is no light effect.

Still working from light to dark, but this time in the shaded areas, use a mix of cobalt blue deep and potters pink to paint in the shadow falling on the market hall wall surface. Modify the mix with small touches of ivory black and brown madder for variety.

Next, start to put in the darker brick surfaces at this point using a size 6 round and a mix of cadmium red, raw sienna and cobalt blue deep. This has a dramatic effect on the sense of lighting and contrast within the painting.

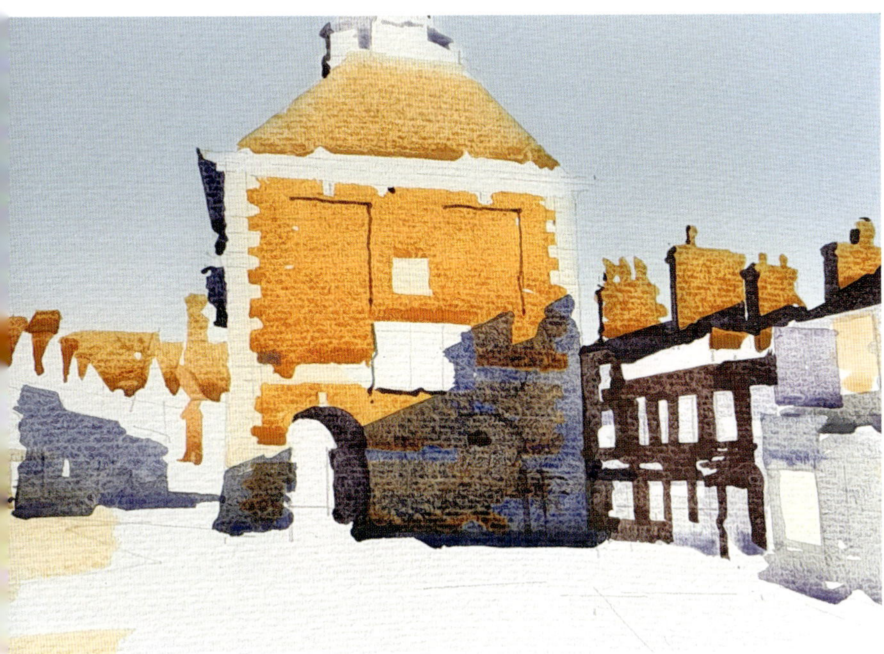

The areas of shadow are used to create volume and depth. Be careful not to make distant shadows too strong as they will come forward and this will affect the depth within the painting. A little ivory black added to your mixes will make them a little greyer and keep a cool colour range.

The darker sides of some of the chimneys were put in with a mix of cadmium red and cobalt blue deep with a round number 6 brush.

Stage 5

At this stage, concentrate on adding more shadows. The shadow across the street was put in with a wash of cobalt blue deep and potters pink in a lighter tone to that of the shadow falling on the market hall – this helps to make it recede slightly, and keeps the focus on the shadow on the market hall. Use a size 8 round brush to apply this wash – a little control is needed to paint the form of the left side of the shadow.

Smaller shapes can be put down with a mix of cobalt blue deep and potters pink, using a size 6 round to apply the paint.

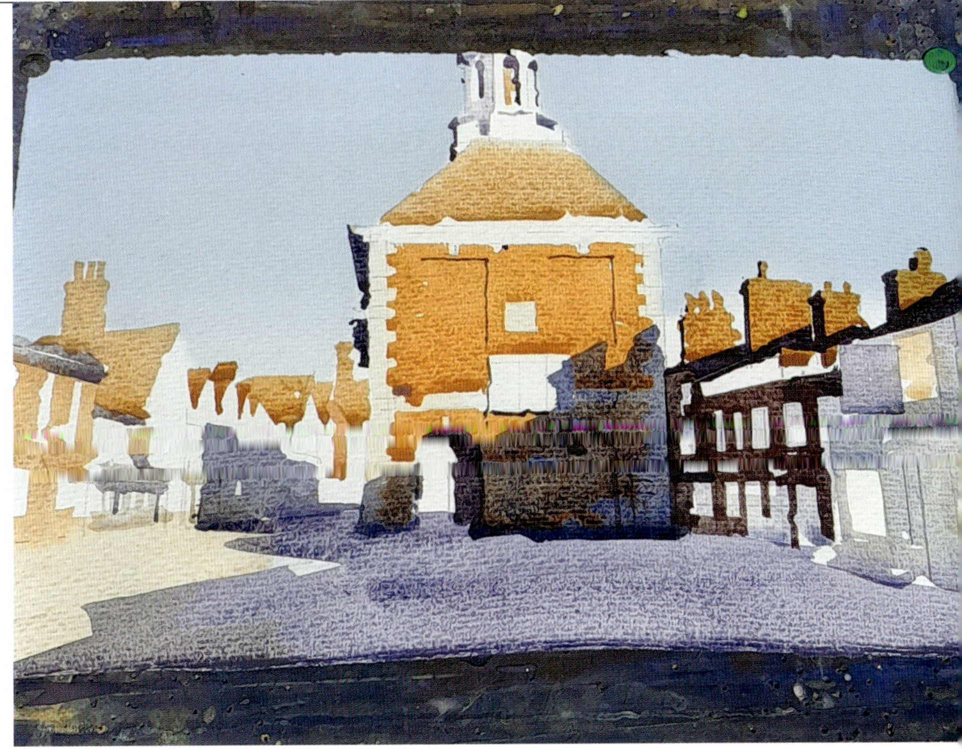

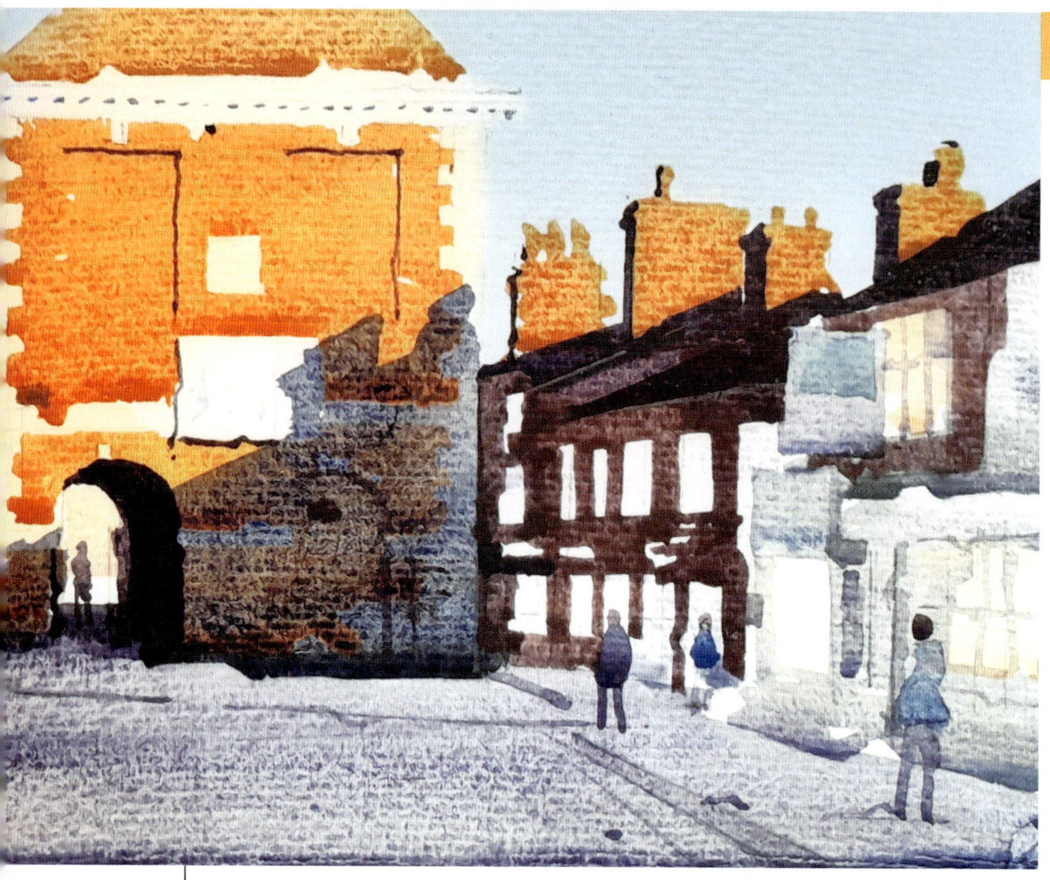

Building skills

- Where the architecture is of primary importance, figures can be useful in giving scale and an indication of the level of activity.

- The presence of figures, even small in scale and number will offer the viewer a 'way into' the painting – but should not be used arbitrarily. For a still atmosphere, avoid adding figures at all.

- Figures in an architectural context can be simple abstracted shapes: they need no detail. A natural pose is important as we want the figure to blend in.

- As with all objects the placement and scale is important and must make sense; a really tall or short figure can distract and we must be careful that they look right.

- A well-placed figure can be used to punctuate otherwise empty areas, or break up lines; blocks of colour; or a shape such as a hedge or wall.

Stage 6

Finish the painting by adding a few figures to heighten the sense of atmosphere. Before painting in figures, note the height of them and draw in the height with top and bottom marks.

For the figure on the right, use the size 6 round to paint a blob for the head using a mix of cobalt blue deep and brown madder. Once dry, paint in the top with cobalt blue, wait for that to dry then put in the leg shapes with any neutral mixes on your palette.

Keep the shapes of the other figures even simpler. Choose empty areas to put them in, and where they are further away, ensure they are smaller. Here, the figure under the arch was the perfect place for a silhouette and created a feature of interest. The pencil marks can be removed using a soft eraser once dry.

The finished painting can be seen on page 97.

Further challenges

Most subjects will offer many options and vary depending on the changing light. It is worthwhile visiting the same subject matter at different times of day to see what those possibilities are.

Weather conditions too will dramatically change a subject and will offer a new range of colour harmonies.

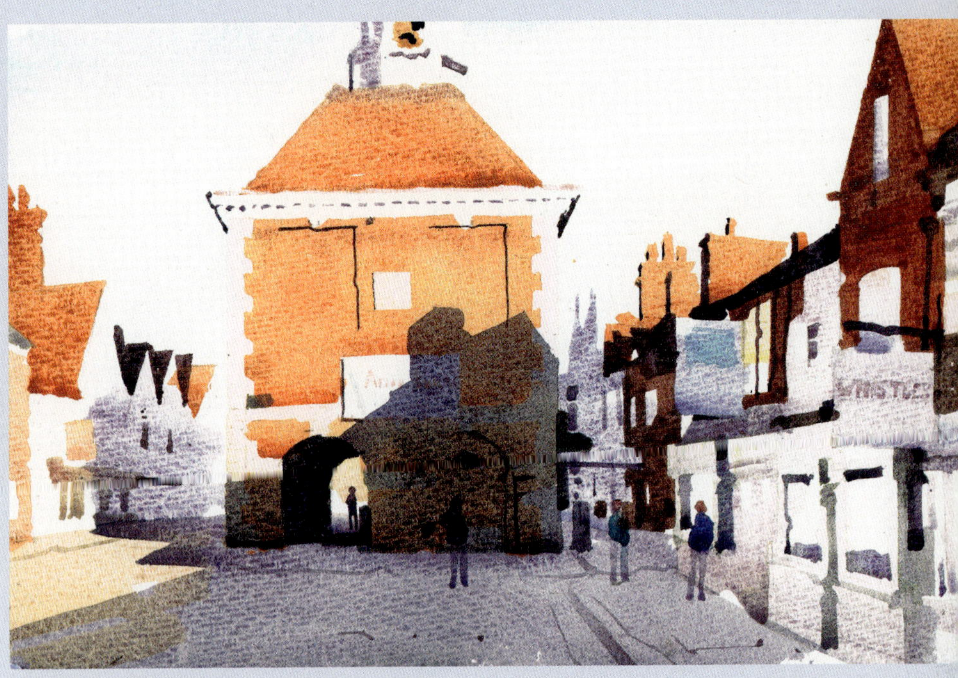

Old Amersham Market Hall 2

28 × 19cm (11 × 7½in) 300gsm (140lb) Saunders Waterford Rough surface paper

In this compositional variation, I placed the market hall to the left of the composition. This had the effect of including more reflected light in the buildings to the right that became a more important aspect of the painting.

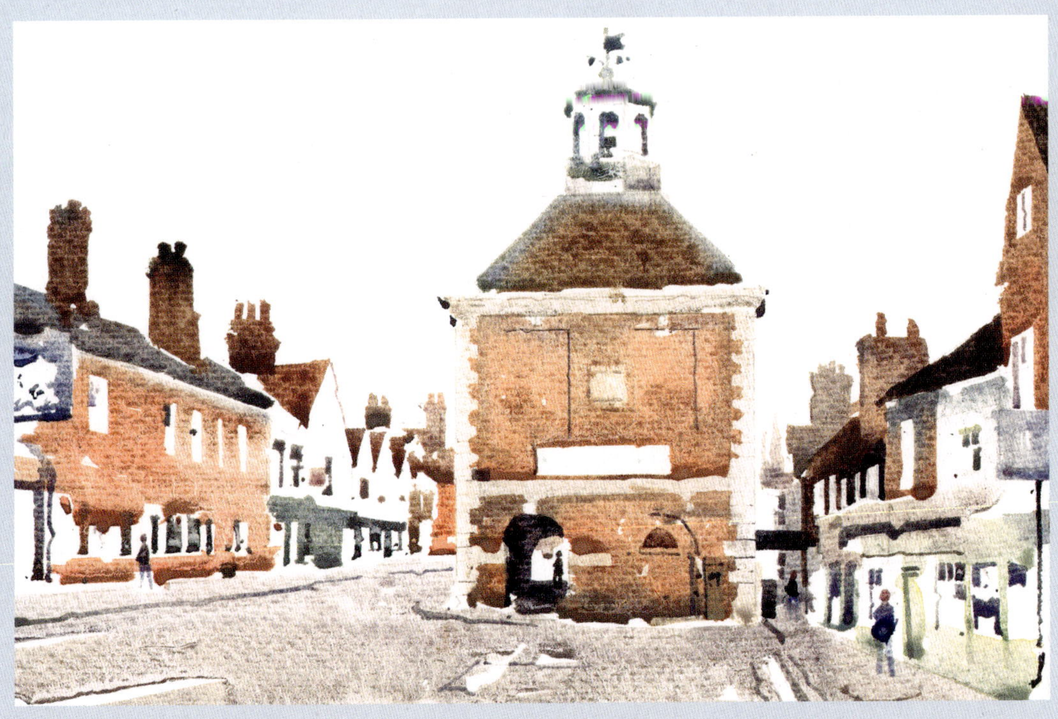

Grey Day, Old Amersham

28 × 18cm (11 × 7in) 300gsm (140lb) Saunders Waterford Rough surface paper

The same scene on a grey day looks totally different. Poor lighting isn't necessarily a problem, as long as there is sufficient contrast to establish forms and features.

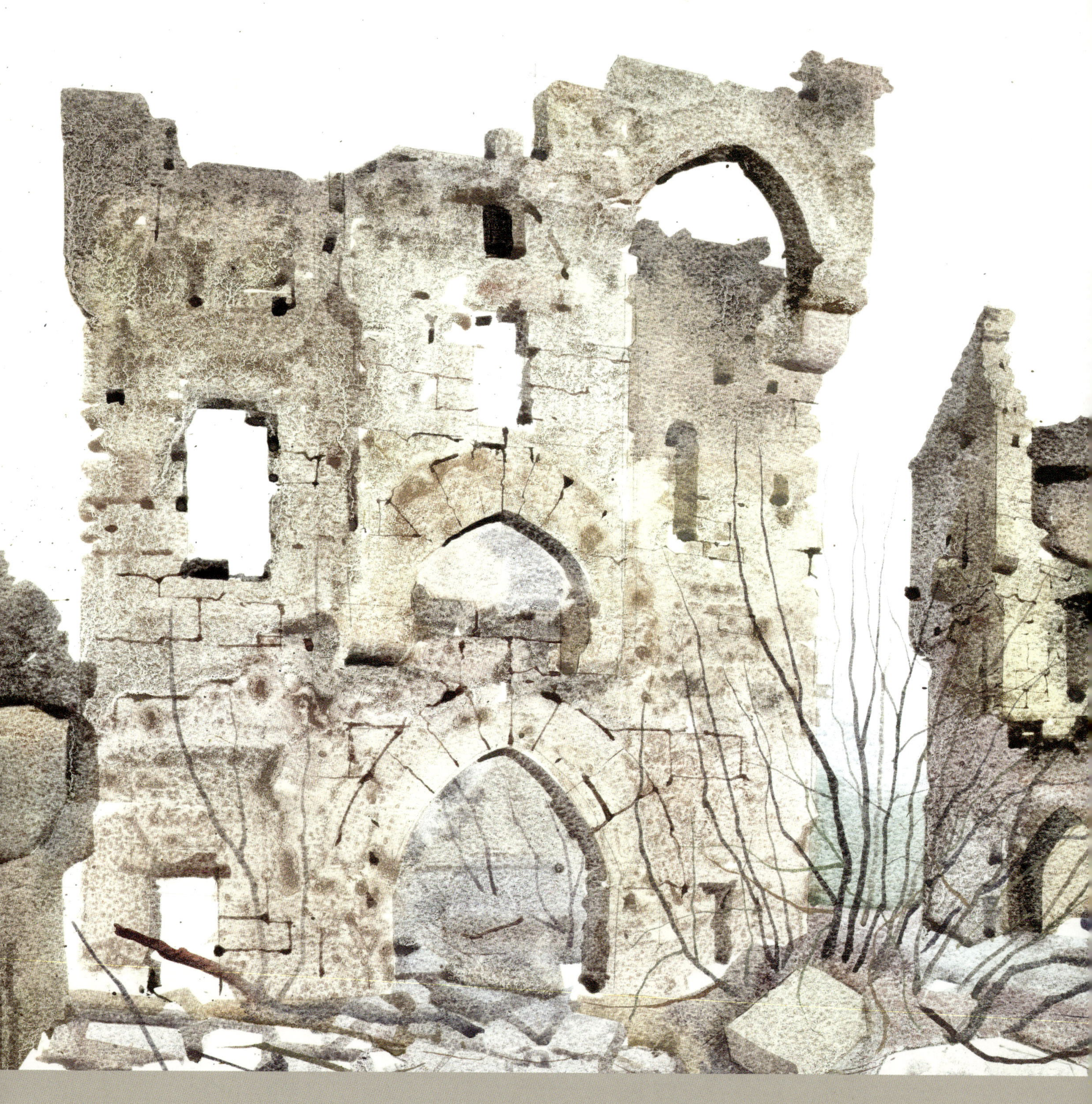

The order of painting

To paint a white circle using acrylics or oils, you can simply paint a white circle on a darker ground. The transparent nature of the medium, however, makes this impossible in watercolour – you must instead leave the white paper surface as a circle and paint around it in some contrasting colour.

The order of painting the different elements of a scene is therefore critical, because it allows us to preserve and create the shapes we wish to appear in the finished painting. Pure watercolour techniques respect the order of painting, and this is how a luminous and fresh painting is accomplished.

For success in watercolour, we must plan – and the more complex the subject the more we must consider the lights and various shapes that we would like to preserve. It is helpful to analyse a scene and visualize it as a watercolour.

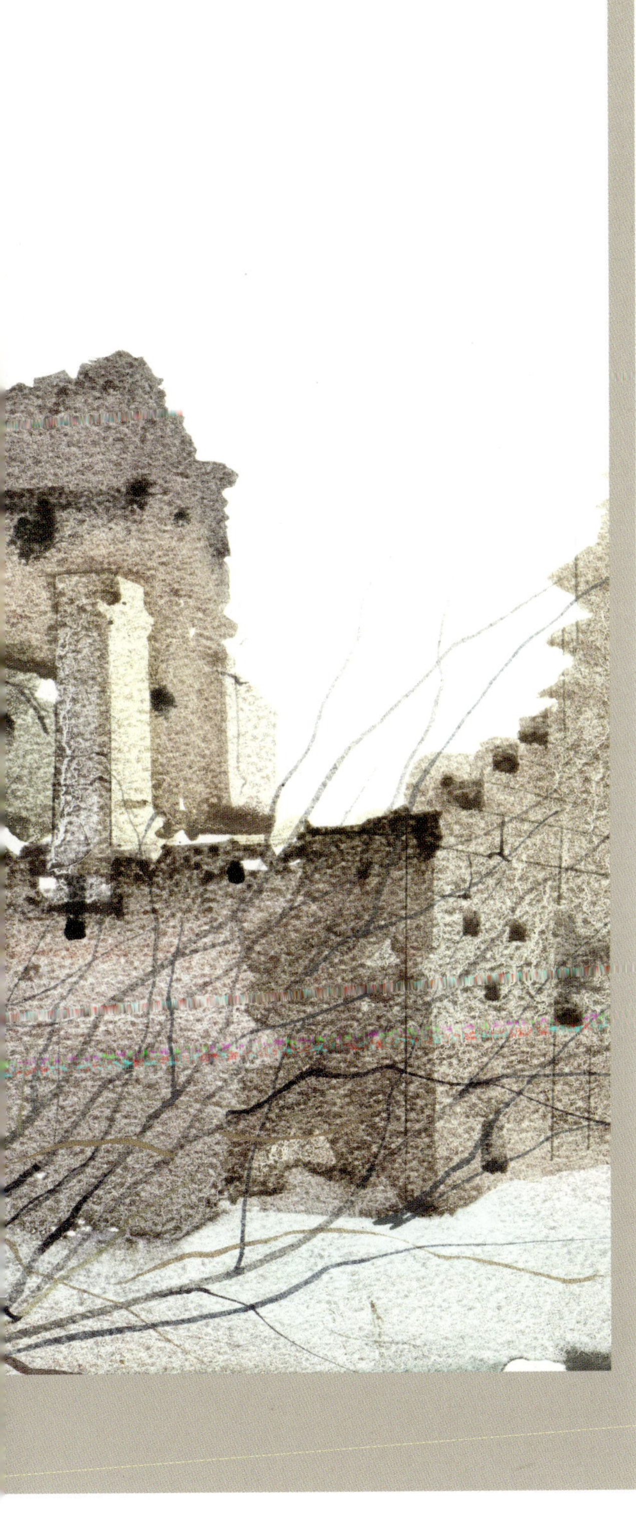

Moulin de Bessan 1

56 × 38cm (22 × 15in) 300gsm (140lb) Saunders Waterford Rough surface paper

The sky was left white to increase contrast with the forms of the building, and the light and dark tones of the building's surfaces were painted in at the same time.

Half-tones were then added along with the trees, followed by the darkest shapes of the sides of the buildings and features.

The ground with wet in wet shadows was then added. Details such as architectural features were last to go on.

Painting from light to dark

Because watercolour is transparent and the white of the paper is used as the white, the paint is put down in order from lightest to darkest tones. Darker tones mask what they cover and so are placed around shapes you wish to create.

The objective of this approach is to paint in a way that creates shapes and gives form to the subject while preserving the fresh, clean colours that are crucial to a successful watercolour. This process will help you to analyse and simplify the subject – and that is key to capturing the atmosphere while describing the subject.

The three wash stages

When faced with the subject, think in terms of areas of paint and work out how you can place the washes in a logical order. Identify within the scene three separate degrees of tone and paint these in three stages: lights, half-tones, and darks.

Pure highlights can be preserved and finishing details can be added, but all the important contrast, balance and atmosphere in the painting is created within these stages.

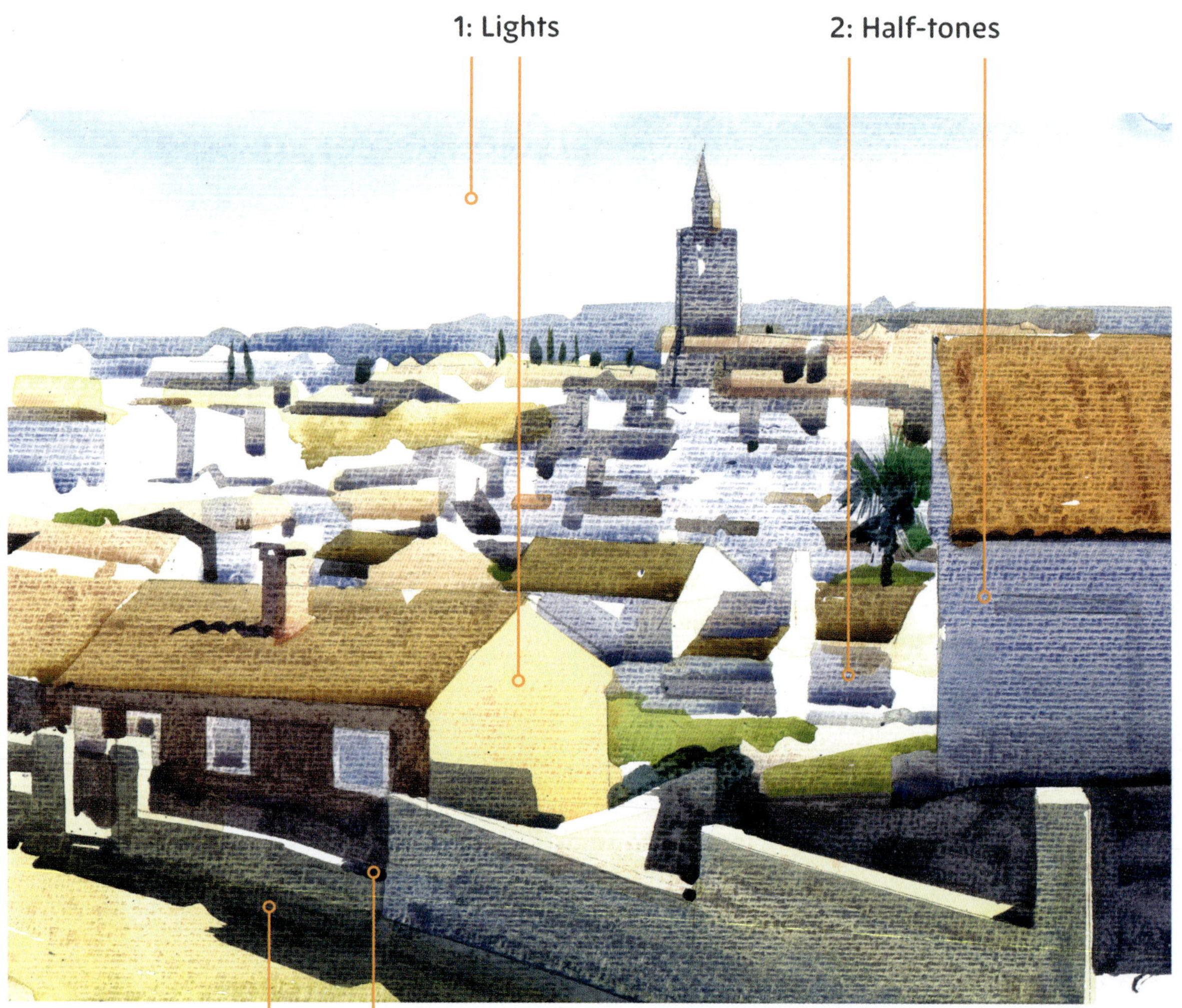

View over Montagnac, Morning Light
30.5 × 25.5cm (12 × 10in) Hahnemühle 300gsm (140lb) Rough surface paper
The sky went on first, followed by the lightest tones – mostly yellow – after which half-tones, such as the blue in the shadows of the buildings, were added. These were followed in turn by the darker tones of the shadows.

Wash stage 1: Lights

The first stage places the lightest tones of the landscape or architecture, leaving the white areas untouched. This crucial stage preserves the lightest tones and shapes we will paint around later. It therefore also includes any underpainting – so lay down any colours here that you want to show through subsequent layers.

Foundations: Lights

- Washes of pure un-mixed colour can sometimes be used to establish lights.
- Because we are working with the lightest tones, it is important to use clean water, palette, and brushes.
- In terms of colour, these tones are usually towards the yellow or red end of the spectrum but can also include off-whites and other colours.

Foundations: Half-tones

- As with the lights, the purity of these washes is important to the overall result, so mix these using as few colours as possible.
- Start with the largest areas and work down to the smallest.
- Prepare your paints beforehand – and make sure you mix enough in advance.

Wash stage 2: Half-tones

Here we place half-tones: those just strong enough to cover areas either completely or partially (to leave the underpainting showing as required). This stage can involve an entire range of tonal values.

While completing these stages, work from large to small areas while using an appropriate brush size for the area you are covering. Importantly, always mix enough paint to cover the area you wish, in order to avoid having to hurriedly mix more paint half-way down a wash.

Wash stage 3: Darks

The next stage is to add the dark tones. These completely cover up the previous layers and create the greatest contrast in the painting.

Every time an area of paint is added the contrast and focus within the painting alters. For these reasons, this last stage is associated with the balance of the painting as the distribution of details and strength are mostly assigned at this point. This is often the stage associated with the dark shadows and at this point we really can emphasize a sense of lighting.

Foundations: Darks

- All the strongest tonal contrast will be established with the darks.
- When mixing darks, remember that paint dries substantially lighter than the colour we can see mixed in our palette.
- Achieving a sufficiently dark tone to create contrast is critical. If you are struggling, double the strength of your mix, then apply and see the results.
- Purity of dark mixes is important, but less so than with the lighter tones.

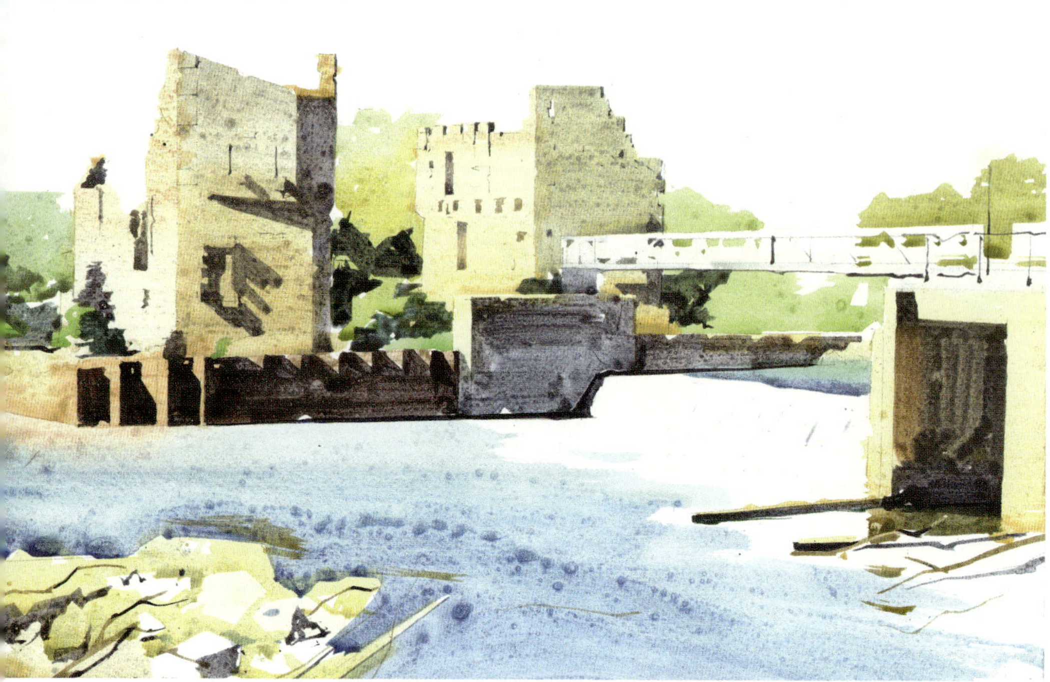

Moulin de Bessan 3

56 × 38cm (22 × 15in) Fabriano 165gsm (90lb) Not surface paper

Dramatic lighting here is key to the atmosphere and interest. The lightest areas – the sky and lighted sides of the structure – went on first, while the lighter surfaces of the mill were reserved by painting around them with the greenery. The half-tone stage helped to create the form and was an important aspect of capturing the light.

Conviction and confidence

In addition to the colour we can add with the three wash stages, we can preserve highlights and add details. In watercolour we cannot make changes, so we must consider carefully before putting brush to paper. A strong plan will help, so as you make your initial drawing (that is, before you start painting), identify the lighter tonal areas that must go on first and the white areas to be preserved.

Once you begin, paint with total conviction. Indecision in watercolour is punished badly. Likewise, spend more time observing and mixing than applying the paint – that part should be done quite quickly, and with clear intent.

Whenever we paint, there will be areas of our picture that we feel surer about than others – and so it is almost inevitable that we reach a point where we need to think about what to do next. At this point, pause and let everything dry. Spend the time considering your next steps and finding a clear way forward. When you start working again in the unresolved areas, continue working from light to dark, and preserving or enhancing the contrast.

While under way, a watercolour is seconds away from disaster or success. Whatever the result, it is important to finish each painting – only then can it be evaluated as a success or failure; only then can you draw worthwhile lessons from it.

Building skills

- The finished picture must make sense, with consistent shadows. It can therefore be helpful to draw in shadows at the start to note their position in your composition, even as the sun moves.

- If in doubt over what you have just applied, do not tinker with it while wet. Let it dry and then start working light to dark on any unresolved areas.

- If you find areas of paint are lacking the desired intensity, try using a stronger mix and a slightly smaller brush.

- Conversely, if areas risk being too fussy, try using a larger brush.

- To create a design and organize the painting, try to think in terms of areas of wash.

- The moment we paint a detail the eye will be drawn to it.

Contrasts

Contrast is crucial to the success of the painting, and can be created by different means during the process of painting. This needs to be planned for in advance so it can be incorporated into the three wash stages.

Contrast can be tonal, it can also be in colour, or it can be textural, for example the difference between a dry brush area and a flat wash area or the material difference between, for example, the pattern of bricks on a wall or the reflections on water.

The rocks in the detail shown here were established during the light stage by painting round the white paper. Their form was developed with half-tones as the water was added with overpainting; and then refined with a few dark touches. Note the contrast in texture between the rocky area, created with brushwork, and the water, where the granulating quality of the paint itself has created visual texture. These contrasts in quality help to highlight the contrasts in tone.

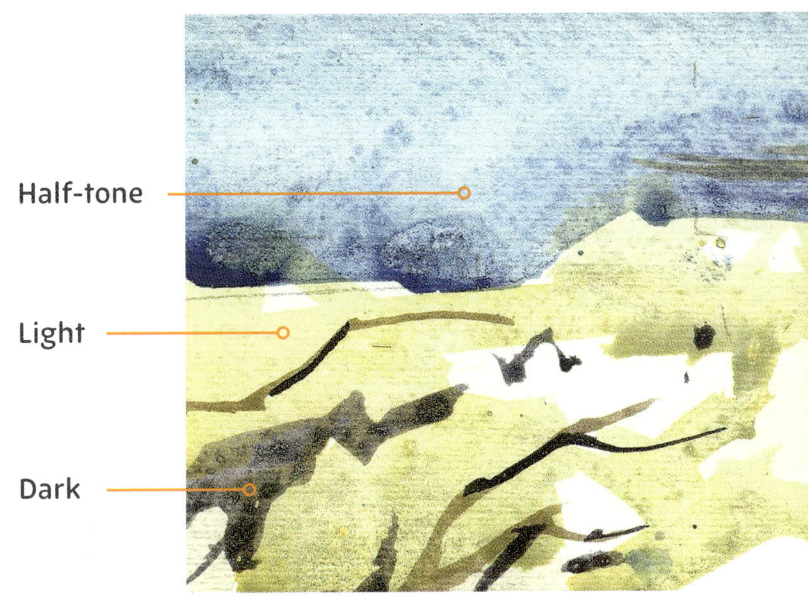

Preserved highlights and details

Finishing touches and details should be made at the very end, using a small brush. In this stage the judgement of balance becomes particularly important. The distribution and weight of these details are important in making the composition look right.

Details are also important in the description of the subject, so aim to choose what is relevant to the character of the subject and do not include anything that will distract.

Note that the details added do not have to be very dark: they can fit into the half-tone values too. The crucial thing is that a detail is always a stronger tone than the layer on which it is painted.

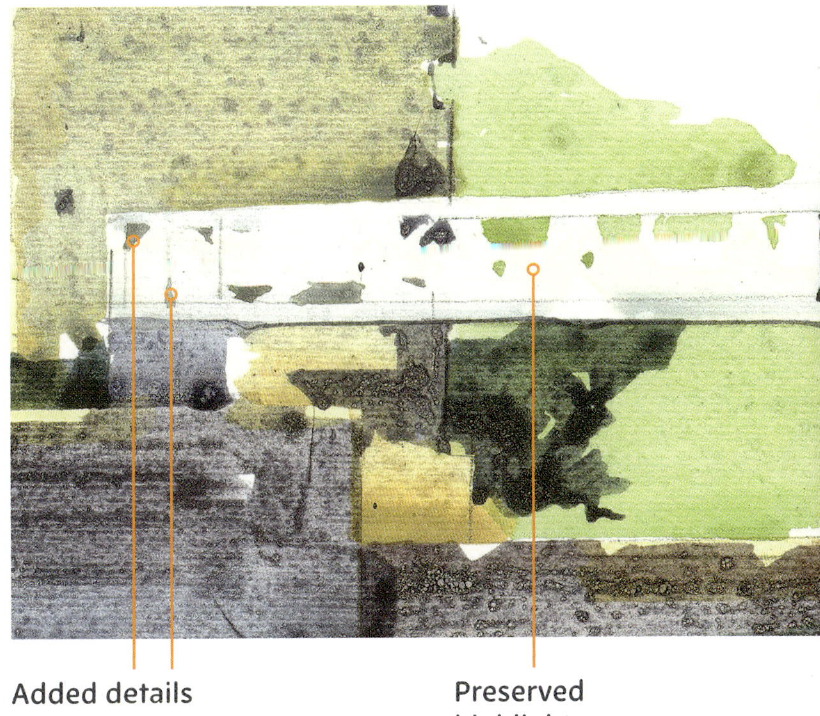

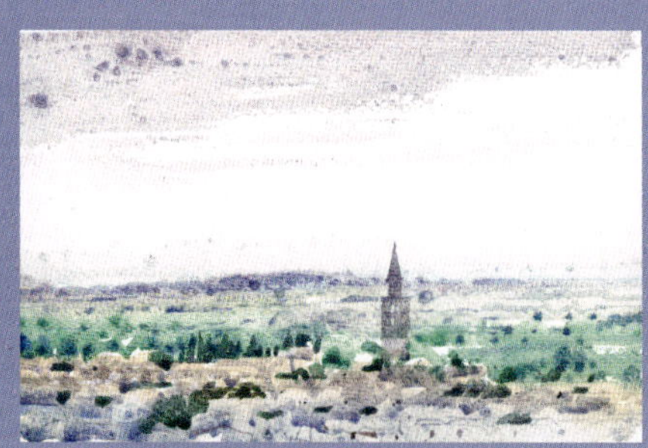
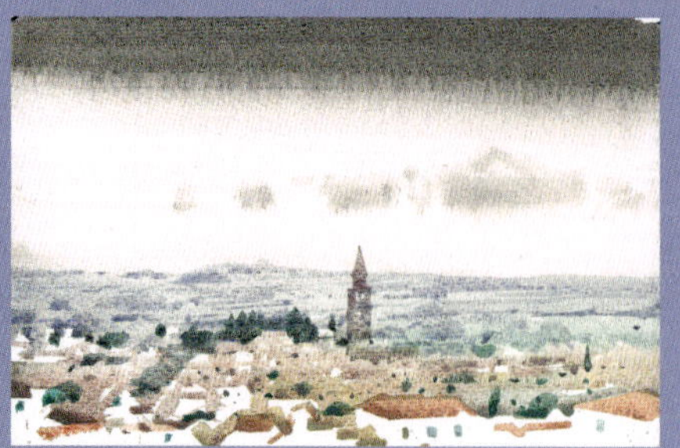
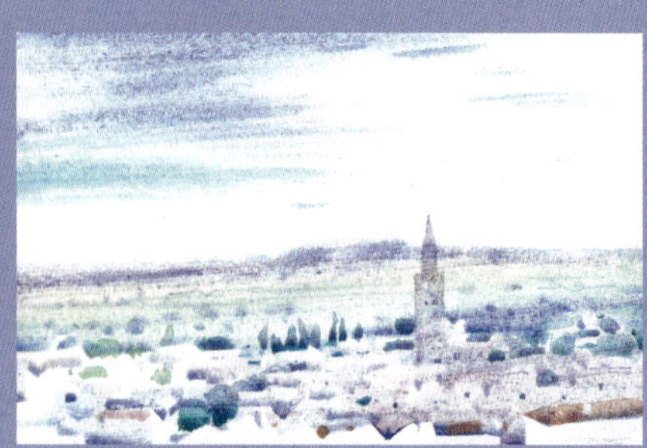

A sky a day

'Old school' watercolourists encouraged their students to paint a sky a day. Broad washes are used and drawing is not essential to capture the general nature of clouds, so it's a very forgiving exercise and great for beginners.

Painting a sky is perfect for helping you to evaluate tone and learn how to put down different tones of washes in the right order while preserving the forms of lighter shapes.

This practice can also help you to learn something about the character of watercolour and will improve your observation and simplification skills.

Skies over Montagnac

I recommend combining the exercise with painting a landscape. The three very different skies shown above were painted on successive occasions from the same point of view, overlooking a town called Montagnac near where I live.

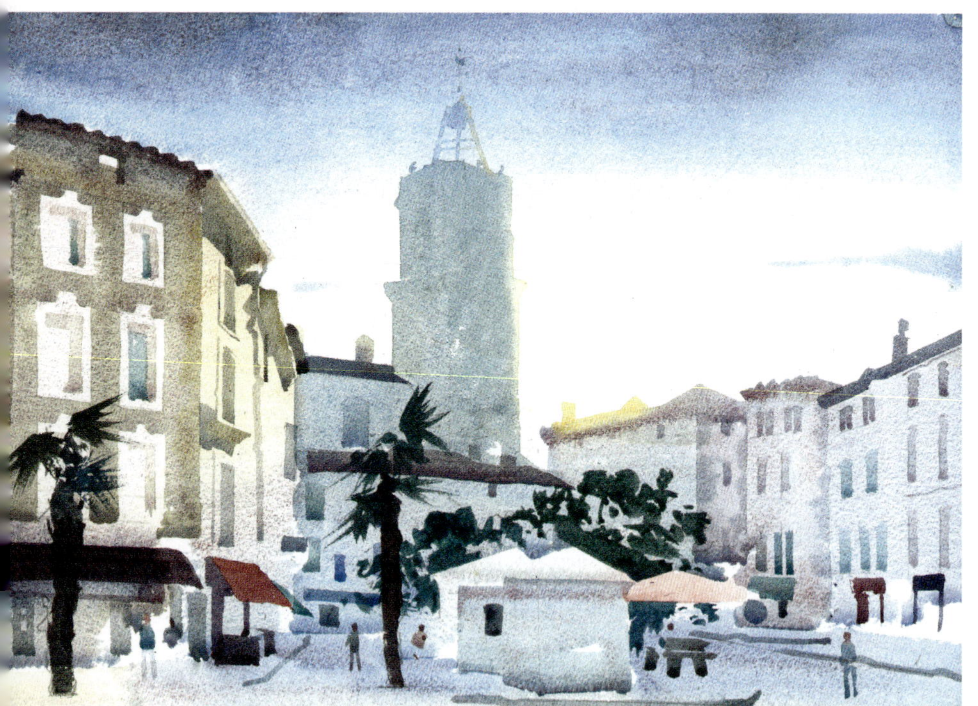

Place de la République, Pézenas

38 × 28cm (15 × 11in) Milford 300gsm (140lb) Rough surface paper

Underpainting was used on the left to make the window shapes. Darker shapes were used to create contrast and give form. The sky went on first as darker shapes would be going on top. The underpainting was added at the same time as the lightest tones. In watercolour you must always think a couple of moves ahead and work out what will be covered up by subsequent layers, and what you wish to preserve.

Style and freedom

There is obviously freedom in the working order I have outlined. For example, lighter and darker tones can be placed down at the same time with areas left as white paper, if you wish. This will depend on the particular painting – and on your own painting style.

When painting the sky, I often place light and darker tones simultaneously. Depending on where in the painting and how vague I wish to keep an area, painting wet against wet, light, and dark tones, can be highly effective. There are additional methods designed to preserve or reveal the highlights, than those described here, that I do not use but that I am not critical of. Some artists choose to use body colour or acrylic for the whites, some scrape out to reveal the white of the paper – David Cox (1783–1859) used a sharp knife and J.M.W. Turner (1775–1851) a sharpened thumbnail. Some artists like to wash a layer over the whole surface, described as a unifying wash, while leaving highlights painted in with latex resist. I prefer to paint around the highlights, but I don't think there is necessarily a better or worse approach. However, the choice of subject is important if you really wish to apply a certain technique.

Ideally, it is the subject that determines the techniques rather than the artist imposing them on the subject.

Fashions

As with all things, working methods go in fashions so if you look at watercolours from the mid-sixties for about thirty years the 'line and wash' technique was probably the dominant working method and was used brilliantly by artists such as Rowland Hilder, Arthur Sheldon Phillips, Edward Wesson and James Fletcher-Watson.

We are inevitably artists of our time, but I think it important that we have confidence in our own view and way of working and keep in mind that the painting is the artists' personal vision, and you can paint your picture however you want. It is good to be open to influences while remaining faithful to ourselves and to what we love in the medium and subject. The moment we put a picture on a wall we must accept that people looking at it will have an opinion. In terms of critique, I find it helpful to listen to everything, but I only consider following the advice I agree with.

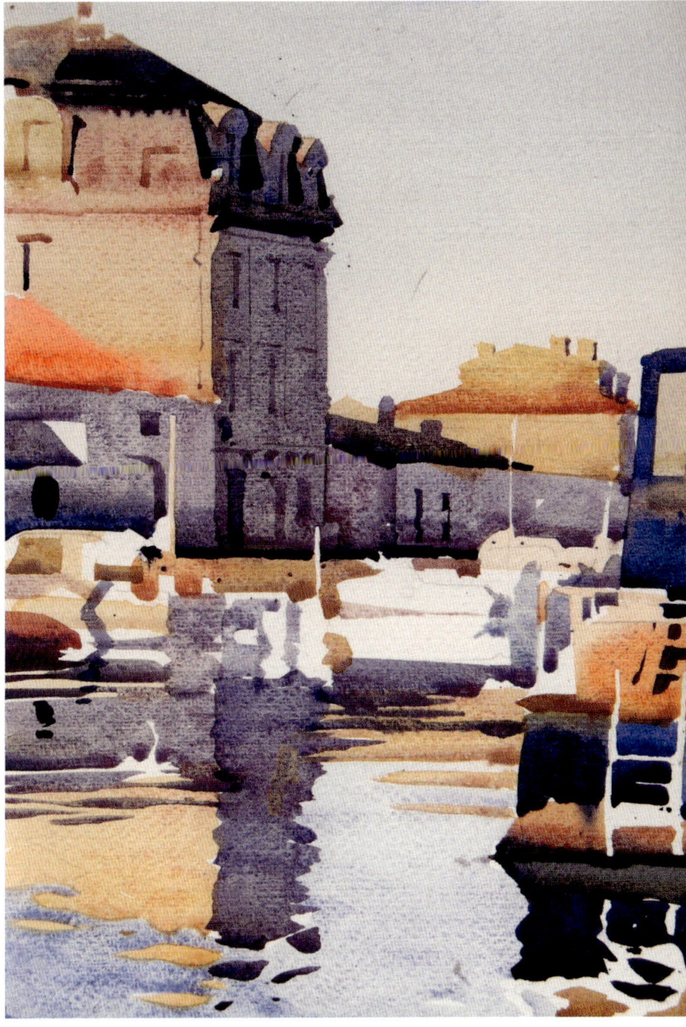

Marseillan Port

9 × 18cm (3½ × 7in) Canson 300gsm (140lb) Not surface paper

In this attractive coastal subject, the lights went on first, with the white of the paper reserved for the various slightly abstract forms of the boats and the little ladder to the right.

Most of the painting was put on in separate areas of wet on dry which helped create clearly defined shapes.

Deconstructing a painting

I found this subject in the Northeast of Spain in the town of Figueras. It is what I would think of as a natural composition. There are many elements that made this view a complex and absorbing subject. Due to the angle of lighting, there were many half-lights (half-tones) where the sunlight skimmed along various surfaces and shadows. Due to the materials within the subject – shiny surfaces, like the pavement on the left that leads to the Dali Museum – there was a lot of reflected light. A tonally light sky and strong sunlight created areas with a high tonal key on the right. The strong tones of the trees also helped create depth and contrast in the painting.

Planning and lights

The first stage was the tonally light wash of the sky which is ultramarine blue. I painted around the lighter areas of the buildings. The lightest tones of the buildings were then put on. These were created by the light falling on the side of the tower and to the surface of the buildings to the right of the painting. On the flat side of the buildings facing us, a half-light was created by the angle of the sun. This was a mix that included a touch of cobalt blue to cool it down a little, and to help give form to the structures.

Half-tones

The next stage was the shadows that were added in quite quickly as they were changing. These gave form to much of the architectural features in the subject, such as the windows and archways.

Darks

The strongest tones went on including the trees and the darker tones on the left. Whenever we add a darker tone, we change the range within the painting and in this case, the trees pushed back the rest of the subject and increased the effect of the lighting.

Details

The last stage included the darkest tones that helped give more form. The figures were added for life and to give scale.

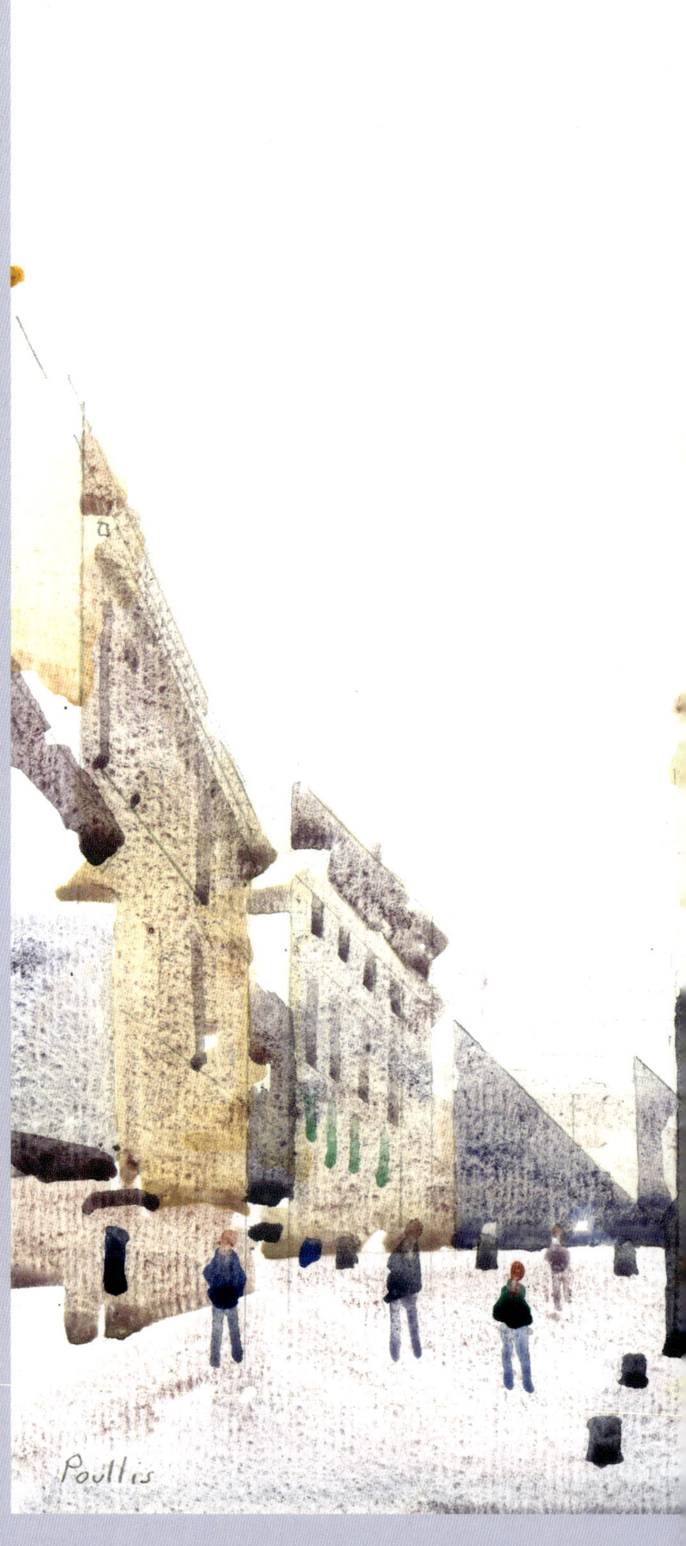

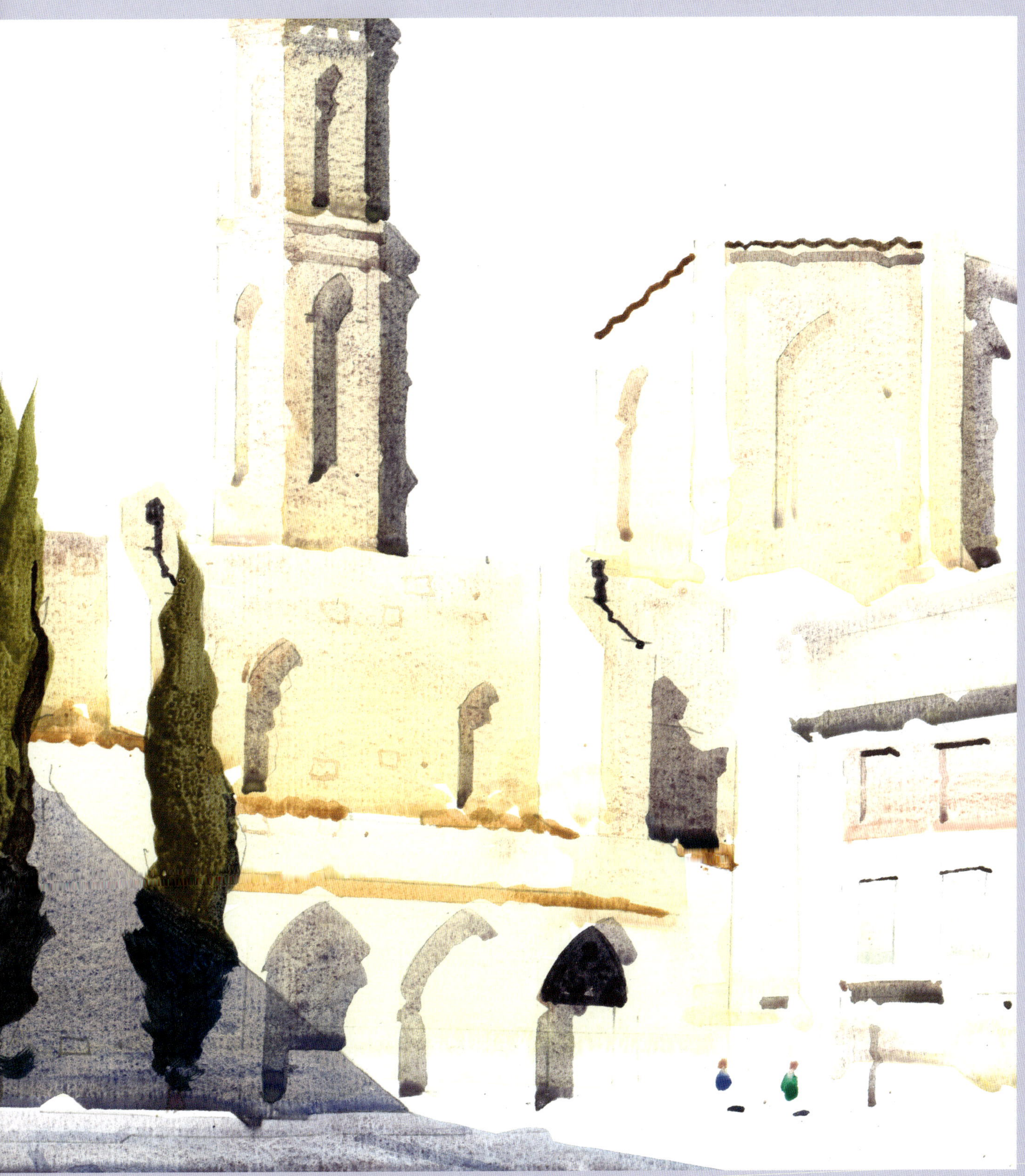

Figueras, Spain
51 × 30.5cm (20 × 12in) Hahnemühle 300gsm (140lb) Rough surface paper

Market Hall Interior

For this demonstration I have chosen the subject of the interior of the market hall in Marseillan, a town near where I live. The subject is a little complicated, due to the arches and the need to preserve the lights.

The key to making the view a success is to simplify without losing any of the key ingredients. Working from light to dark helps me to organize the painting and, in so doing, to simplify the scene.

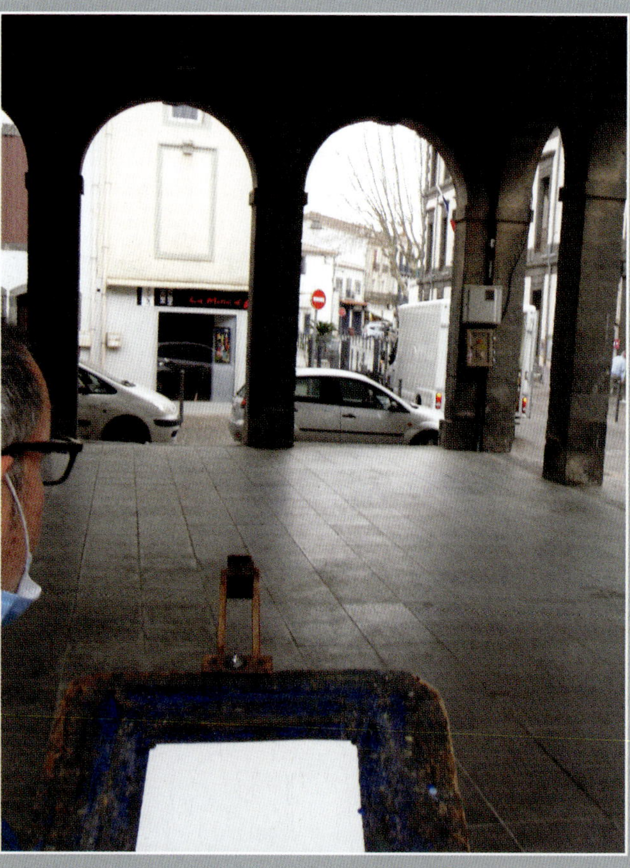

Setting up

The position in which you set up, particularly when at close range, will dramatically affect the composition and resulting picture. In this painting the view through the arches was important and so I positioned myself so I could see something interesting beyond the market. The arches themselves were important because they provided interesting shapes, setting and contrast that helped create depth.

I positioned myself at a distance where I was not straining to see the top of the arches, and could see clearly through them to the streets beyond. Had I positioned myself further to the right, the arches on that side would have a more acute perspective and the gaps through them would disappear, forming a solid mass.

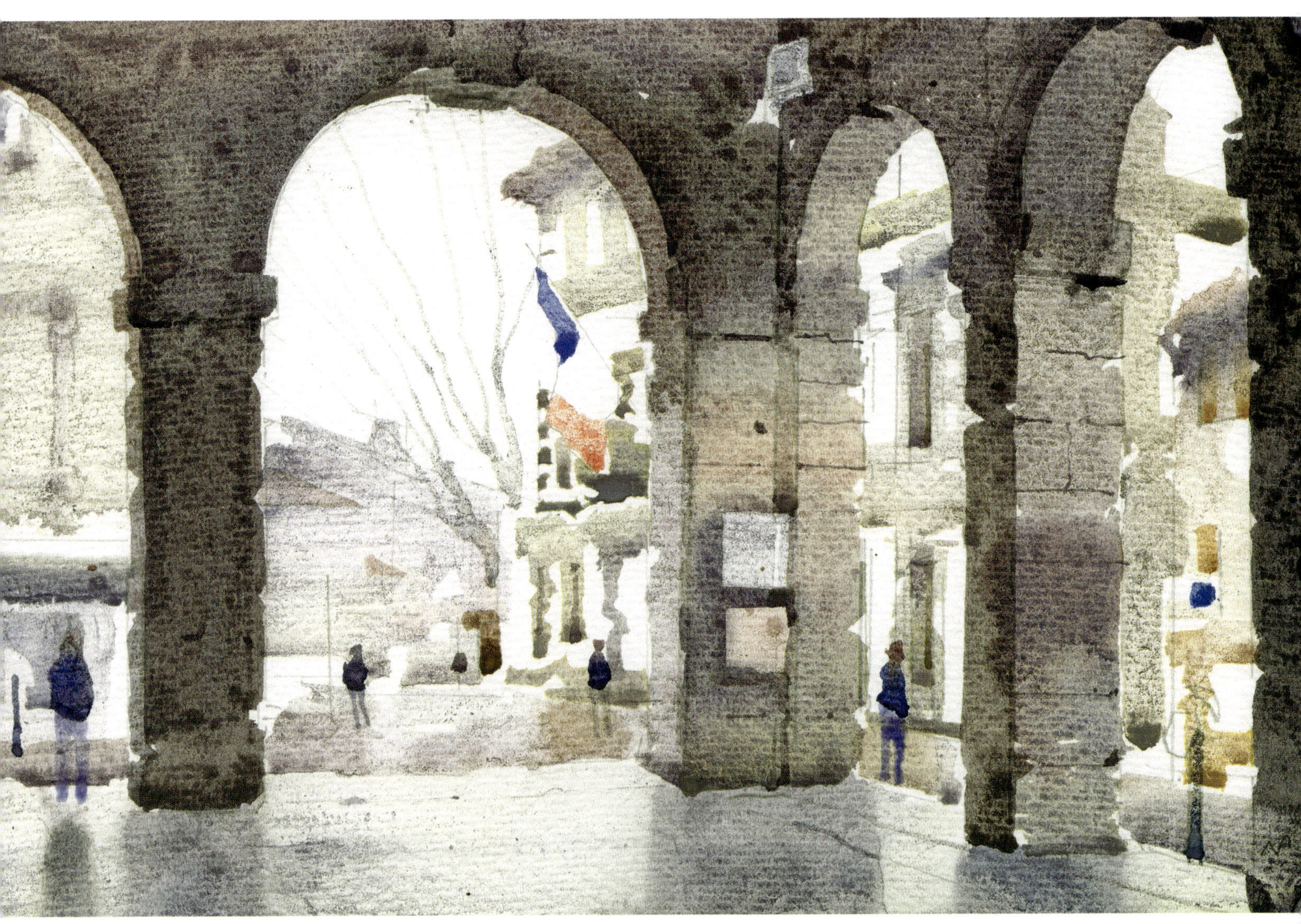

The finished painting

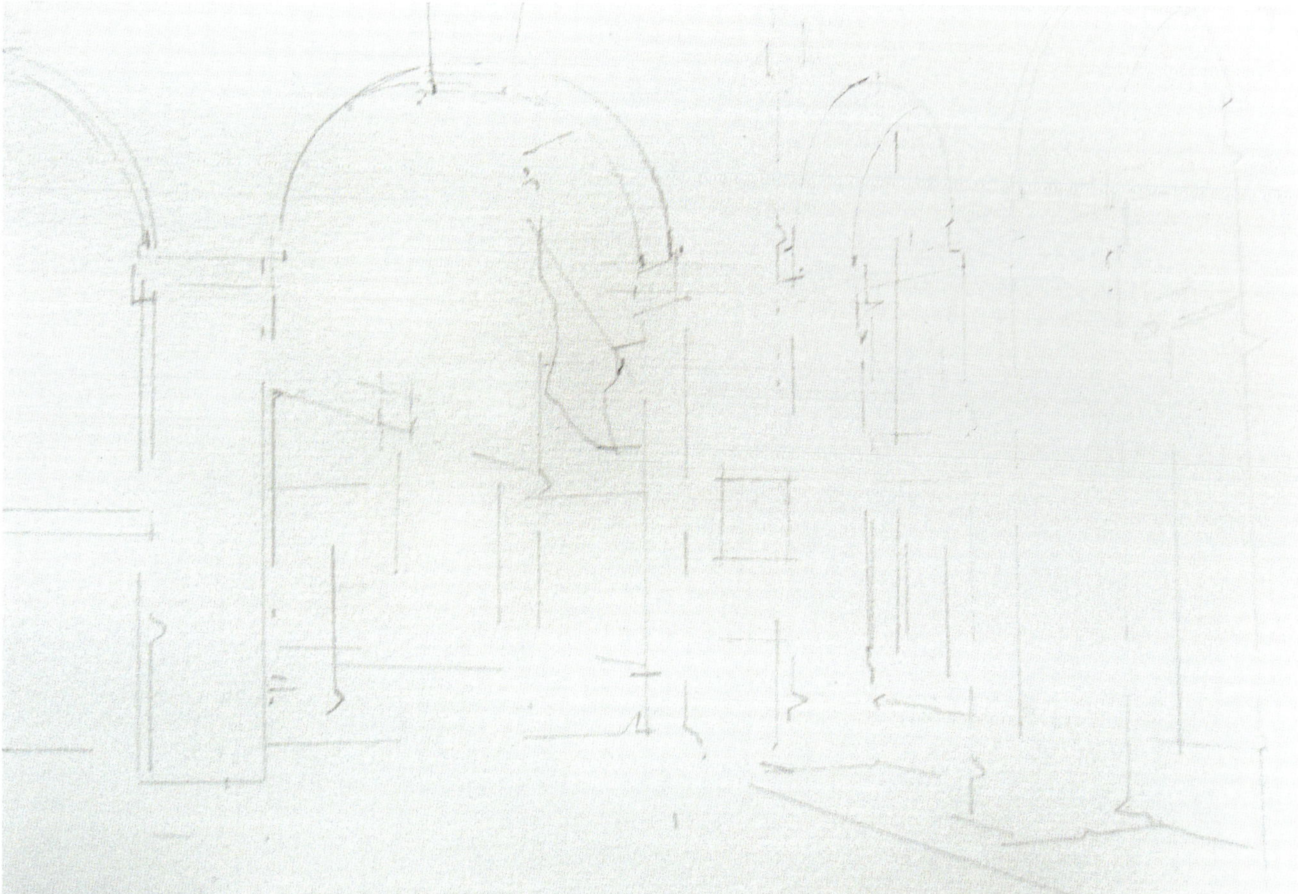

Stage 1

The first step is always the drawing: try to include the key shapes and leave out the detail. The drawing needs to focus on the structure and composition, so at this point start your selection. Be ruthless – it is essential. Here, the arches themselves provide interest, so be sure to include some details of their features.

A well-established compositional device is creating a frame within the frame – and here we can use the arch to create this. This frame can serve several purposes, such as providing information about the setting of the view. It also offers a view out of the picture plane, and when used as part of an interior, it can help to avoid a composition seeming claustrophobic or flat by providing depth.

Building skills

- Choose an unobstructed view of your subject.
- Draw simplified major features.
- Draw accurately but simply.
- Draw in details as and when they are required. Don't be afraid to draw in between subsequent wash stages if needed.
- The frame in this example is an arch, but the device can take the form of many features. These include windows, doorways, or even less obvious forms like trees that provide a shape to view through.

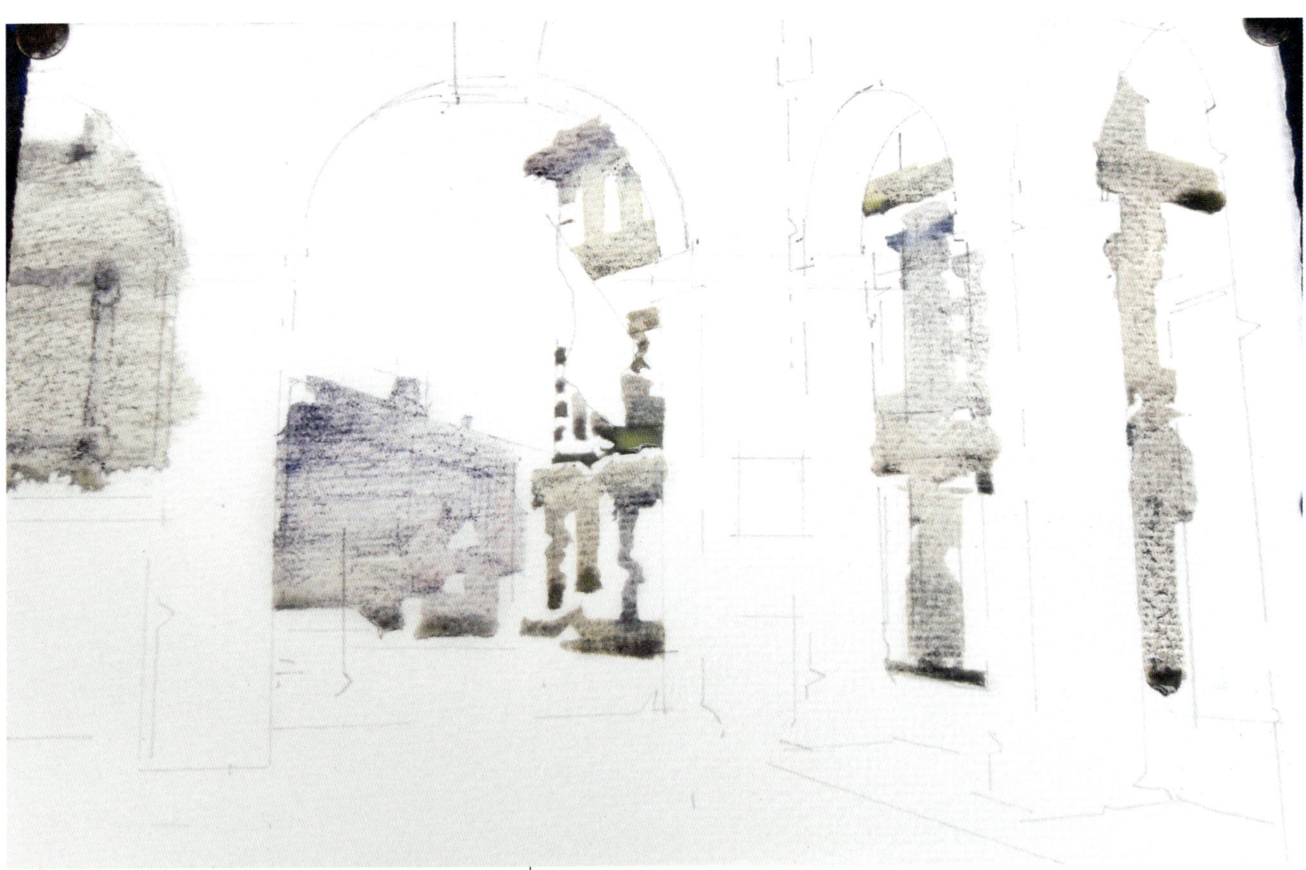

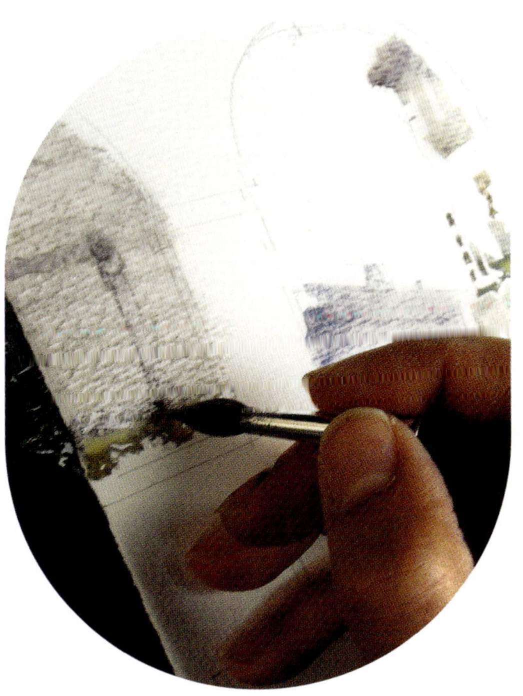

Stage 2

Using a size 8 round brush, start by painting in the background using mixes of Naples yellow, potters pink and ivory black – vary the proportions to create interest. Create a limited colour range of cool and warm greys using varying amounts of raw sienna, potters pink and cobalt blue deep, and use these for further variation.

Paint the view through the arches first – this will help you to balance the overall tones because the arches and pillars are of stronger tone. It will also help you keep things neat, as you can paint over them later. Finally, the arches will help to frame what is seen beyond – so it's important to get this stage right.

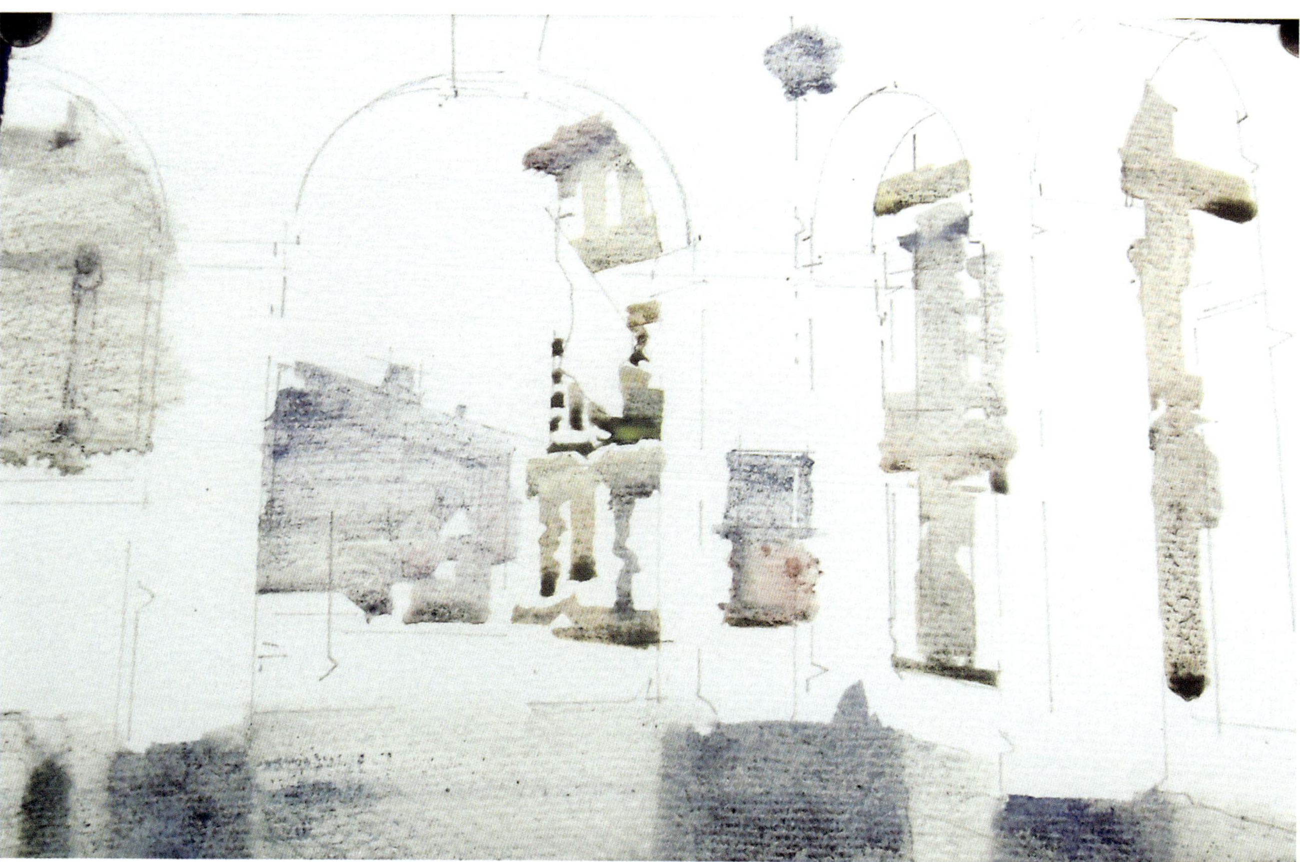

Stage 3

Using a size 8 round brush, paint in the reflections on the ground starting with a mid-tone wash of a Naples yellow, cobalt blue deep and potters pink mix. Change to a size 6 round brush and add the darker reflections into this wet in wet. This will create reflections with soft edges, as shown. The reflections are important for creating depth, and to ensure that the arches and pillars do not appear to float.

Prepare a lighter-toned mix of cobalt blue deep and light red, and a slightly deeper-toned mix of French ultramarine and light red. Using these in concert, and working wet in wet, paint the reflections. To ensure an even wash, draw the brush across the surface of the paper and do not press hard. Any form of stabbing motion should be avoided – ensure the brush is not bent and pushed towards the surface.

Building skills

- Whenever there is a fault that needs correcting in watercolour it will take time and persistence – any technical difficulty the student has, such as with drawing, (arches in this instance, are a difficult form to draw) must be worked on and will only be resolved over time – there is no quick fix.

- Persistence is important. I have seen students work at something to reach a point where they 'get it' and progress is made – while quick fixes are usually temporary.

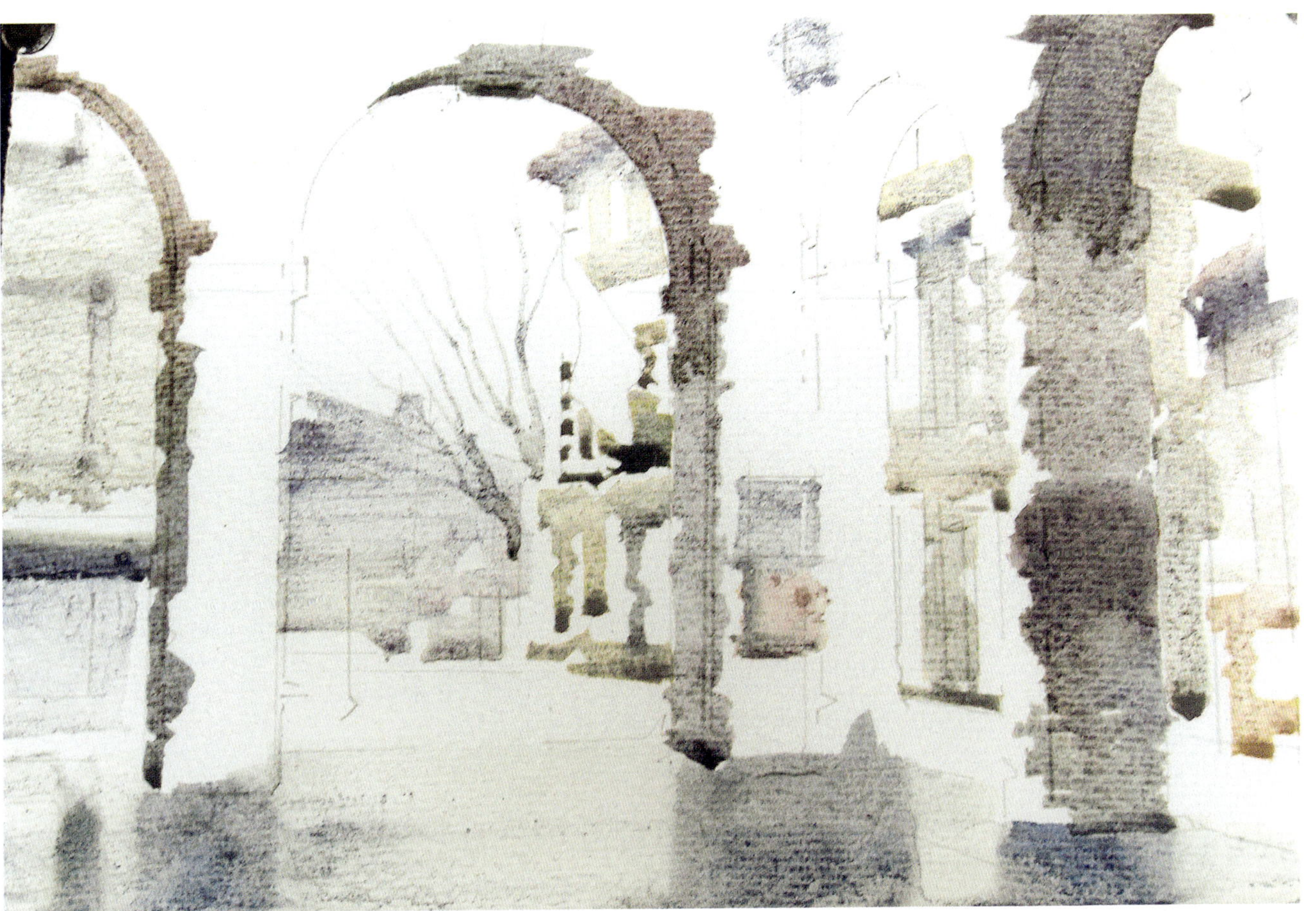

Stage 4

Once the background and previous layers have dried, it's time to add the lighter areas. It is important to use clean water for watercolour, and especially so for lights, so this is a good stage to refresh your water.

Be aware of overworking – the end of this stage is when you have stated what you wish; no more, no less.

Paint in the lighter sides of the pillars with a graduated wash, using a mix of cobalt blue deep, potters pink and light red for the darker areas, and a lighter tonal mix of Naples yellow, cobalt blue deep and potters pink for the lighter areas.

Once the lighter sides of the pillars have dried, add the tree in the background with a mix of cobalt blue deep and light red, using a size 4 rigger.

Building skills

- Work on larger areas first and use a brush the right size for the area you wish to paint.

- Be decisive. When you find yourself in doubt about how to proceed, stop work, let the paint dry and start again once you have a plan

- Our judgement is not at its best when we are painting as it is easy to fixate on one aspect we perceive has not worked.

- The only way to properly evaluate a watercolour, where there are so many elements that must work together, is when it is complete, so when things do go wrong it is always important to carry on and complete the painting. It is easy to get into the habit of not finishing paintings, but this habit makes it impossible to improve.

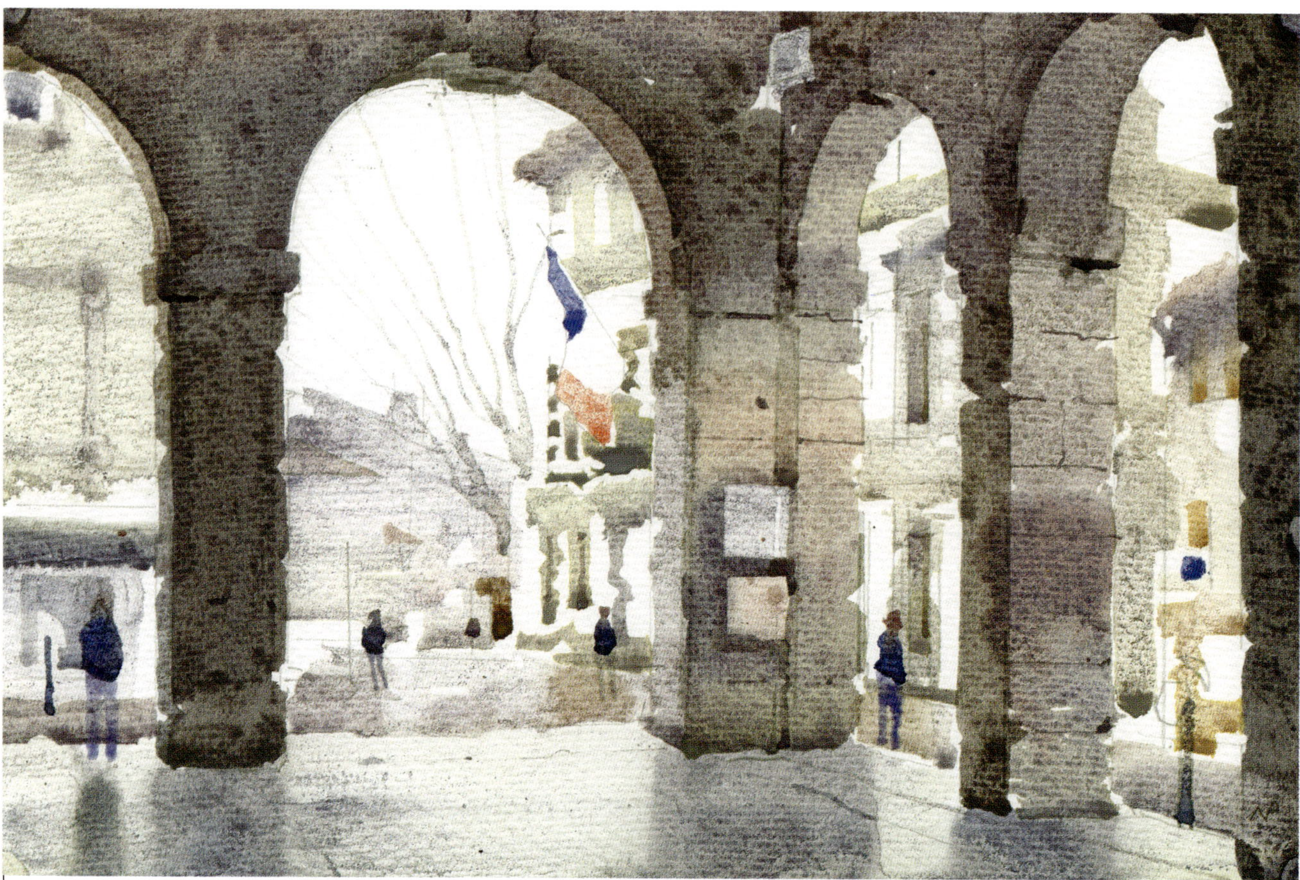

Stage 5

To finish, paint in the darker side of the pillars with a size 8 round brush. Put in a mix of cobalt blue deep and potters pink next to a mix of French ultramarine, light red and raw sienna. Once dry, add one or two details in the background such as the flag and windows using a size 6 round brush.

The painting is finished with the addition of figures that give scale and life to the scene. These can be added with a size 6 round brush, and the colours on your palette, along with cadmium red, cadmium yellow and/or brown madder. Finally, unwanted pencil marks can be rubbed out once everything is dry – remember that it is important to use a soft eraser, and rub gently to avoid damaging the paper surface or removing the paint.

Further challenges

As with all subjects, different lighting conditions offer different opportunities.
In terms of lighting most of the difference in this subject concerns the contrast
between the interior and exterior. Different angles on the subject and paper shapes
will also add to the range of what can be done with the subject.

Seasonal differences can dramatically affect views as well, particularly where
trees are involved, as leaves will hide potential subject matter that is revealed in
winter. The forms of winter trees are interesting, and I find they combine well with
buildings as we can see through the trees – and the branches can form part of the
overall design.

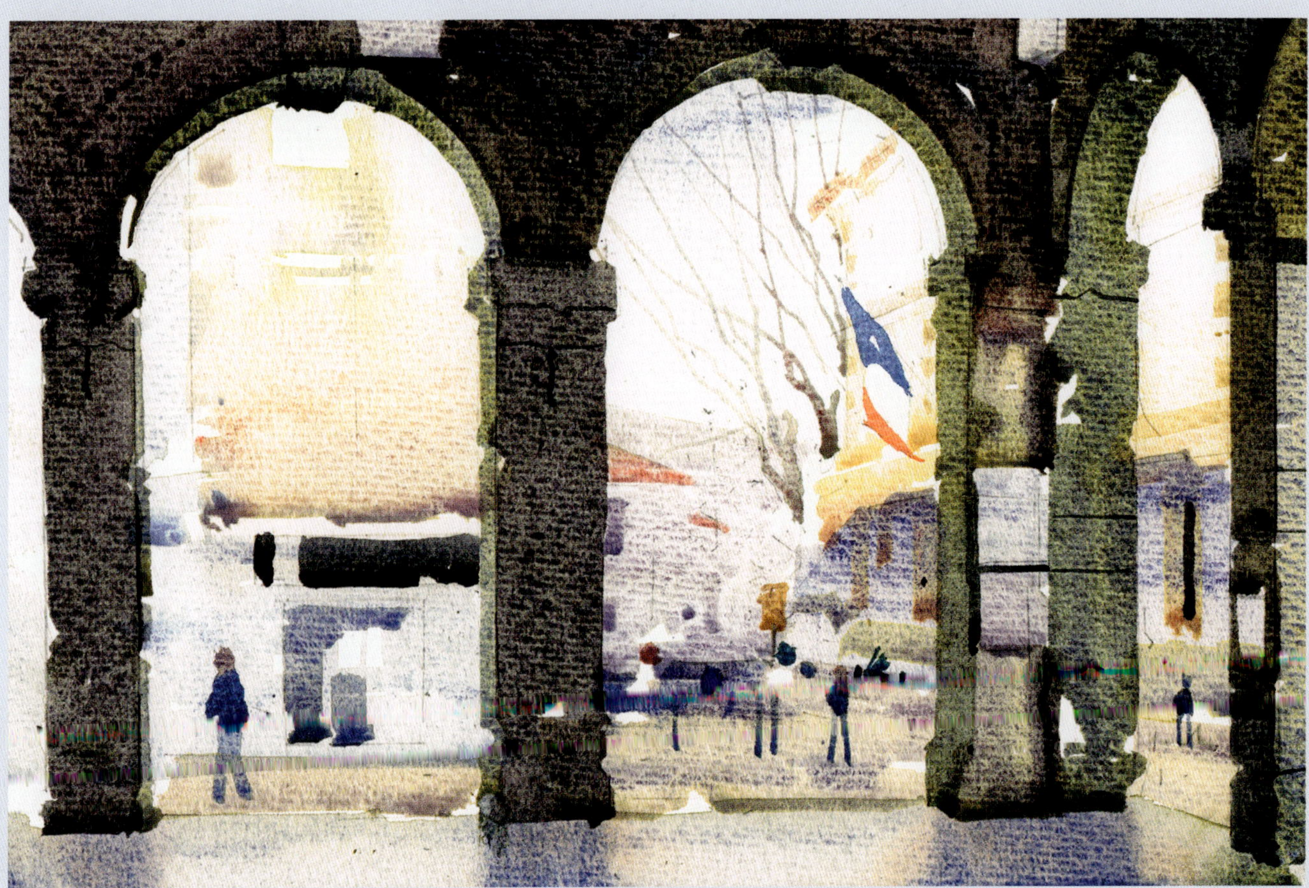

Marseillan Covered Market
28 × 18cm (11 × 7in) Saunders Waterford 300gsm (140lb) Rough surface paper

*In the same subject, with different lighting, the contrast and colour
range increases. The composition is very similar to the demonstration
piece, but with sunlight and shadows the atmosphere is different.*

*In the project, I used the arch to help create depth and contrast in order to
bring the eye to the exterior beyond where there is plenty of interest.*

*Due to the lighting in this version, the arches are darker, and so provide more
contrast. It's because of this that the viewer is drawn to look through the
arches, making the covered market the focus, rather than the pillars.*

How to develop your painting

Developing your painting is about the continual enjoyment and exploration of subject matter and the medium. Development should ideally mean improvement. You can develop your art in many ways: by working on your observation skills, honing your technical skills, or perhaps simply making better choices in subject matter or the angle of approach. In that sense it is developing an 'eye', and this chapter explores some of these different aspects of picture-making to give you new avenues to explore.

Identifying areas to improve

Something crucial to improvement is to identify what you need to work on. This is where good tuition or feedback can really help, but being self-critical is essential to improvement. When artists are not self-critical, and therefore believe everything they do is brilliant, they stop improving – after all, why would you work at what you think is perfect?

Perfection never arrives and is always something to which to aspire and work towards. Something can always be expressed better, with more clarity and with more economy. Paintings can always be improved.

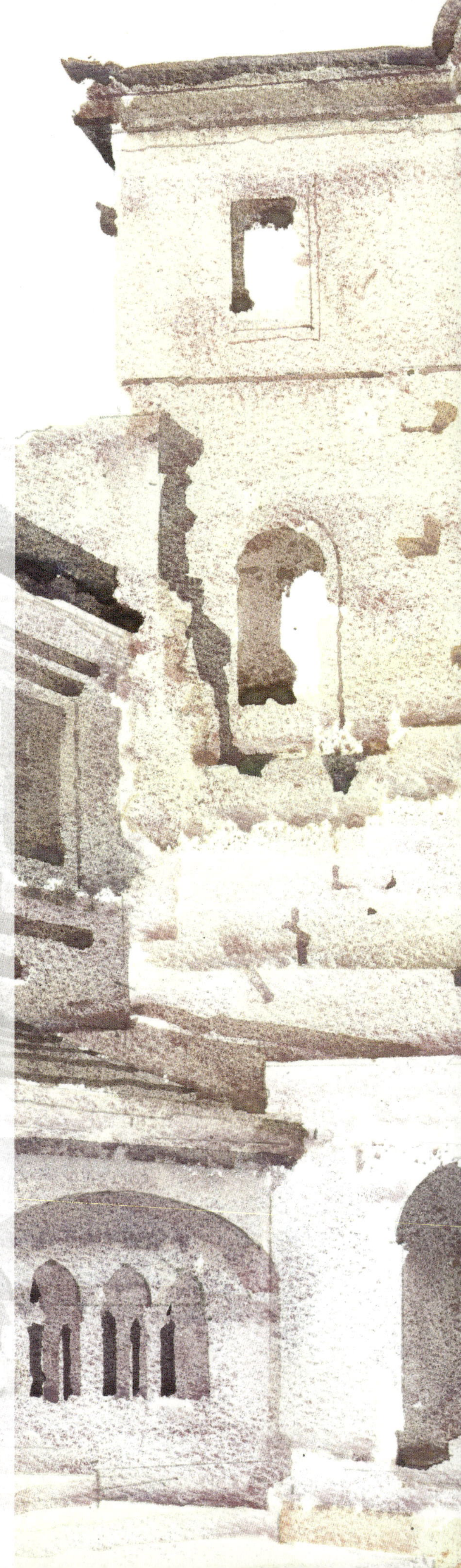

Abbaye de Montmajour
56 × 38cm (22 × 15in) Saunders Waterford 300gsm (140lb) Rough surface paper
In this complicated subject, contrast was important to help define the separate elements of architecture. The expression of texture had a significant role to play in the finished painting and helped create contrast and interest. Details and the dark shapes in the shadows were painted last.

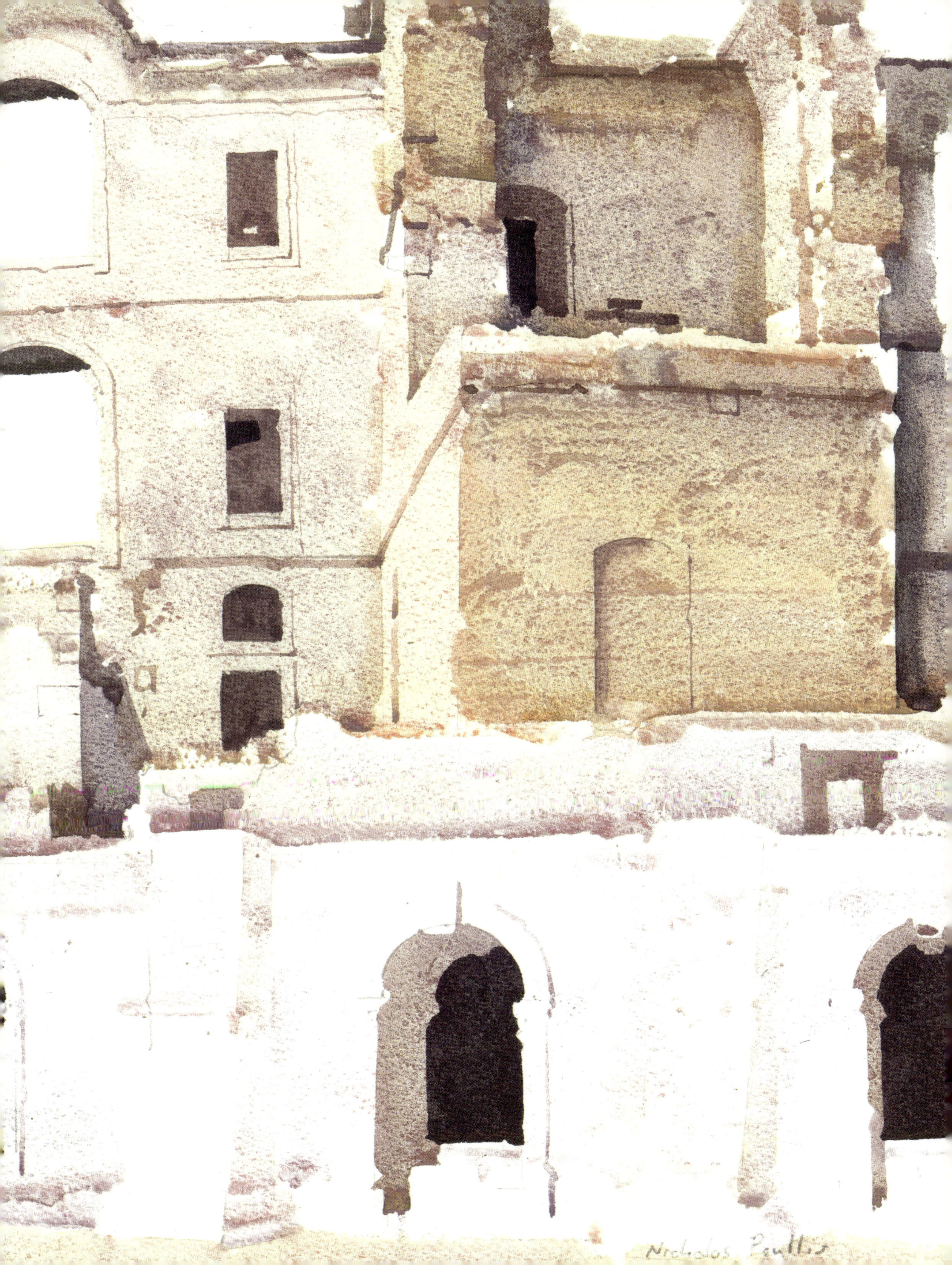
Nicholas Poullis

Looking beyond your subject

Aside from incremental technical improvements brought about through practice in drawing and painting in general, an exciting way of developing is through exploring diverse subject matter. In painting something other than buildings, you will find that you produce something that surprises and challenges you, and takes you in a new direction.

I decided one year to follow the Tour de France cycle race, and produced work of the various sites that the race passed through. These pictures were mostly in line with what I would normally produce, but I also produced some paintings of the cyclists themselves – as in *Tour de France, Alignan-du-Vent*, below. I used sketches and memory and painted this in the studio.

These paintings were concerned with movement and atmosphere, and were more abstract than my architectural work. This helped me to realize the potential of abstraction in capturing moving elements of a subject – but also as a means of simplification for other subjects.

This led to a more general interest in movement and later, when I saw the opportunity, I painted the subject of the *Abrivado* (see opposite) in the south of France. Here, I applied the lessons learned to showing the combined movement of the horses and bulls.

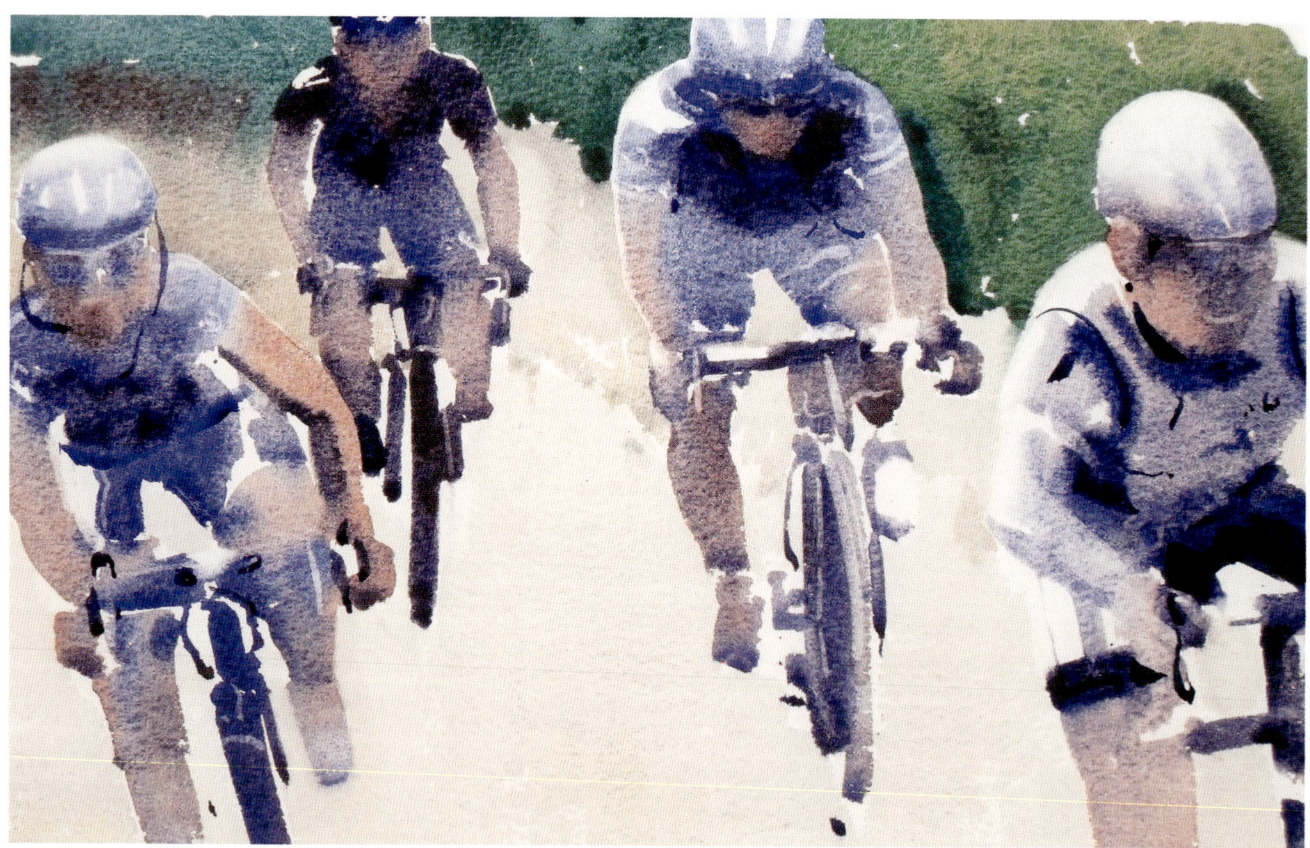

Tour de France, Alignan-du-Vent
38 x 23cm (15 x 9in) Saunders Waterford 300gsm (140lb) Rough surface paper
This painting is about movement and uses abstraction as a means of simplification and expression. Some subject matter lends itself to abstraction and can be used to develop that aspect of your work.

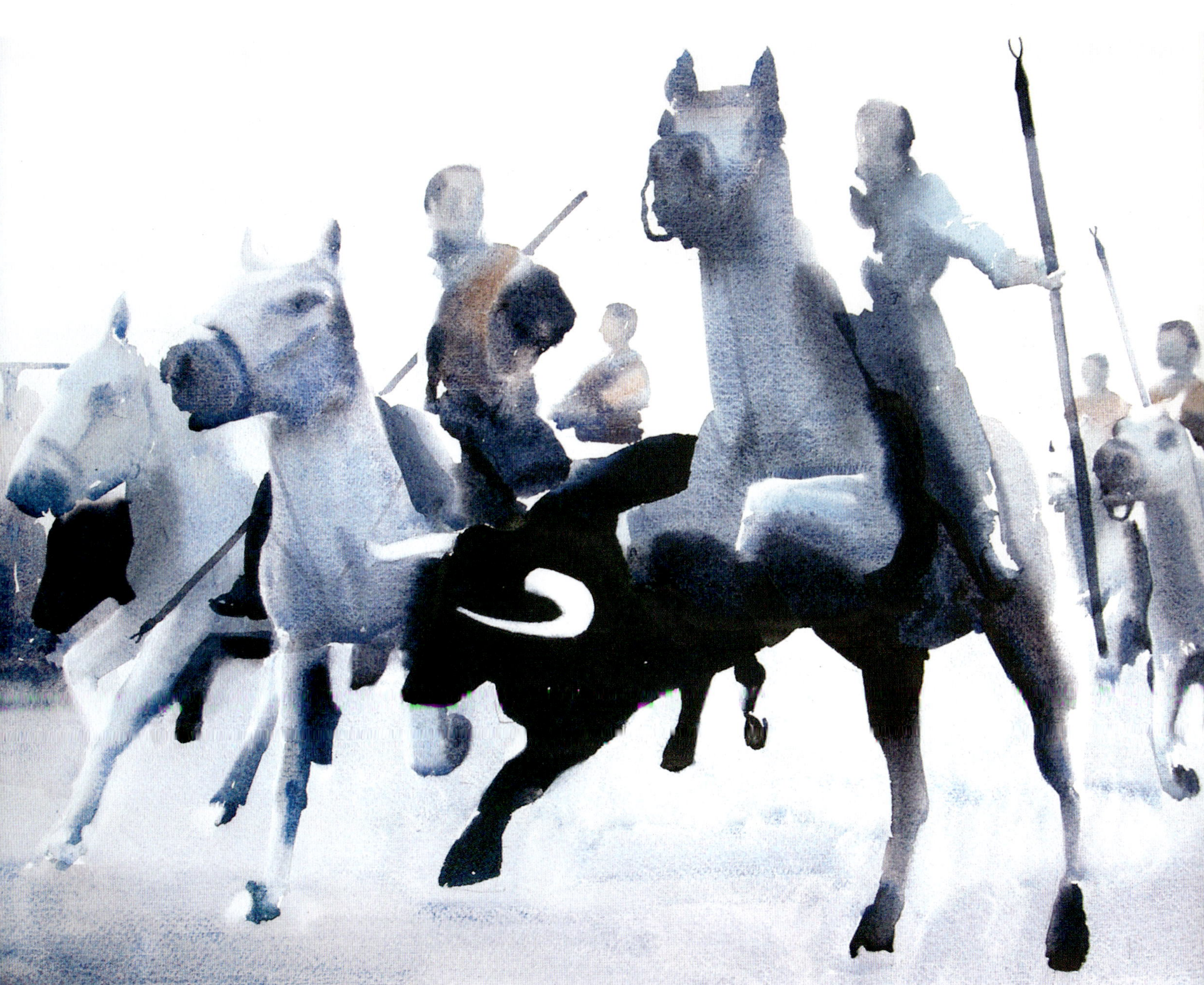

Abrivado

76 × 56cm (30 × 22in) Hahnemühle 300gsm (140lb) Rough surface paper

This painting is about movement and captures a dramatic moment when the guardians on horseback try to steer and control the bulls.

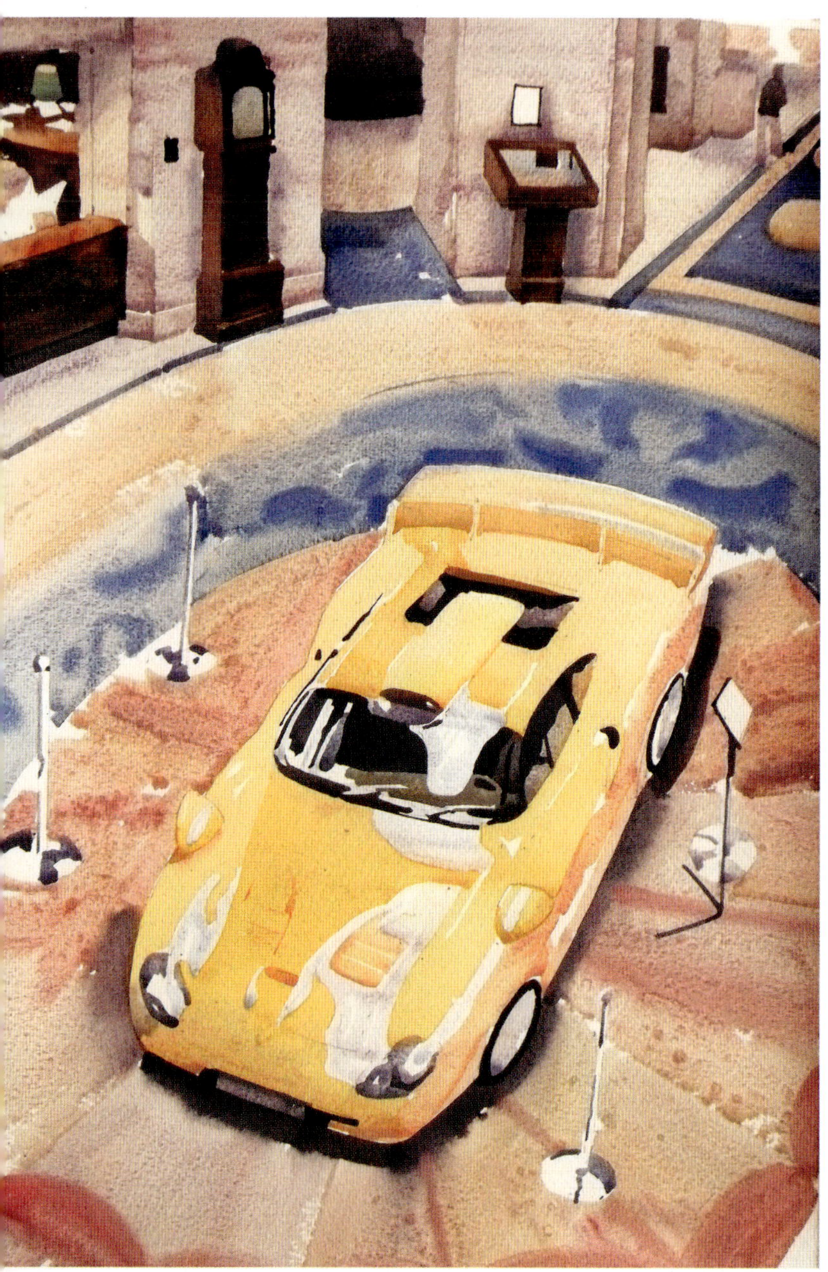

Porsche 911 RAC

*38 × 56cm (15 × 22in) Millford 300gsm
(140lb) Rough surface paper*

*This was a unique opportunity to paint cars from
above in an architectural setting. Reflected light on
the various materials was an important aspect.*

Different routes to success

A new point of view Another way of developing is
to explore various aspects offered by one subject
or setting. Aim to see the potential offered by
each subject. The ruined mill at Bessan helped me
to explore texture and atmosphere and elements
of architecture within a landscape setting – you can
see the various approaches I took on pages 4–5,
104–105, 108 and 128. Sometimes with this subject
I pushed the atmospheric aspect, in others the
textural, in others the detail, and in others the
landscape setting.

Challenge your weaknesses You might look for
a particular challenge. On preparation for a solo
exhibition at the RAC in Pall Mall, London, I took
the opportunity to paint interiors at the club
and the cars on display in the building (see left)
and this was a terrific way of exploring reflected
light and texture. Views within the club building
made fascinating subject matter – particularly the
swimming pool, which you can see opposite.

Follow your interests You can steer your own
development by following your interests. For a
number of years, I explored the theme of cultural
influence in southern Europe, often Roman and
Moorish, that resulted in the look of places we see
today, and this led to a more informed approach
to painting architecture. If you want to develop
the use of light in your work, for example, then
choose a subject that will allow this: a well-lit scene
with architecture with reflective surfaces, perhaps.
If you would like to develop depth and perspective,
choose a subject with a strong architectural
element with some tall buildings or find a dramatic
vantage point.

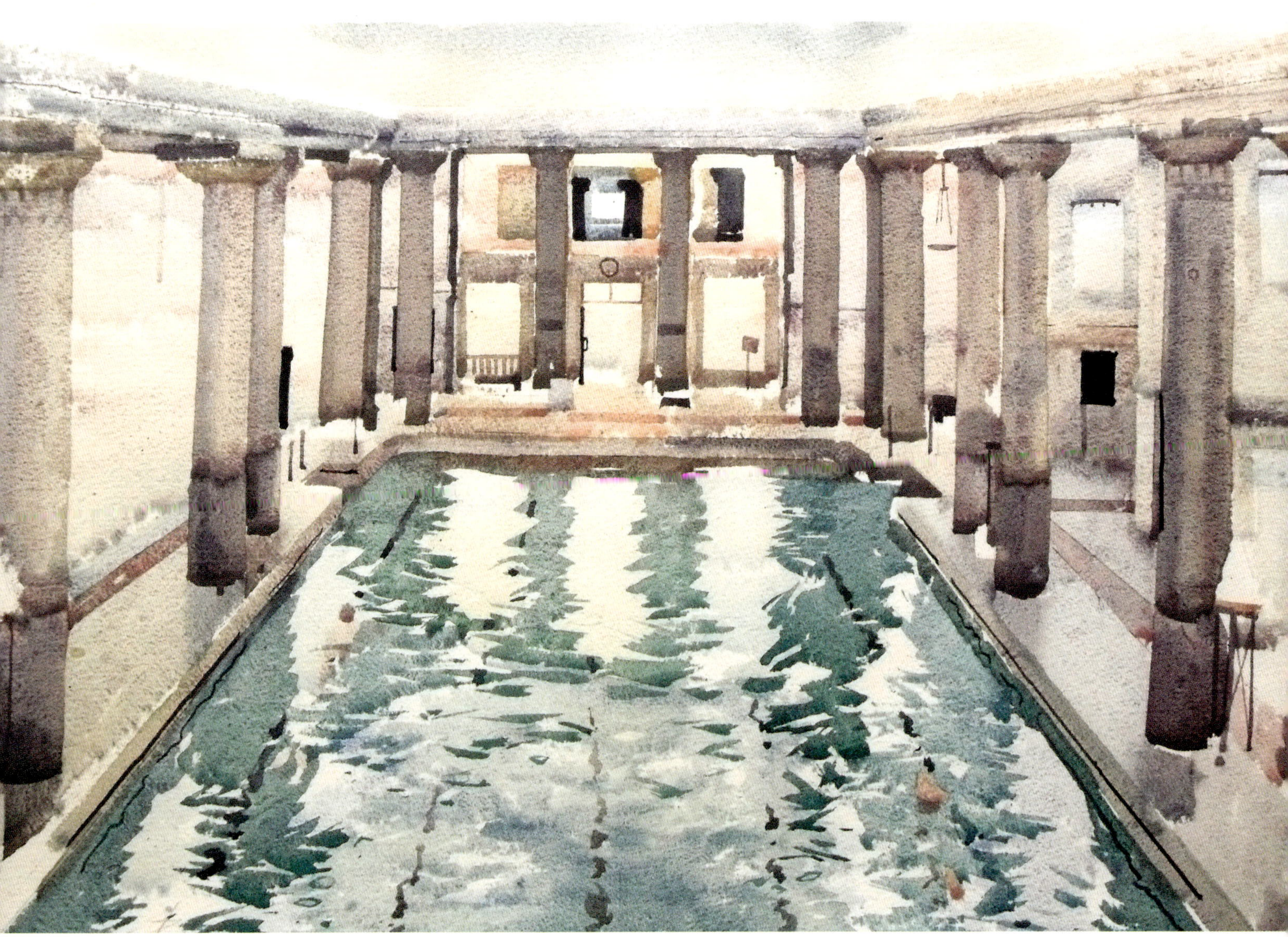

RAC Swimming Pool

56 × 38cm (22 × 15in) Millford 300gsm (140lb) Rough hard-sized paper

The setting, full of reflective surfaces, water and light, made a unique subject for lighting. Like many interior subject matter there were multiple sources of lighting.

The high viewpoint on this subject created an unusual and interesting perspective on the pool. I was so high up, that the ceiling was close to my head. This extreme perspective helped the subject enormously: the angle reduced the amount of ceiling – which held no interest for me – that could be seen, and reduced it to a strip across the top of the picture. Instead, I could give most of the picture space to the pool, the reflections and the surrounding columns and general architectural setting.

Exploring composition

As well as exploring subject matter, a good and straightforward way of developing is to experiment with composition. This will also help you to avoid making formulaic pictures.

Try alternating between assorted sizes and shapes of papers to explore the possibilities of a subject. This also offers a way of better understanding the use of the space in a picture and how to simplify. When I need a fresh approach, I often use a letterbox format of paper (see below) that leads to unusual compositions as it forces me to adapt and create new perspectives.

Moulin de Bessan 2

28 × 10cm (11 × 4in) 300gsm (140lb) Saunders Waterford Rough surface paper

The letterbox format pushed me into using a different sort of composition where I could explore balance. Using a different format is a good exercise and pushes us to find solutions and explore the possibilities of the subject.

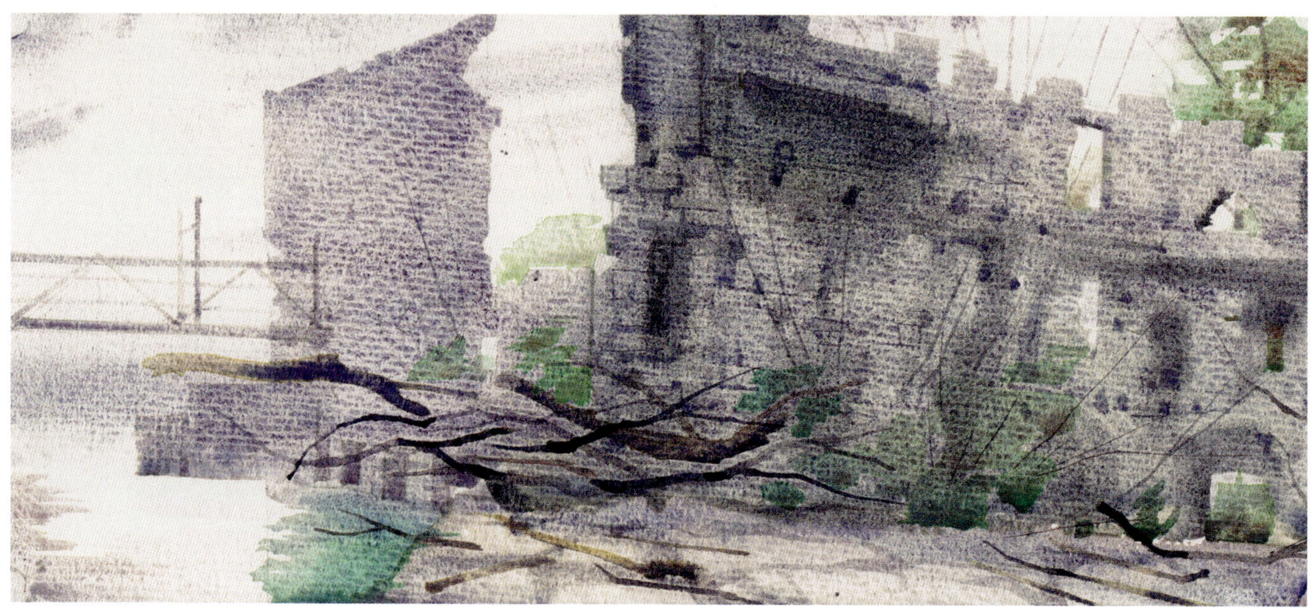

...and materials

You can also develop by simply exploring different paper types. The surface characteristics of papers will behave differently, and so trying something out of your comfort zone can be a really absorbing way to advance.

An effective way to start this experimentation is to use your preferred paper (in my case a hard-sized Rough paper) and alternate with different papers. You might try the same subject on various surfaces to see how this single change makes a difference.

You can also develop your use of colour by adding a new colour to your existing palette and seeing what new colour mixes result or how that colour can be used.

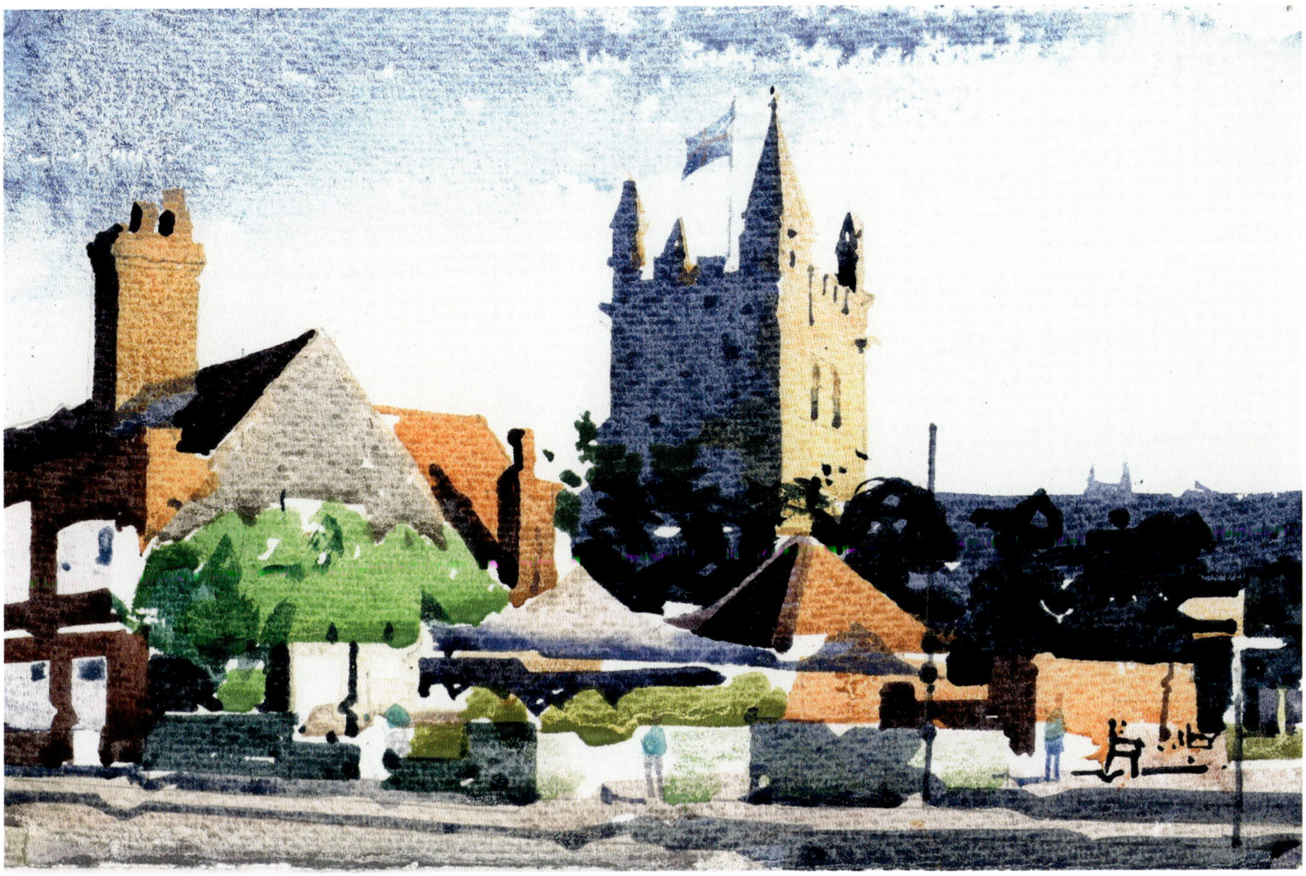

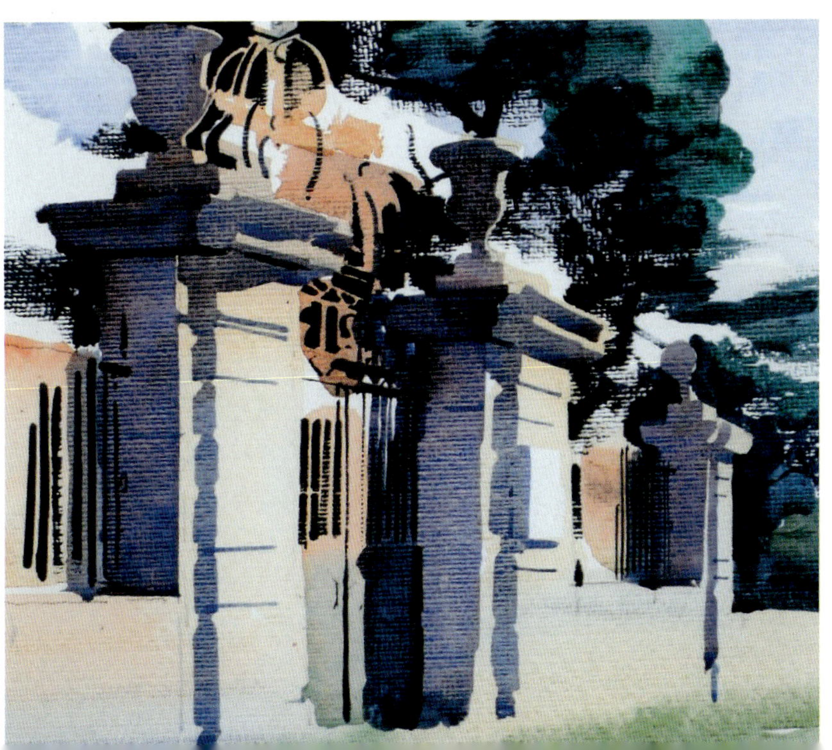

Old Amersham Willow Tree Café

28 × 18cm (11 × 7in) Saunders Waterford 300gsm (140lb) Rough surface paper

With the contrast created by the strong early morning light and the various forms and colour, this is a great little composition with plenty going on.

Parc Moliere, Pézenas

25.5 × 25.5cm (10 × 10in) Hahnemühle 300gsm (140lb) Rough surface paper

This square-format painting shows how even very modest subject matter can provide inspiration. The lighting was important in creating contrast and giving form.

Steady improvement

To develop, confidence is important. When starting out, choose subject matter with simple forms and a light and dark side (see page 41) so you can produce work with the specific objective of building confidence. When you feel brave, move on to tackle a more complex subject. Sometimes I try to paint the most difficult and challenging subject I can find, as I need to get my teeth into something. If you wish to develop it is important to move forward by continually challenging yourself.

It is also important to avoid replicating past successes. This can be a real pitfall for artists who then get locked into a tired way of working, resulting in self-parody. When we push ourselves, often a surprising picture can result that can lead us in a new direction and this is a fascinating, and never-ending, aspect of painting.

You might find lulls in your development – you might even get worse for a little while. Do not be discouraged: this happens to most artists and the only way to deal with this is to paint through it. To stay at the same standard, I must paint once a week and to improve I must paint at least three or four times. Usually, I paint five times a week (fitting in around school runs!).

Whatever approach – or combination of approaches – you choose, you will only develop by actively painting and drawing. An effective way of improving is to have an intensive week of painting. You will not be able to sustain this work rate, but it will lead to a massive improvement in a short space of time.

Building skills

- Develop through subject. Use different subject matter to develop aspects of your work – for example, working on architectural subject matter will help develop skills in perspective. Landscape might help you develop depth.

- Change things if you find yourself in a rut – change paper type and size.

- Always complete paintings: otherwise it is impossible to judge the level of success or failure; and thus your progress.

- It is crucial to be critical of your own work and then to identify and fix problems as this is how to develop and move forward. Identify what has worked and what has not in our work – we always learn more from our mistakes.

- Show your work – listen to criticism – follow advice you agree with.

- It is important to remain self-critical. The painter who thinks they are great will never improve.

- Improve drawing and painting by drawing and painting whatever holds your interest as often as you can.

- Do not copy your subject – interpret it.

- Enjoy. Love painting and be excited – there is nothing mundane about painting on the spot: it is a high-risk way of painting and fun.

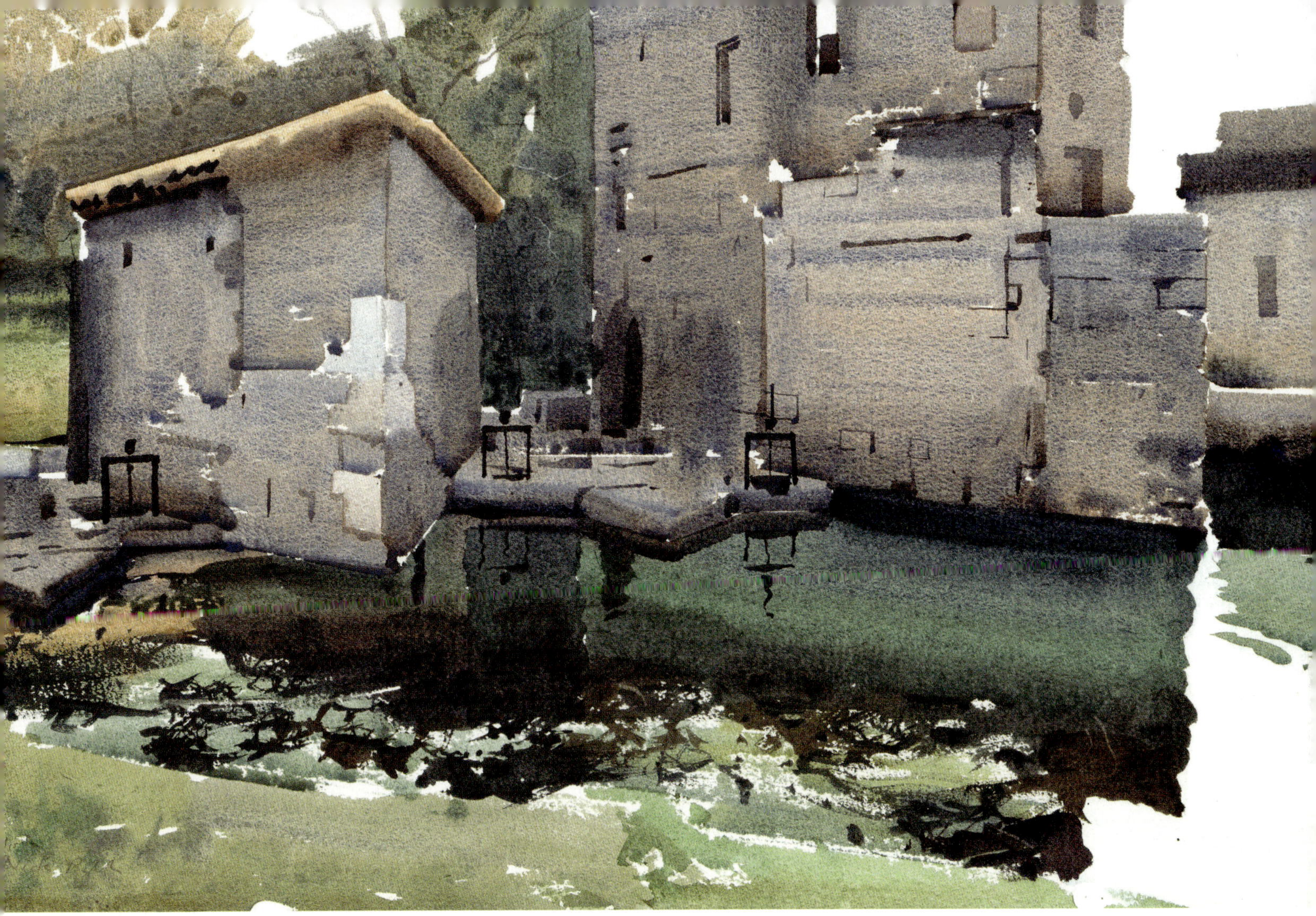

Moulin Cordier

56 × 38cm (22 × 15in) Whatman 300gsm (140lb) Not surface paper

Although architectural, there is a landscape aspect to this view and so this subject allowed an exploration of how buildings fit into a natural (rather than townscape) setting.

A range of techniques were used including dry brush for the greenery sitting on the water surface and looser washes for the larger areas of the mill. Wet in wet was used for the background.

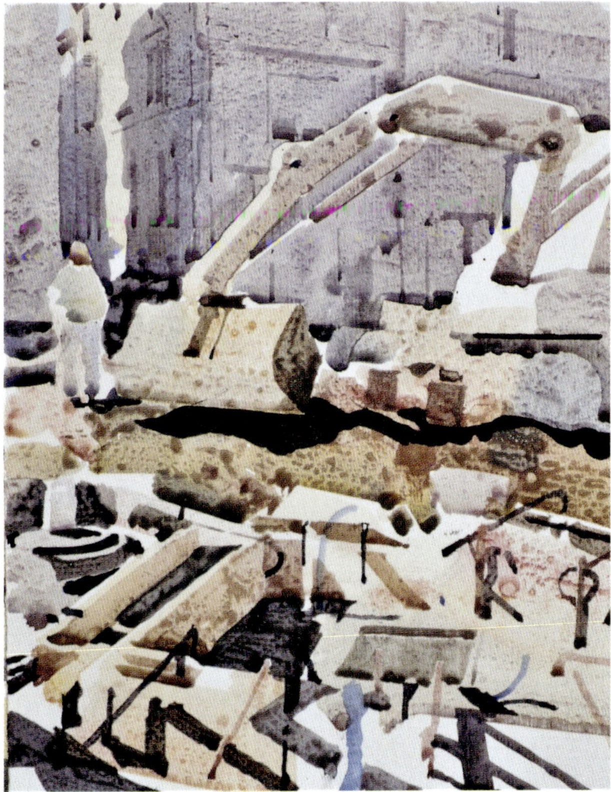

Roadworks

25.5 × 30.5cm (10 × 12in) Hahnemühle 300gsm (140lb) Rough surface paper

This subject offered an unusual perspective on painting architecture. The various shapes created an abstract design with the buildings providing a cool background.

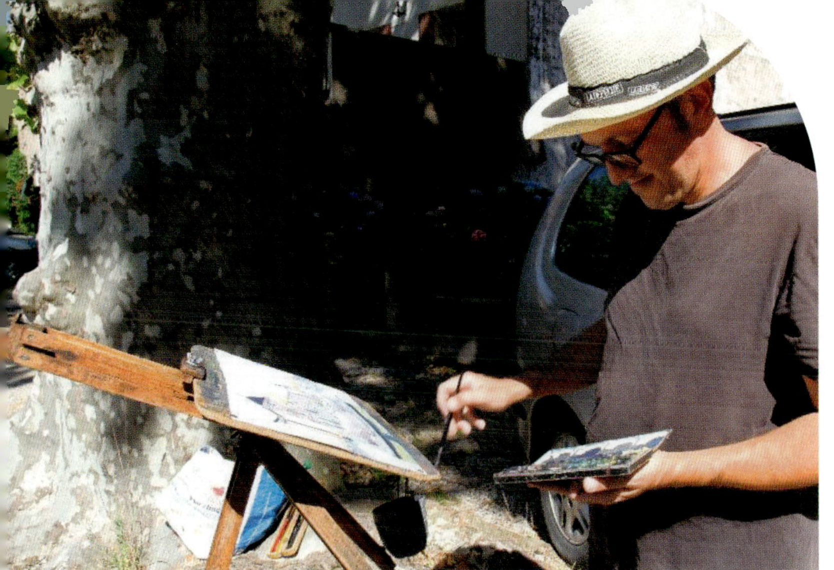

A personal style

Students often ask me how they might develop their own style. We must be cautious about the value that we put on it, and avoid pursuing a particular preconceived style. Painting only a narrow range of subjects or using only a particular brush or technique will be constraining, limiting the range of expression and subject that you can tackle.

It is important to 'own' your painting. As every decision and mark will be yours it will be your style. If you want to change the way you work – into a broader approach, for example – the change must be gradual if it is to be anything other than a superficial departure. There might not be anything wrong with what you are doing if what you are doing is true to yourself and the subject. Just because a particular approach might not be in fashion does not mean there is anything wrong with it.

Style will develop naturally as you work out your own way of tackling subjects, learning the fundamental techniques, and developing the drawing and picture-making skills outlined in this book. My advice is this: learn the simple techniques and apply them appropriately to your chosen subject. In effect, you can develop your style by not worrying about it – it will become apparent in the way you deal with the subject.

A natural style

I have always felt that watercolour works best when broader areas of paint create depth, volume and atmosphere within a composition, while smaller areas of detail add definition and interest. As a result, I have always used watercolour very freely. With practice, this has developed into a considered working method – and this has naturally come to be a recognizable style.

You can develop your style through technical improvement, and as you refine what you wish to express about a subject in a more studied way.

My style

When I started using watercolour, I used to begin with a black ink drawing that would form part of the finished painting – a practice called line and wash. This is a challenge, and I found it an excellent foundation. Working in this way helped to cement discipline in drawing and composition, but eventually I found it limiting, as the drawing was either extraordinarily strong or not there.

I eventually stopped using line and wash technique as I developed a way of making paint say what the lines were saying (and more). This opened more possibilities of what could be done with the painting – though this was a gradual process.

The lines I drew in Indian ink allowed for no lost or found edges, and no edge softer than the hard drawn line. Feeling restricted, I experimented and found using a lighter ox gall ink gave a pale grey-brown result. While allowing me more options and freedom, the painting was still fundamentally line and wash, a way of working that I wished to move away from. To make use of the painting more than the line drawing, I started using pencil to draw – and changed what I was drawing, so the lines became purely functional.

The pencil lines I now use do not form part of the finished picture and are purely for my understanding of the subject. Sometimes I do not draw at all, and this has helped push all the process onto the painting stages. As my technique developed, I found that I added new approaches to my repertoire: broad, loose, tighter, detailed – but the results are all distinctly in my style.

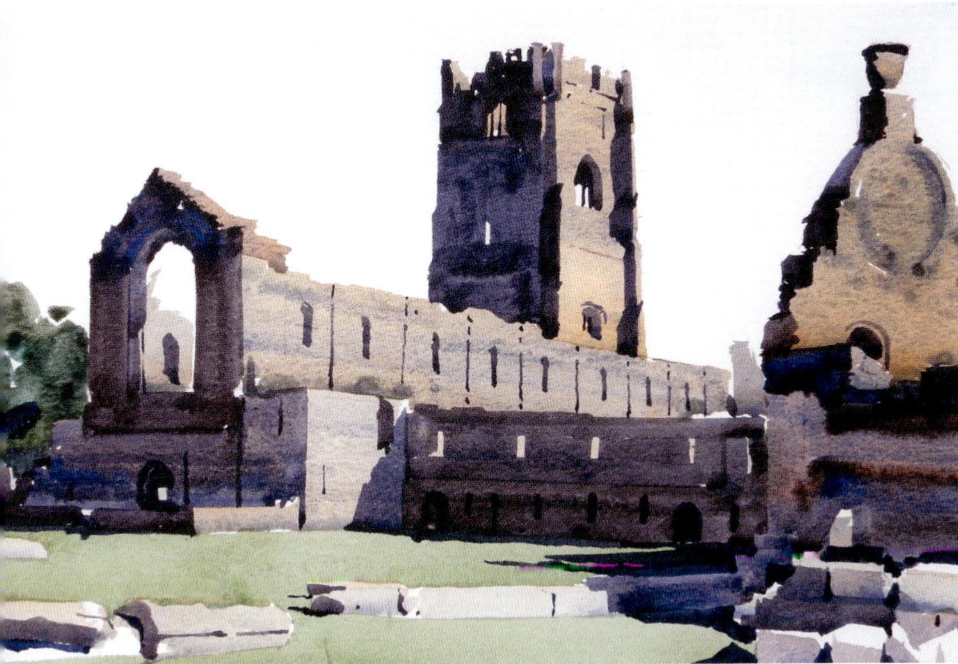

Fountains Abbey

38 × 28cm (15 × 11in) Saunders Waterford 300gsm (140lb) Rough surface paper

For the first stage of painting this subject I used simple washes. This helped me to establish the forms and atmosphere and then once this stage was dry, I added stronger tones to help define shapes. The lighting on the day I painted this was perfect and was used in the contrast and tonal range of the painting.

Compare this piece with that of the same subject on page 32. While each is a different treatment, the underlying style remains consistent.

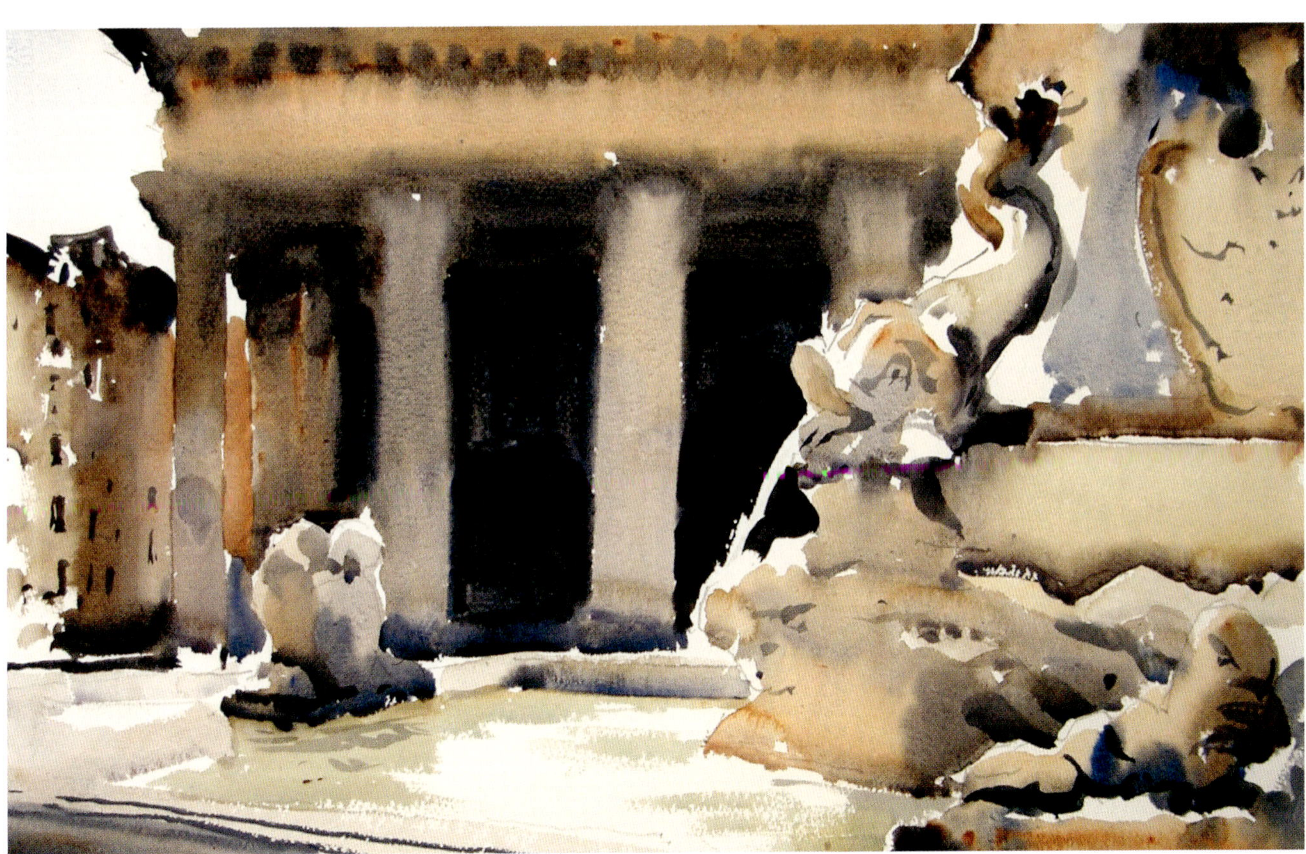

The Pantheon, Rome

56 × 38cm (22 × 15in) Whatman 300gsm (140lb) Rough surface paper

This painting was produced as part of a series looking at ancient cultural influences seen along the route of ancient Roman roads running from Cadiz to Rome.

Ancient Bridge

An effective way to refresh your approach is to mix things up a bit by using a variety of paper sizes and dimensions. A different format forces us to re-evaluate a subject and often a range of compositions will become possible, that you might not have noticed previously. Sometimes you find a particular format works well with the shapes and forms offered by an especially interesting and unusual subject, like this ancient bridge at Saint-Thibéry.

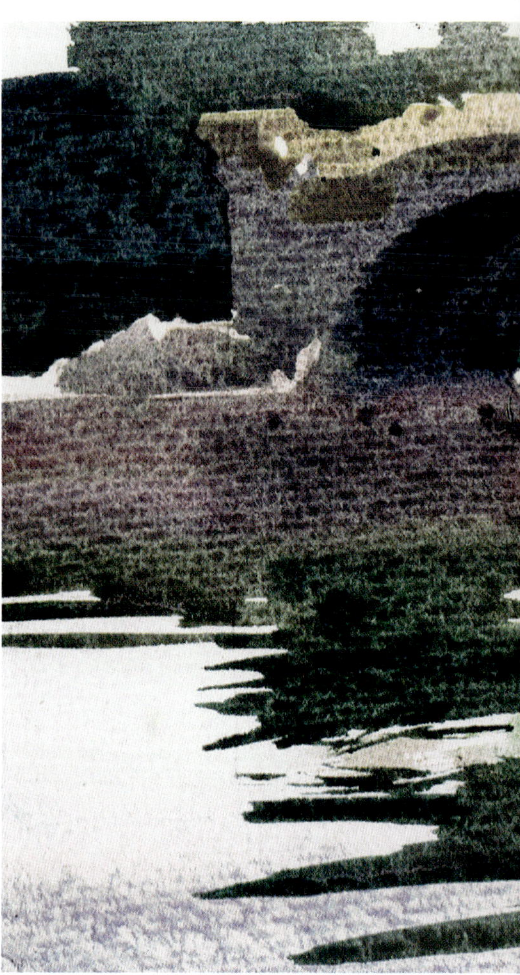

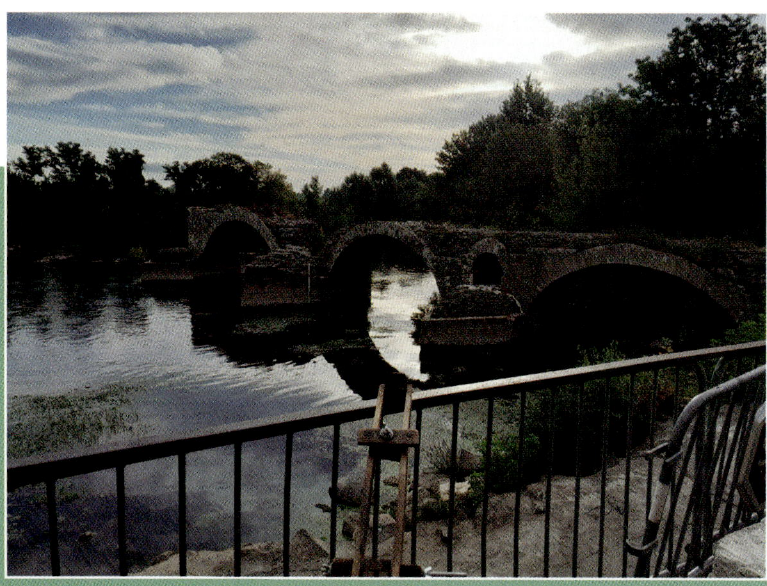

Setting up

On seeing this bridge, the idea of a letterbox composition came to me – this shape works well for a panoramic view and would suit the overall shape of the bridge.

The water appealed to me far more than the sky, so I set up so that I could see the bridge at a bold diagonal. This would allow me to make a composition where the proportion of the paper allowed for the sky to be mostly omitted and for the water with its reflections to play a prominent role.

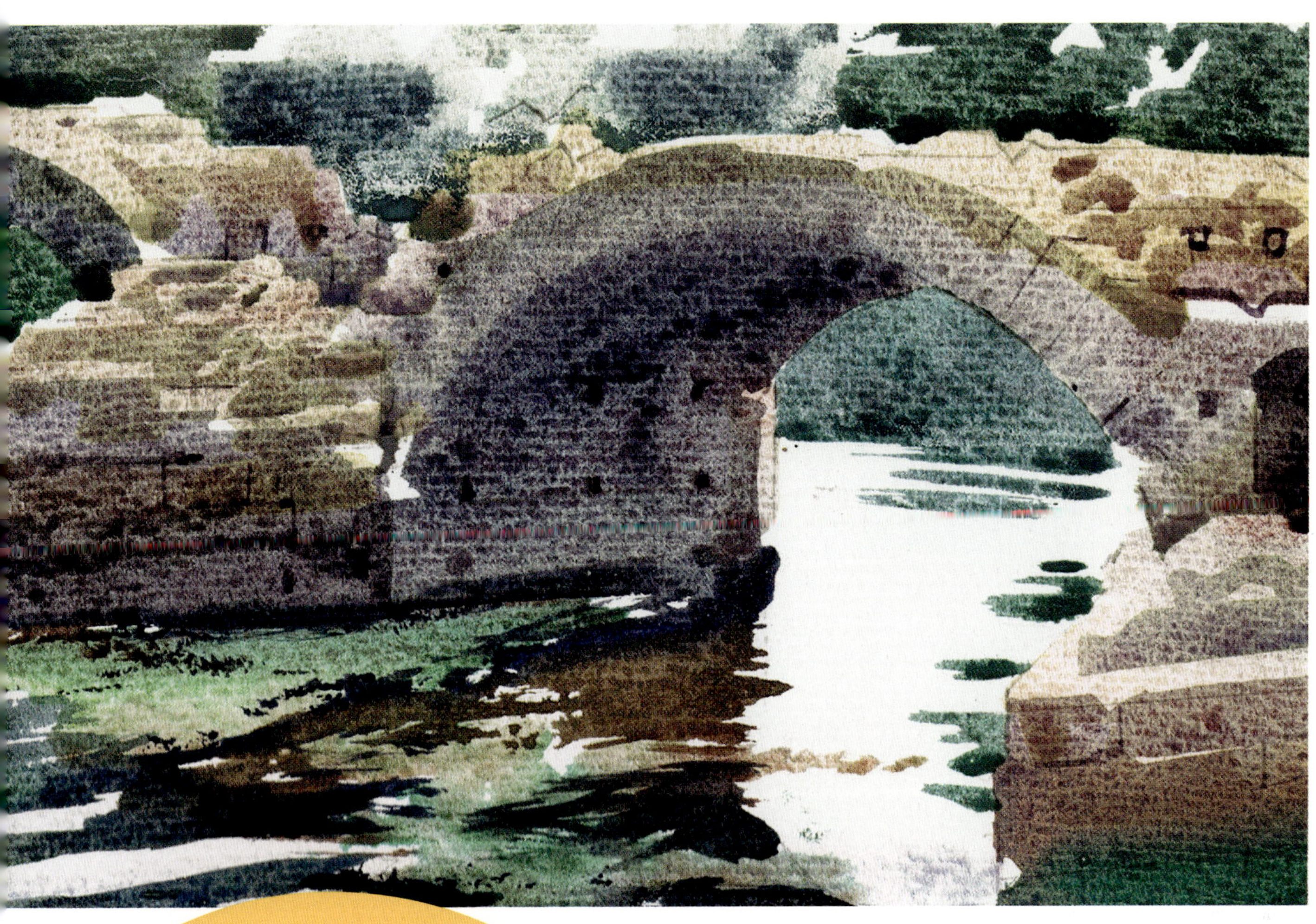

The finished painting

YOU WILL NEED

Watercolour paints: potters pink, light red, raw sienna, Naples yellow, viridian, cobalt blue deep, French ultramarine, ivory black, brown madder

Brushes: size 8 round, size 6 round, size 4 rigger

Paper: Rough surface watercolour paper, 28 × 12.5cm (11 × 5in)

2B pencil and soft eraser, gum arabic

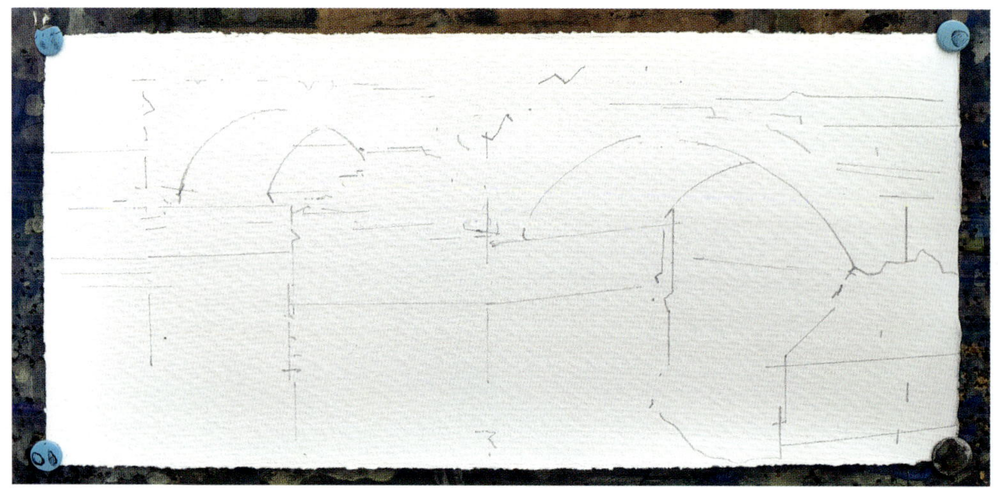

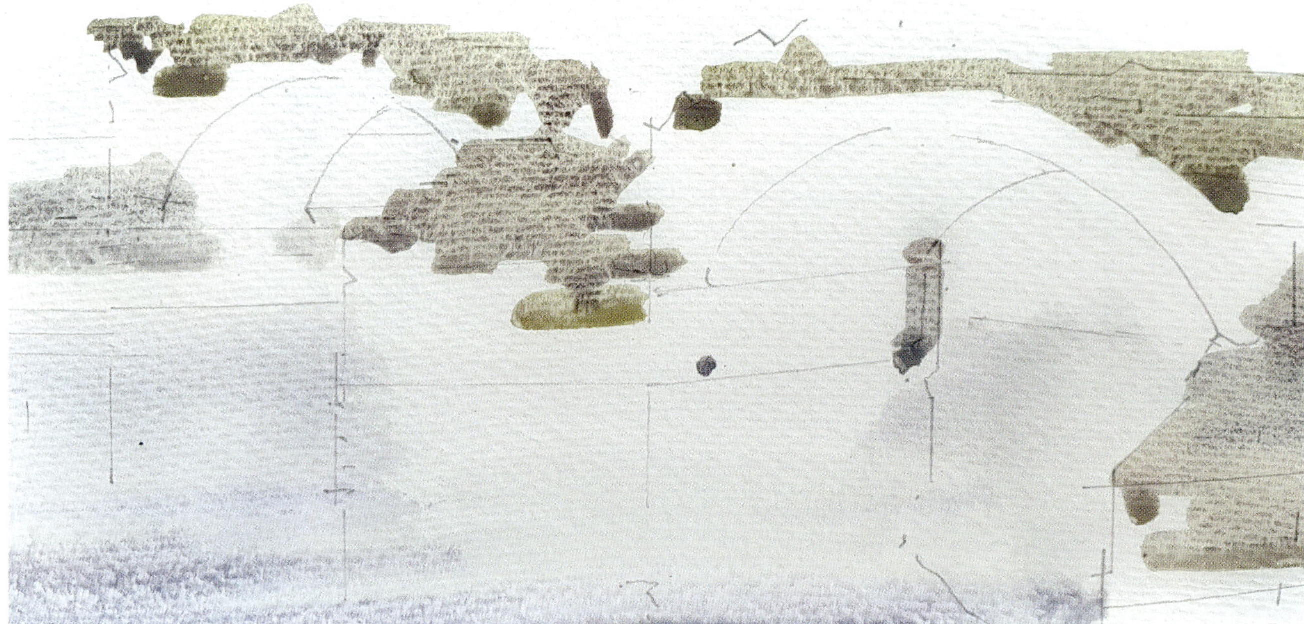

Stage 1

I had considered going straight in with the painting, but decided that it was best to draw first due to the complex form and the arches. Use a 2B pencil to make your basic drawing. By placing the bridge itself high up on the paper, you will be able to include a large part of the water, with the reflections and surface weeds providing interest.

All the paint in this stage was put on with a size 8 round brush. Working wet in wet, apply Naples yellow, raw sienna, potters pink and cobalt blue deep to add the lighter parts of the stone on the bridge, allowing the colours to partially blend and merge.

Leaving spaces of clean dry paper around the bridge, to ensure the areas do not run into each other, add the lighter shade of the water with a reverse graduated wash and a mix of cobalt blue deep and potters pink.

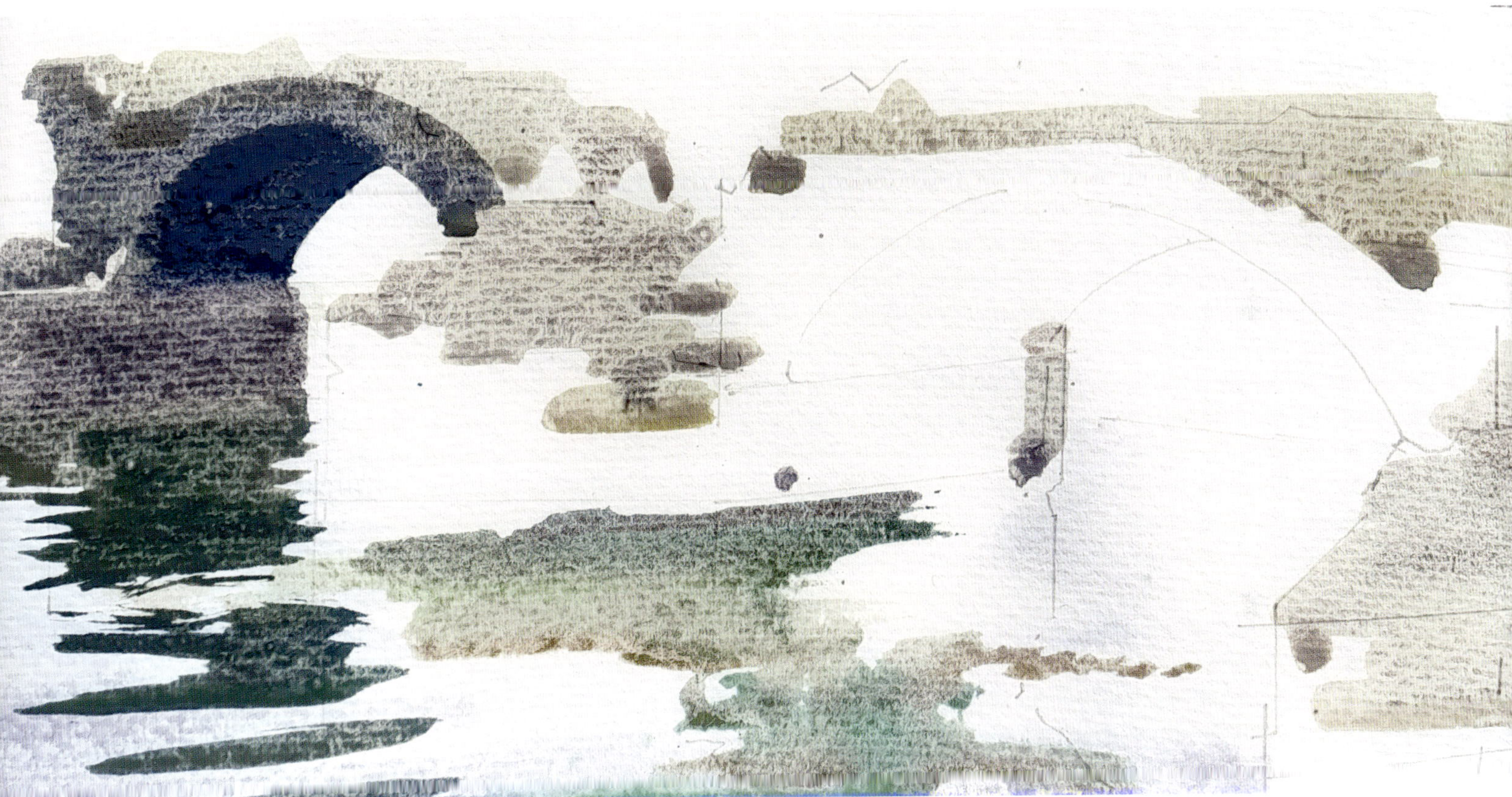

Stage 2

The green of the surface weed is darker nearer the bridge, and this helps to create the effect of depth. Add it to your painting by using a size 6 round brush to apply a graduated wash. Start with a tonally darker mix of viridian, potters pink and cobalt blue deep near the bridge, and work downwards into a lighter tonal mix of Naples yellow and potters pink. Add a little viridian to the lighter tonal mix as you near the bottom of the paper.

Next, add the shaded side of the structure with a mix of varying amounts of cobalt blue deep, potters pink, brown madder and raw sienna, and for the darkest tones (as under the furthest arch), a mix of French ultramarine and brown madder was added wet against wet. Start by painting the furthest arch and draw the wash straight into the water. Keep the effect vague as this will help to simplify and create depth.

Look for patterns of reflections in the water and be careful when painting around the surface weed. Next, paint in the nearer arch with the same colours and mixes.

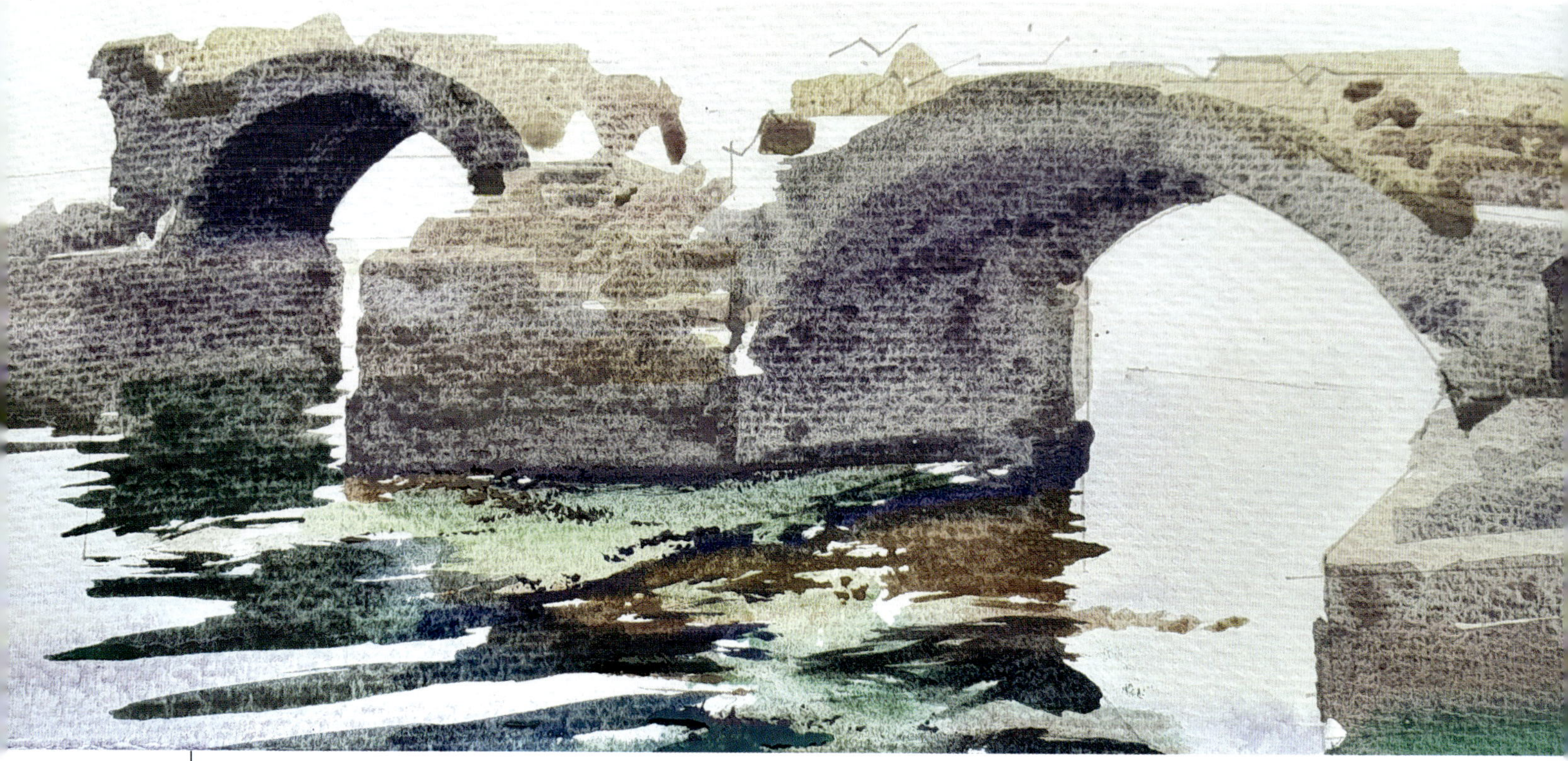

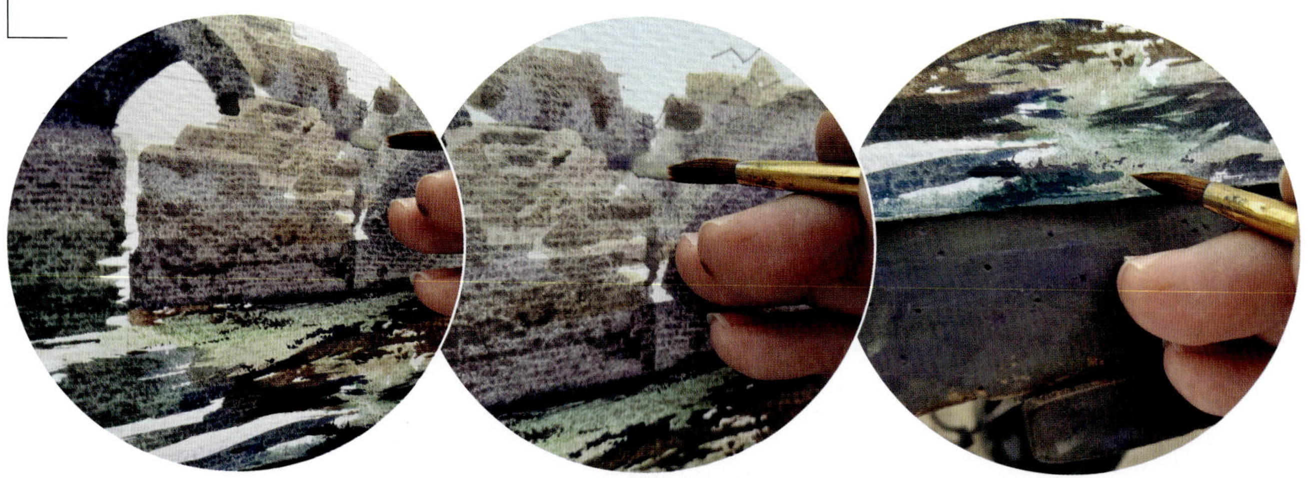

Stage 3

Paint in the other structures of the bridge, using a lot of wet into wet technique to keep things vague. Avoid being drawn into detailed work: it is important to interpret rather than copy.

Add defining details to the stonework using a size 6 round brush and the viridian, potters pink and cobalt blue mix. Swap to a size 8 round brush and paint the water using a similar mix, but swapping cobalt blue for French ultramarine for added depth of colour.

Consider carefully where to add details to the stonework – don't overdo it.

Be careful to make sure the picture is dry wherever you might need to touch the painting, to avoid smearing wet patches of paint.

The water being painted on – note that even a relatively large size 8 round brush can be used, as long as it has a good point.

Stage 4

Swap to a size 8 round brush for all the painting in this stage. Start to put in the background using muted tones of a mix of viridian, cobalt blue deep and potters pink. Working wet in wet, couple this with a mix of Naples yellow, viridian and potters pink.

Still working wet in wet, suggest shaded areas by adding a tonally darker mix of cobalt blue deep and potters pink. This will provide depth and contrast that also helps to define the shape of the bridge.

In the background, place other reflections beneath the arch of the bridge on the right, using the same wash of viridian, cobalt blue deep and potters pink. Continue bringing this down the painting and, at the bottom edge, make reflection shapes.

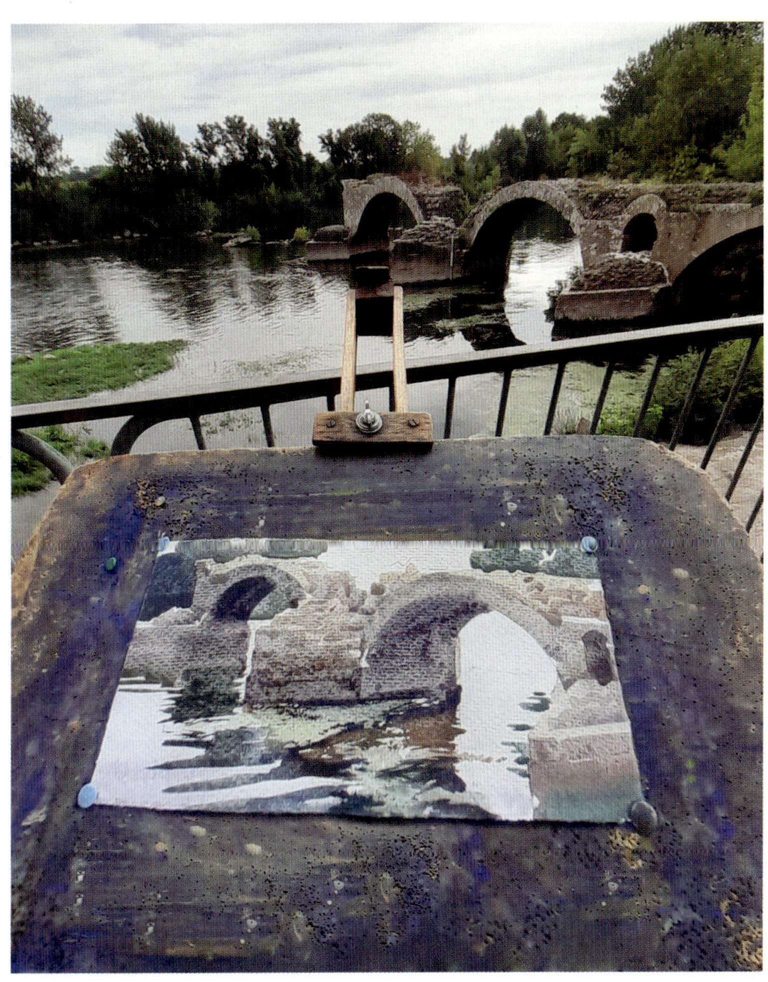

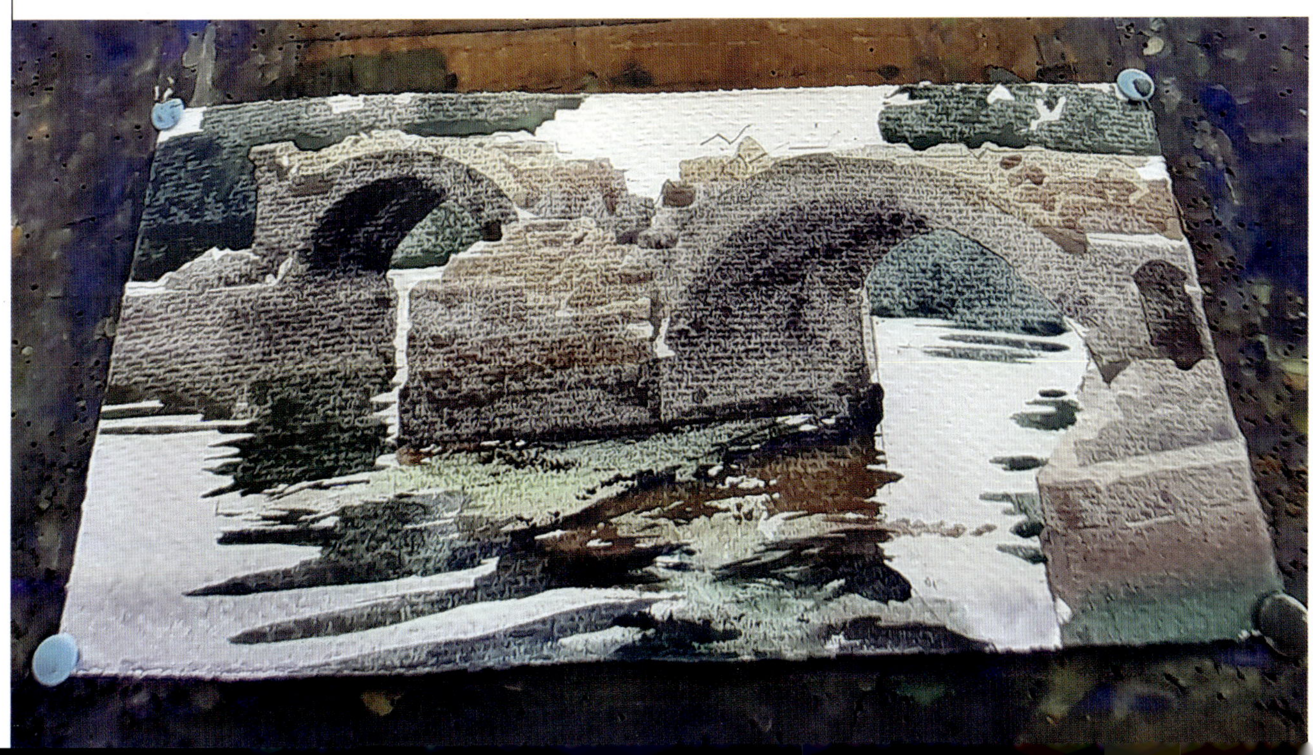

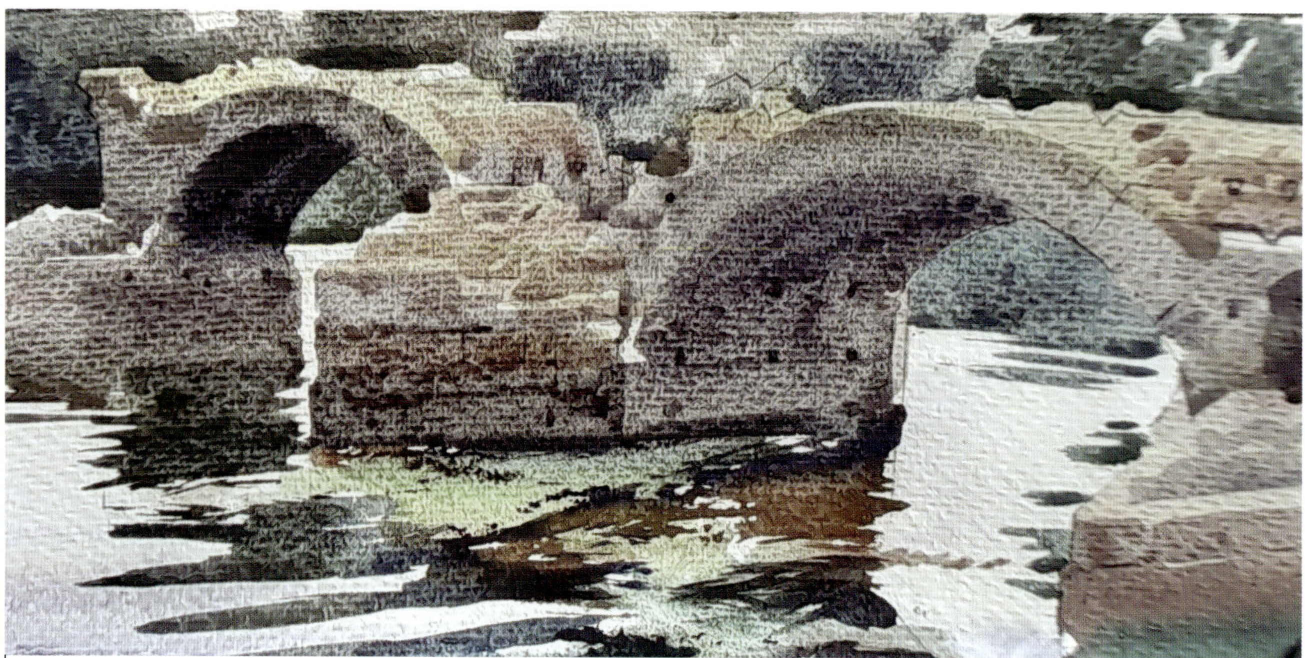

Stage 5

Use a rigger to add a small number of lines to define some of the stones and texture. When completely dry, fill in a couple of the white circles left by the drawing pins, then gently rub out the pencil using a soft eraser. The finished painting can be seen on page 135.

Another approach

Various things will affect how we approach a subject: atmospheric conditions, lighting and viewpoint will affect the appearance of a subject and the content, while changing paper size and proportions will affect composition and structure.

Exploring the same subject under varied lighting conditions will reveal new possibilities and will result in dramatically different paintings.

Changing viewpoint will change what we include and therefore the focus and content of the painting.

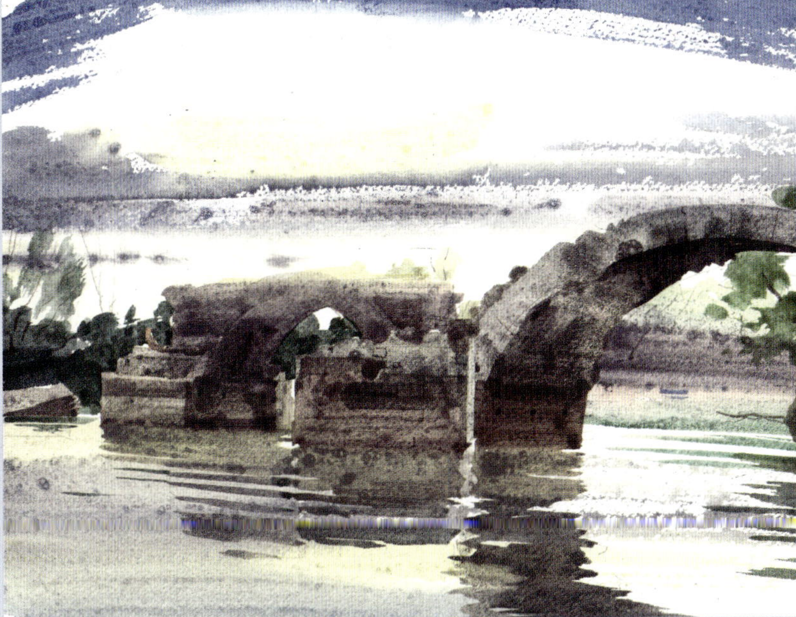

Top

Ancient Bridge, Saint-Thibéry

28 × 12.5cm (11 × 5in) Saunders Waterford 300gsm (140lb) Rough surface paper

In this version I included more of the sky and painted the architecture as an integral part of the landscape setting, rather than as the focus.

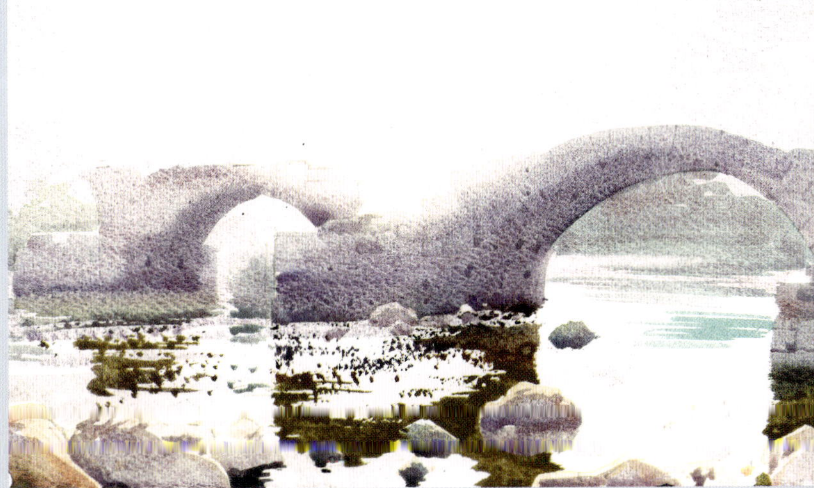

Middle

The Bridge at Saint-Thibéry, *Contre-jour*

28 × 18cm (11 × 7in) 300gsm (140lb) Saunders Waterford Rough surface paper

A change in viewpoint left me looking into the sun, which allowed me to concentrate on lighting. The forms of the bridge were painted with a light touch, meaning that the rocks, reflections and shadows on the water become more important to the composition. These were tackled with more controlled, smaller areas of wash to balance the ethereal appearance of the bridge.

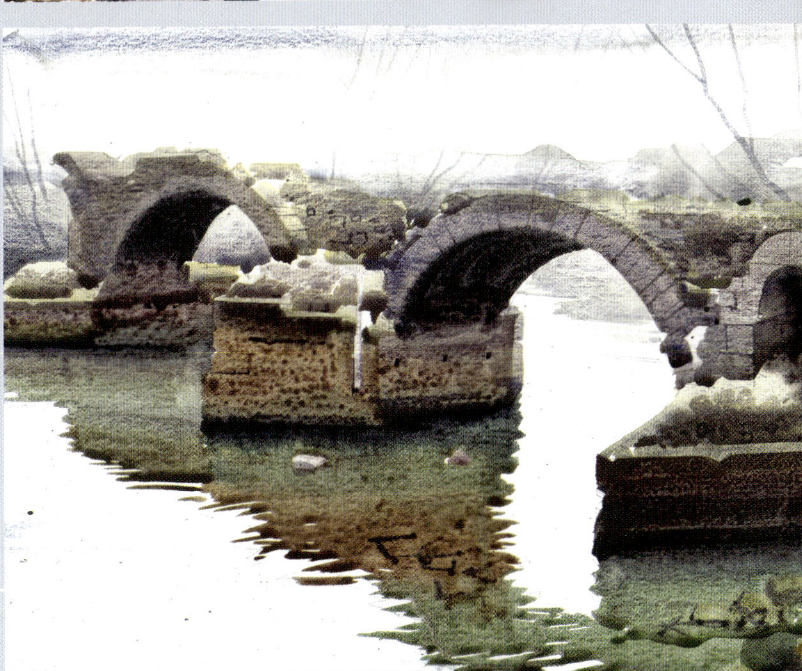

Bottom

The Bridge at Saint-Thibéry

20.5 × 25.5cm (12 × 10in) Hahnemühle 300gsm (140lb) Not surface paper

A seasonal change allowed a different approach to the subject; grey winter lighting altered the colour range. More obviously, the different format means more of the water, reflections and setting of the bridge can be included.

In this version the reflections form a much more important – indeed crucial – role in the painting.

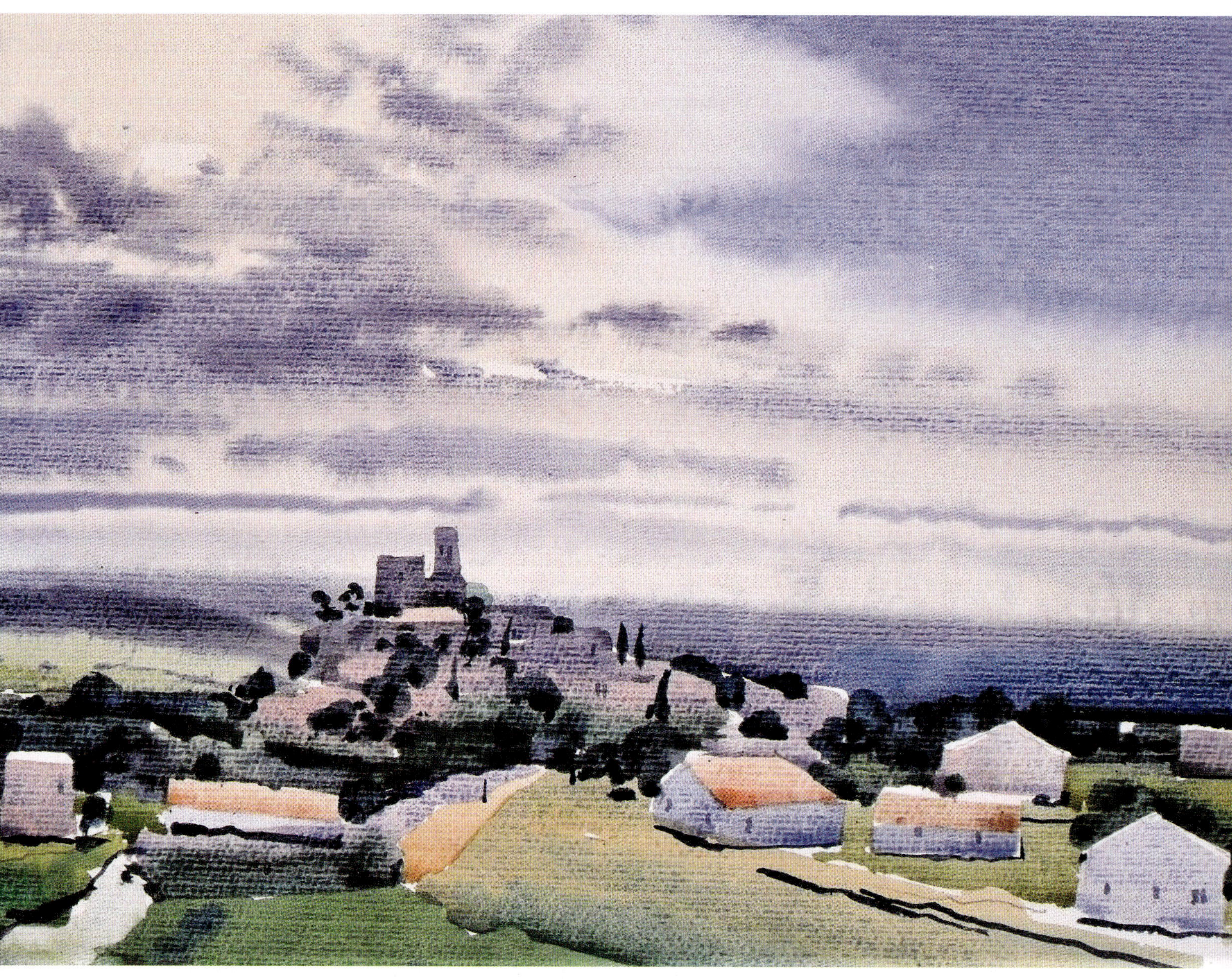

St Pons

30.5 × 25.5cm (12 × 10in) Hahnemühle 300gsm (140lb) Rough surface paper
In this subject, the buildings help to explore and give interest to the landscape in which they sit.

Afterword

You are in great company. The painting of architecture, also known as topography, has a long history. The most notable topographer was Turner but there have been many great exponents including Girtin, Cotman, De Wint, Cox, Bonington, Flint, Seago, Wesson and Hilder to name but a few, and this tradition continues into the present. The questions and challenges watercolour brings up perhaps explain why watercolourists are often, (and in a positive way) obsessive. For us, no other activity could replace it – artists never retire!

Buildings, as we have seen, provide enormous scope for great subject matter. As well as demonstrating the practical side of how to capture atmosphere in your architectural paintings, my hope for this book is that it inspires you, by showing how traditional methods and techniques can be given a contemporary and personal spin.

Painting with dedication brings enjoyment. The more you paint, the more you will find success; which in turn leads to the drive to paint more. This virtuous circle will show in your work. It is my hope that this book has equipped you to find your own path towards painting atmospheric buildings successfully, and that as you continue to explore, your pictures grow more and more personal to you.

Acknowledgements

Books like this are the result of the work of many people and I thank everyone at Search Press for their contribution. Especial thanks to Edward Ralph, for guidance and making things straightforward, and improving the text and content. Thanks also to Samantha Warrington and to Katie French for their confidence in me.

I would like to give special thanks to Sally Bulgin for her help and support over the years and for the foreword.

I would like to express my gratitude for the inspiration, kindness and generosity of several artists, all of whom represent so many great qualities associated with this artform we love so much: thanks to David Curtis ROI RSMA, Trevor Chamberlain ROI RSMA, Mike Chaplin RWS RE FRSA and to the late Ken Howard OBE RA.

A big thanks also to my family and friends for their love and support.

Index

abbey 28, 32, 34, 122, 133
arch(es) 46, 61, 62, 65, 78, 102, 114, 116, 118, 121, 136, 137, 139
atmosphere 12, 14, 36, 40, 45, 52, 53, 82, 89, 102, 106, 108, 121, 124, 126, 132, 133, 143

background 27, 36, 47, 51, 52, 62, 94, 117, 119, 120, 131, 139
balance 42, 44, 45, 46, 47, 49, 53, 54, 56, 58, 59, 61, 62, 89, 96, 106, 107, 109, 117, 128, 141
boats 40, 111
bricks 51, 53, 99, 100, 109
bridge 56, 59, 61, 62, 134, 136, 137, 138, 139, 141

cathedral 56, 58, 61, 62, 63
change in viewpoint 141
character 8, 14, 34, 40, 49, 50, 51, 52, 109, 110
church 36, 42, 59
columns 65, 127
combining the techniques 34
common perspective traps 78
composition 8, 39, 40, 41, 42, 44, 45, 46, 47, 53, 56, 58, 61, 66, 68, 70, 82, 87, 89, 90, 91, 96, 103, 108, 109, 112, 114, 116, 121, 128, 129, 132, 134, 141
    natural 39, 41, 44, 47, 96, 112
    sketches 44
confidence 8, 93, 108, 111, 130
contre-jour 30, 93, 141
counterchange 54
cross-hatching 69

darks 106, 107, 112
depth 26, 36, 40, 42, 45, 46, 47, 49, 51, 52, 67, 69, 70, 84, 87, 93, 96, 98, 101, 112, 114, 116, 118, 121, 126, 130, 132, 137, 138, 139
details 61, 75, 105, 109, 112, 122
direct painting 36
drama 16, 56, 65, 70, 82, 90, 94, 96, 100, 125, 126
drawing from life 68
dry brush 27, 28, 131
drying time 14, 32, 54, 56, 98

easel 10, 70
edge(s) 22, 25, 27, 29, 30, 51, 52, 65, 67, 72, 73, 79, 81, 85, 94, 118, 132, 139
    lost and found 94
en plein air 8, 12, 66
evaluating tone 69
experimentation 128

figure(s) 29, 53, 67, 78, 87, 102, 112, 120
flocking 32, 33 *see also* granulation
focus 8, 39, 42, 44, 45, 46, 47, 50, 53, 56, 68, 81, 86, 87, 98, 101, 107, 116, 121, 141
foliage 61, 63, 108, 131
foreground 26, 36, 42, 49, 51, 61, 87

granulation 14, 32, 33, 86
green 18, 54, 61, 137
greenery *see* foliage
gum arabic 29, 35, 56, 57, 96, 98, 135

half-tones 105, 106, 107, 109, 112
hatching 69
highlights 34, 58, 87, 106, 108, 109, 111
    see also lights
    clean paper 34
    preserved 109
horizon 27, 78, 82

impact 8, 36, 56, 88
improvement 122, 130, 132
incline, working at a 10, 16, 19, 25, 30, 79, 84
indirect painting 20, 36
interior 42, 95, 114, 116, 121, 127

keeping colour clean 19

lifting out 10, 12, 29, 30, 87, 94
lighting 8, 36, 41, 46, 47, 51, 52, 84, 87, 89, 91, 92, 93, 94, 95, 96, 98, 100, 103, 107, 108, 112, 121, 127, 129, 133, 141
    artificial 42
    early morning 55, 96, 129
    indoor 95
    reflected light 25, 31, 61, 87, 95, 99, 103, 112, 126
    sunlight 16, 27, 91, 94, 112
lights 54, 58, 59, 63, 76, 90, 99, 100, 105, 106, 107, 111, 112, 114, 119
    see also highlights

making changes 53
market 69, 96, 98, 99, 100, 101, 103, 114, 121
measuring 68, 72, 79, 80
mill 7, 70, 72, 74, 76, 77, 85, 88, 90, 91, 92, 95, 105, 108, 126, 128, 131
mood 89, 91

off lights 58 *see also* highlights
overpainting 31, 34
overworking 54, 119

paintbrushes 12
    care of 23
    handling 22
    hog hair 12, 23
    large brush 12, 19
    my choice 23
    rigger 12, 23, 84, 87, 114, 119, 135, 140
pencil lines 62, 132
    unwanted marks 68, 120
perspective 16, 40, 42, 45, 46, 65, 68, 70, 71, 72, 73, 75, 78, 79, 81, 82, 83, 84, 85, 114, 126, 127, 130, 131
    aerial perspective 42
pillars 117, 118, 119, 120, 121
proportions 67, 68, 72, 78, 79, 117, 141

reflections 42, 47, 52, 56, 62, 67, 82, 87, 90, 109, 118, 127, 134, 136, 137, 139, 141
roofs 49, 55, 92, 99

scratching out 14, 111
setting up 16, 56, 70, 84, 96, 114, 134
shadows 25, 55, 60, 61, 75, 83, 87, 88, 90, 96, 101, 105, 106, 107, 108, 112, 121, 122, 141
shutters 84, 85, 86

simplification 8, 47, 49, 50, 51, 52, 53, 54, 55, 56, 63, 87, 106, 110, 114, 124, 128, 137
sizing 14
sketch(ing) 10, 44, 58, 67, 76, 80, 81
sky(-ies) 26, 27, 30, 34, 36, 51, 59, 62, 86, 95, 98, 99, 105, 106, 108, 110, 111, 112, 134, 141
stone 34, 36, 51, 53, 87, 95, 99, 136, 140
street 42, 65, 66, 82, 84, 86, 87, 101
style 14, 36, 111, 132, 133
sun, looking into *see contre-jour*
surface texture *see* watercolour paper, tooth

techniques 10, 12, 20, 21, 24, 25, 26, 27, 28, 30, 34, 36, 74, 94, 105, 111, 131, 132, 143
time limit 54, 67, 68
tone 18, 19, 26, 27, 31, 36, 44, 49, 50, 58, 62, 69, 70, 87, 95, 101, 106, 107, 108, 109, 110, 112, 117
    darkest 69
    lightest 69
    mid-tones 54, 69, 76, 118
tower 36, 39, 42, 45, 52, 68, 72, 73, 74, 112
treeing 19, 21, 30, 32
trees 12, 51, 52, 56, 105, 112, 116, 121

underpainting 31, 36, 54, 61, 63, 99, 107, 110
unusual subject matter 42

wash(es)
    flat 26, 34, 98, 109
    graduated 26, 27, 30, 34, 61, 86, 87, 88, 98, 119, 136, 137
    three stages 106, 108, 109, 116
    unifying 111
watercolour paints 12, 57, 84, 96, 114, 135
    choosing colours 18
    ensuring freshness 18
    handling 52
    my palette 19
watercolour paper 14
    highly textured 20
    my choice 20
    stretching 14, 21
    tooth 14, 24, 28, 34
    weight 14
weather 103
wet in wet 27, 30, 52, 86, 105, 118, 131, 136, 138, 139
wet on dry 24, 25, 27, 31, 34, 52, 111
windows 50, 61, 75, 78, 84, 85, 86, 87, 99, 112, 116, 120

First published in 2024

Search Press Limited
Wellwood, North Farm Road,
Tunbridge Wells, Kent TN2 3DR

Copyright © Search Press Ltd 2024
Photographs author's own, except
for pages 11, 13–15, 18–19, 21–23
by Mark Davison at Search Press
Studios, and the author's
photograph, by Coraligne –
Pascale Servent.
Author's photograph copyright ©
Coraligne – Pascale Servent

ISBN: 978-1-80092-042-2
ebook ISBN: 978-1-80093-035-3

Suppliers
For details of suppliers, please visit
the Search Press website:
www.searchpress.com

You are invited to the author's
website: www.nicholas-poullis.com

Bookmarked
For further ideas and inspiration,
and to join our free online
community, visit
www.bookmarkedhub.com

Publisher's note

All the step-by-step photographs
in this book feature the author,
Nicholas Poullis, demonstrating
watercolour. No models have
been used.

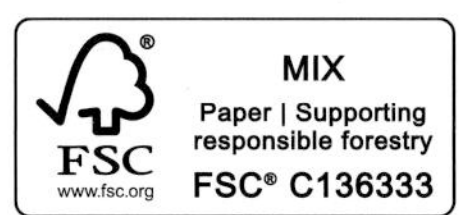